SHE
SAID

Hey Mom!

These two authors are the same reporters that we listened to during our ride in Michigan this summer. Very smart women and a fascinating + critical topic. Also a fantastic memory for me. I'm so grateful we got to spend that quality time together talking + learning. Can't wait for the next trip. Love you very much,

Kiera

SHE
SAID

SHE
SAID

BREAKING THE SEXUAL HARASSMENT STORY

THAT HELPED IGNITE A MOVEMENT

Jodi Kantor and Megan Twohey

PENGUIN PRESS ▪ NEW YORK

2019

PENGUIN PRESS
An imprint of Penguin Random House LLC
penguinrandomhouse.com

ISBN: 9780525560340 (hardcover)
ISBN: 9780525560357 (ebook)
ISBN: 9781984879202 (international export)

Printed in the United States of America

BOOK DESIGN BY LUCIA BERNARD

TO OUR DAUGHTERS:

MIRA, TALIA, AND VIOLET

CONTENTS

SHE SAID

I n 2017, when we began our investigation of Harvey Weinstein for the *New York Times*, women held more power than ever before. The number of jobs once held almost exclusively by men—police officer, soldier, airline pilot—had narrowed almost to a vanishing point. Women led nations including Germany and the United Kingdom, and companies such as General Motors and PepsiCo. In one year of work, it was possible for a thirtysomething-year-old woman to make more money than all of her female ancestors had made in their combined lifetimes.

But all too often, women were sexually harassed with impunity. Female scientists and waitresses, cheerleaders, executives, and factory workers had to smile past gropes, leers, or unwelcome advances to get the next tip, paycheck, or raise. Sexual harassment was against the law—but it was also routine in some jobs. Women who spoke up were frequently dismissed or denigrated. Victims were often hidden and isolated from one another. Their best option, many people agreed, was to accept money as some form of reparation, in exchange for silence.

The perpetrators, meanwhile, frequently sailed to ever-higher levels of success and praise. Harassers were often accepted, or even cheered, as mischievous bad boys. Serious consequences were rare. Megan wrote some of the original articles in which women alleged that Donald J. Trump preyed on them—and then she covered his triumph in the 2016 election.

After we broke the story of Weinstein's alleged sexual harassment and abuse on October 5, 2017, we watched with astonishment as a dam wall broke. Millions of women around the world told their own stories of mistreatment. Large numbers of men suddenly had to answer for their predatory behavior, a moment of accountability without precedent. Journalism had helped inspire a paradigm shift. Our work was only one driver of that change, which had been building for years, thanks to the efforts of pioneering feminists and legal scholars; Anita Hill; Tarana Burke, the activist who founded the #MeToo movement; and many others, including our fellow journalists.

But seeing our own hard-won investigative discoveries help realign attitudes left us asking, Why this story? As one of our editors pointed out, Harvey Weinstein wasn't even that famous. In a world in which so much feels stuck, how does this sort of seismic social change occur?

We embarked on this book to answer those questions. Nothing about the change was inevitable or foretold. In these pages, we describe the motivations and wrenching, risky decisions of the first brave sources to break the silence surrounding Weinstein. Laura Madden, a former assistant to Weinstein and a stay-at-home mother in Wales, spoke out just as she was reeling from divorce and about to undergo post-cancer breast surgery. Ashley Judd put her career on the line, spurred by a little-known period in her life when she stepped away from Hollywood to immerse herself in big-picture thinking about gender equality. Zelda Perkins, a London producer whose complaints against Weinstein had been suppressed by an agreement she had signed two decades before, spoke to us despite potential legal and financial retribution. A longtime Weinstein employee, increasingly troubled by what he knew, played a key, and previously undisclosed, role in helping us to finally unmask his boss. We intend the title, *She Said*, as a complicated one: We write about those who did speak out, along with other women who chose not to, and the nuances of how and when and why.

This is also a story about investigative journalism, beginning with the first uncertain days of our reporting, when we knew very little and almost no one would speak to us. We describe how we coaxed out secrets, pinned down information, and pursued the truth about a powerful man even as he used underhanded tactics to try to sabotage our work. We have also, for the first time, reconstructed our final showdown with the producer—his last stand—in the offices of the *New York Times* right before publication, as he realized he was cornered.

Our Weinstein reporting took place at a time of accusations of "fake news," as the very notion of a national consensus on truth seemed to be fracturing. But the impact of the Weinstein revelations was so great in part because we and other journalists were able to establish a clear and over-whelming body of evidence of wrongdoing. In these pages, we explain how we have documented a pattern of behavior based on first-person accounts, financial and legal records, company memos, and other revealing materials. In the wake of our work, there was little public debate about what Weinstein had done to women; it was about what should be done in response. But Weinstein has continued to deny all allegations of non-consensual sex, and has repeatedly asserted that our reporting is incorrect. "What you have here are allegations and accusations, but you do not have absolute facts," a spokesman said when we asked for a response to the revelations presented here.

This book toggles between what we learned during the course of our original work on Weinstein in 2017 and the substantial amount of information we've gathered since. Much of the new reporting we present about Weinstein helps illustrate how the legal system and corporate culture has served to silence victims and still inhibits change. Businesses are co-opted into protecting predators. Some advocates for women profit from a settlement system that covers up misdeeds. Many people who glimpse the problem—like Bob Weinstein, Harvey's brother and business partner, who granted extensive interviews for this book—do little to try and stop it.

As we write this, in May 2019, Weinstein awaits a criminal trial for alleged rape and other sexual abuse and faces a volley of civil suits, in which actresses, former employees, and others are seeking to hold him financially accountable. No matter the outcome of those cases, we hope this book will serve as a lasting record of Weinstein's legacy: his exploitation of the workplace to manipulate, pressure, and terrorize women.

In the months after we broke the Weinstein story, as the #MeToo movement exploded, so did new debates about topics ranging from date rape to child sexual abuse to gender discrimination and even to awkward encounters at parties. This made the public conversation feel rich and searching, but also confusing: Were the goals to eliminate sexual harassment, reform the criminal justice system, smash the patriarchy, or flirt without giving offense? Had the reckoning gone too far, with innocent men tarnished with less-than-convincing proof, or not far enough, with a frustrating lack of systemic change?

Nearly a year to the day after our Weinstein story was published, Dr. Christine Blasey Ford, a psychology professor from California, appeared before a U.S. Senate committee and accused Judge Brett Kavanaugh, then nominated to the Supreme Court, of sexually assaulting her while drunk in high school. He furiously denied the allegation. Some saw Ford as the ultimate hero of the #MeToo movement. Others saw her as a symbol of overreach—a living justification for the mounting backlash.

We saw her as the protagonist of one of the most complex and revealing "she said" stories yet, especially once we began to learn how much about her path to that Senate testimony was not publicly understood. Jodi watched from the hearing room, observed some of her legal team as they worked, and met her the next morning. In December, Megan conducted the first post-hearing interview of Ford, over a breakfast in Palo Alto. In the following months, she had dozens of hours of additional interviews with Ford about how she came to raise her voice and what the consequences were. We also spoke with others who shaped and witnessed her experience. We tell the story of Ford's journey to Washington and how an overwhelming array of viewpoints, institutions, political forces, and fears all came to bear on her.

Many people wonder how Ford has fared since her testimony. The final chapter of this book consists of a unique group interview, in which we brought together some of the women we reported on, including Ford, across these different stories. But something larger is at stake in Ford's odyssey too: that continued question of what drives and impedes progress. The #MeToo movement is an example of social change in our time but is also a test of it: In this fractured environment, will all of us be able to forge a new set of mutually fair rules and protections?

This book recounts two astounding years in the life of women in the United States and beyond. That history belongs to all of us who lived it: Unlike some journalistic investigations that deal with locked-away government or corporate secrets, this one is about experiences many of us recognize from our own lives, workplaces, families, and schools. But we wrote this book to bring you as close as we could to ground zero.

To relate those events as directly and authentically as possible, we have incorporated transcripts of interviews, emails, and other primary documents. There are notes from the first conversations we had with movie stars about Weinstein, a searching letter that Bob Weinstein wrote to his brother, excerpts from Ford's texts, and many other firsthand materials. Some of what we share was originally off the record, but through additional reporting, including returning to the parties involved, we were able to include it here. We were able to depict conversations and events that we did not witness firsthand through records and interviews. All told, this book is based on three years of reporting and hundreds of interviews conducted from London to Palo Alto; the endnotes give a detailed accounting of which information we learned from which sources and records.

Finally, this book is a chronicle of the partnership we developed as we worked to understand these events. To avoid confusion, we write about ourselves in the third person. (In a first-person account of our reporting, which was collaborative but often involved us following separate threads, "I" could be either Jodi or Megan.) So before we slip into that way of telling the story, we want to say, in our own voices: Thank you for joining our partnership for the duration of these pages, for puzzling through these events and clues as we have, for witnessing what we witnessed, and hearing what we heard.

CHAPTER ONE

THE FIRST PHONE CALL

The *New York Times* investigation into Harvey Weinstein began with the most promising source refusing even to get on the phone.

"Here's the thing, I have been treated quite shabbily by your paper at times and I believe the root of it is sexism," the actress Rose McGowan wrote on May 11, 2017, responding to an email from Jodi asking to talk. McGowan listed her criticisms: a speech she had made at a political dinner was covered in the Style section instead of the news pages. An earlier conversation she'd had with a *Times* reporter about Weinstein had been uncomfortable.

"The NYT needs to look at itself for sexism issues," she responded. "I'm not that inclined to help."

Months earlier, McGowan had accused an unnamed producer—rumored to be Weinstein—of having raped her. "Because it's been an open secret in Hollywood/Media & they shamed me while adulating my rapist," she had tweeted, adding the hashtag #WhyWomenDontReport. Now she was said to be writing a memoir intended to expose the entertainment industry's mistreatment of women.

Unlike almost anyone else in Hollywood, McGowan had a history of risking her own career prospects to call out sexism, once tweeting out the insulting clothing requirements on a casting notice for an Adam Sandler movie: "tank that shows off cleavage (push up bras encouraged)." In general, her tone on social media was tough, confrontational: "It is okay to be angry. Don't be afraid of it," she had tweeted a month earlier, later adding: "dismantle the system." If McGowan, as much an activist as an actress, would not have one off-the-record conversation, who would?

Harvey Weinstein was not the man of the moment. In recent years, his moviemaking magic had faltered. But his name was synonymous with power, specifically the power to make and boost careers. First he had invented himself, going from a modest upbringing in Queens, New York, to concert promotion to film distribution and production, and he seemed to know how to make everything around him bigger—films, parties, and most of all, people. Over and over, he had propelled young actors to stardom: Gwyneth Paltrow, Matt Damon, Michelle Williams, and Jennifer Lawrence. He could turn tiny independent movies like *Sex, Lies, and Videotape* or *The Crying Game* into phenomena. He had pioneered the modern Oscar campaign, winning five Best Picture statues for himself and armloads for others. His record of raising money for Hillary Clinton, and flanking her at countless fund-raisers, was almost two decades long. When Malia Obama had sought an internship in film, she worked for "Harvey"—first name only, used even by many strangers. By 2017, even though his movies were less successful than they used to be, his reputation remained outsized.

Rumors had long circulated about his treatment of women. People had joked about them publicly: "Congratulations, you five ladies no longer have to pretend to be attracted to Harvey Weinstein," the comedian Seth MacFarlane said at the Oscar nomination announcements in 2013. But many people had dismissed the behavior as philandering, and nothing had ever been publicly documented. Other journalists had tried and failed in the past. A 2015 investigation by the City of New York Police Department (NYPD) into a groping accusation against Weinstein had ended without any criminal charges. "At some pt, all the women who've been afraid to speak out abt Harvey Weinstein are gonna have to hold hands and jump," Jennifer Senior, a journalist, had tweeted back then. Two years had passed. Nothing had happened. Jodi had heard that two more reporters, a writer at *New York Magazine* and NBC's Ronan Farrow, had tried, but no stories had appeared.

Were the whispers about Weinstein's interactions with women wrong? Had McGowan's tweet referred to someone else? In public, Weinstein boasted of feminist credentials. He had just given a large donation to help endow a professorship in Gloria Steinem's name. His company had distributed *The Hunting Ground,* a documentary and rallying cry about campus sexual assault. He had even participated in the historic women's marches of January 2017, joining the pink pussyhat throngs in Park City, Utah, during the Sundance Film Festival.

The point of the *Times* investigations department, tucked away from the hum of the rest of the newsroom, was to dig for what had never been reported, bringing to account people and institutions whose transgressions had been deliberately concealed. The first step was often careful outreach. So how to reply to McGowan so as to motivate her to pick up the phone?

Her email had openings. First, she had written back. Lots of people never did. She had put thought into her note and cared enough to offer a critique. Maybe she was testing Jodi, jabbing at the *Times* to see if the reporter would defend it.

But Jodi wasn't looking to have an argument about her own workplace of fourteen years. Flattering McGowan ("I really admire the bravery of your tweets . . .") also was not the way to go. That would sap what little authority Jodi had in the interaction. And there was nothing to be said about the investigation to which McGowan would be contributing: If she asked how many other women Jodi had spoken to, the answer would be none.

The note would need to be phrased just so, with no mention of Weinstein's name: McGowan had a history of posting private communications on Twitter, like the Adam Sandler casting notice. She was someone who wanted to blow things open, but that impulse could backfire in this situation. ("Hey, world, check out this email from a *Times* reporter.") The subject matter made the response even trickier. McGowan had said she was an assault victim. Pressuring her would not be right.

In 2013, Jodi had started investigating women's experiences at corporations and other institutions. The gender debate in the United States already seemed saturated with feeling: opinion columns, memoirs, expressions of outrage or sisterhood on social media. It needed more exposure of hidden facts. Especially about the workplace. Workers, from the most elite to the lowliest, were often afraid to question their employers. Reporters were not. In doing those stories, Jodi had found that gender was not just a topic, but a kind of investigative entry point. Because women were still outsiders at many organizations, documenting what they experienced meant seeing how power functioned.

She wrote back to Rose McGowan, calling on those experiences:

> Here's my own track record on these issues: Amazon, Starbucks, and Harvard Business School have all changed their policies in response to gender-related problems I exposed. When I wrote about the class gap in breastfeeding—white collar women can pump on the job, lower paid women cannot—readers responded by creating the first-ever mobile lactation suites, now available in 200+ locations across the country.
>
> If you'd rather not speak, I understand, and best of luck with your book publication.
>
> Thank you, Jodi

McGowan wrote back within a few hours. She could talk any time before Wednesday.

The call seemed like it could be tricky: McGowan appeared tough, with a buzz cut and that call-to-arms Twitter feed. But the voice on the phone belonged to someone impassioned and game, who had a story and was searching for the right way to tell it. Her tweets about being raped had just been hints, with few details. Generally, the rule in interviews was that they were on the record—meaning the material could be published—unless otherwise discussed. But any woman with an assault complaint against Weinstein would probably be reluctant to have even an initial conversation. So Jodi agreed that the call would be kept private until they decided otherwise, and McGowan started in.

In 1997, she had been young and newly triumphant, on a heady trip to the Sundance Film Festival, where she alternated between premieres and parties and a TV camera crew followed her around. She had only been in four or five films, like the teen-horror flick *Scream*, but she was becoming one of the ingenues of the moment, with multiple new movies at the festival alone. "I was the belle of Sundance," she said. Independent films were at the center of the culture, the festival was the place to be, and Harvey Weinstein was sovereign: That was where the producer-distributor had bought small films like *Clerks* and *Reservoir Dogs*, which he had turned into cultural touchstones. In her telling, McGowan didn't remember which year this was; many actresses chronicled the past not according to date but instead to which movie of theirs was filming or being released at the time. McGowan recalled the screening where she had sat right near Weinstein: The movie was called *Going All the Way*, she said with an incredulous laugh.

Afterward, he had asked for a meeting with her, which made sense: The top producer wanted to get together with the rising star. She went to see him at the Stein Eriksen Lodge Deer Valley, in Park City, where they met in his room. Nothing happened except the usual talk about films and roles, she said.

But on the way out, Weinstein pulled her into a room with a hot tub, stripped her on the edge, and forced his face between her legs, according to McGowan. She said she remembered feeling like she was leaving her body, floating up to the ceiling and observing the scene from above. "I was just feeling massive shock, I was going into survival mode," she said. To get away, McGowan said, she faked an orgasm and mentally gave herself step-by-step instructions: "Turn the door handle." "Walk out of this meeting."

Within a few days, she said, Weinstein had left a message on her home phone in Los Angeles with a creepy offer: Other big female stars were his special friends, and she could join his club as well. Shocked and distraught, McGowan had complained to her managers, hired a lawyer, and ended up with a $100,000 settlement from Weinstein—essentially, a payment to make the matter go away, without any admission of wrongdoing on his part—which she said she had donated to a rape crisis center.

Did she have her records from the settlement? "They never gave me a copy," she said.

The problem was worse than Weinstein, she said. Hollywood was an organized system for abusing women. It lured them with promises of fame, turned them into highly profitable products, treated their bodies as property, required them to look perfect, and then discarded them. On the call, her indictments came fast, one after another:

"Weinstein—it's not just him, it's an entire machine, supply chain."

"No oversight, no fear."

"Each studio does the victim shaming and payouts."

"Almost everyone has an NDA."

"If white men could have a playground, this would be it."

"The women here are just as guilty."

"Don't step out of line; you can be replaced."

McGowan's words were arresting. It wasn't new to say that Hollywood took advantage of women, forced them into conformity, and dumped them when they aged or rebelled. But hearing a direct account of exploitation from a familiar face, in full disturbing detail, and with one of the most renowned producers in Hollywood as the perpetrator, was entirely different: sharper, more specific, sickening.

The call ended with an agreement to talk again soon. The actress was an unusual character, but the sometimes outrageous things she had done or said or whom she had dated didn't matter for these purposes. The question was how her account would stand up to the rigors of the journalistic process, and, if it got that far, the inevitable challenge by Weinstein, and then public scrutiny. Before the *Times* would even consider publishing McGowan's allegations, they would need to be buttressed, and, finally, taken to Weinstein. He would have to be given an opportunity to respond.

The paper had a duty to be fair, especially given the gravity of the charges. In 2014, *Rolling Stone* magazine described what it called a horrific group sexual assault at the University of Virginia without anything close to sufficient evidence. The ensuing controversy set off a series of lawsuits, almost ruined the magazine's reputation, gave ammunition to those who said women fabricated rape stories, and set back the cause of fighting campus sexual assault. The *Washington Post* reported that police had called the story "a complete crock," the *Columbia Journalism Review* called it "a mess," and the article won an "Error of the Year" award.

On first inspection, McGowan's account seemed vulnerable to challenge by Weinstein. He would easily be able to say that he remembered things differently, that she had appeared to enjoy herself. He would have the perfect evidence: her faked orgasm. The old answering machine tape was potentially significant, showing that Weinstein was using his power as a producer to compel sexual favors. But unless McGowan had the tape from two decades ago, it was just a memory of a long-ago message, also easy to deny.

As a sole account, McGowan's story had a high likelihood of becoming a classic "he said, she said" dispute. McGowan would tell a terrible story. Weinstein would deny it. With no witnesses, people would take sides, Team Rose versus Team Harvey.

But McGowan said she had gotten a settlement. Finding any record of it would be difficult, but there had been lawyers, a signed agreement, money that changed hands, the donation to the rape crisis center. The agreement had to be documented somewhere. It wouldn't prove what had happened in the hotel room, but it could add support by showing that Weinstein had paid McGowan a significant sum at the time to settle a dispute.

Jodi brought everything she had learned to her longtime editor at the *Times*, Rebecca Corbett, who was an expert in complex investigations. They discussed whether McGowan's account could be backed up, and the important question: Did other women have similar stories about him?

Finding that out would require huge effort. Weinstein had produced or distributed hundreds of movies over the decades. With his brother, Bob, he had co-owned and run two companies: Miramax and The Weinstein Company (TWC), his current endeavor. That meant there were a lot of potential sources, a better situation than when critical information was held by just a few people. But there were an overwhelming number of people to contact, actresses and former employees scattered across several continents, most of whom would probably be reluctant to talk.

In mid-June Corbett suggested that Jodi contact a colleague, Megan Twohey, who was relatively new at the paper. Megan was on maternity leave, but she had a real touch with this kind of work, the editor said. Jodi didn't know what help she would be, but she sent off an email anyway.

When Megan got Jodi's email, she was caring for her newborn child and recovering from the most bruising reporting stretch of her career. She had arrived at the *Times* in February 2016 to cover politics, investigating the presidential candidates. Megan had said yes to the job with some hesitation: Politics had never been her assignment or interest.

But within weeks of her arrival, Dean Baquet, the executive editor of the paper, had tapped Megan for a specific line of inquiry that drew on her reporting expertise: Had Donald J. Trump's behavior toward women ever crossed legal or ethical lines? For more than a decade, Megan had been uncovering sex crimes and sexual misconduct. In Chicago, she had revealed how police and prosecutors in the area were shelving rape kits, robbing victims of the chance for justice, and how sex-abusing doctors had continued to practice. Later, she had exposed a black market for adopted children that had delivered some of them to sexual predators.

Trump had long fashioned himself a playboy, or at least a caricature of one. He was on his third wife and had entered the presidential race with a trail of Howard Stern interviews in which he bragged about his sexual exploits and engaged in crude commentary about women, including his own daughter Ivanka.

Baquet saw some red flags beneath the bravado. If Donald Trump had simply been promiscuous, that was not a story—the paper didn't peer into people's sex lives, even those of presidential candidates, without a reason. But some of Trump's comments had been made in the workplace, a possible sign of sexual harassment. On *The Celebrity Apprentice*, a show that he helped produce and starred in, Trump had told a contestant, "That must be a pretty picture, you dropping to your knees." Decades earlier, Trump's first wife, Ivana Trump, had reportedly accused him of marital rape, then minimized the allegation. Baquet had already enlisted another reporter, Michael Barbaro, to investigate Trump's treatment of women, and he wanted him and Megan to answer the question of whether Trump was just crude in his behavior toward women or if the problem was more extensive.

Initially, the reporting was slow: Most of Trump's former employees were bound by nondisclosure agreements, his history of being vindictive toward those who crossed him had left a chilling effect, and so many lawsuits had been filed against him over the years that it was hard to know which to examine.

By May 2016, however, Megan and Barbaro were prepared to write an article, based on hundreds of records and more than fifty interviews with people who had worked with or for Trump, dated him, or socialized with him. Trump was a powerful man who had engaged in contradictory behavior toward women. He could be gracious and encouraging to women he worked with, and he had promoted several to the top positions in his company. But he also had a habit of unending commentary about women's bodies and unsettling workplace conduct.

Most significantly, Megan had pieced together multiple allegations of sexual aggression beyond the Ivana rape allegation. A former Miss Utah had explained in detail how, in 1997, Trump had forcibly kissed her on her mouth twice, at a gala after the Miss USA pageant and later at a meeting at his office to discuss a possible modeling career. In two old lawsuits, a former Trump beauty pageant business partner claimed that Trump had groped her under the table during a work dinner at the Plaza Hotel and had taken her into a room at another work gathering and forcibly "kissed, fondled, and restrained" her from leaving.

Caution was essential. If a single allegation in a story turned out to be shaky, it could undermine the entire article. When a former pageant contestant told Megan that Trump had groped her at his Palm Beach mansion, prompting her to flee to her room and place a panicked call to her father, a colleague tracked the man down in another country. "Got the father," the colleague reported back in an email. "In short—he has no memory of this having happened with Trump." That didn't mean the woman had been lying. But it did mean that they couldn't use her allegation in the story.

The article—in which many women's accounts were told in their own words—was published at dawn (ET) on Saturday, May 14, 2016, and it quickly exploded, eventually becoming the most-read *Times* political article thus far that year. That Trump, known for viciously attacking critical stories about him, said nothing about the article all weekend was seen as a sign of its strength. Before publication, Megan and Barbaro had conducted a lengthy interview of the candidate and woven in his responses, including his denials of any misconduct and his insistence that he had always treated women with respect.

On Monday morning, they were in the green room of the *CBS This Morning* news show, preparing to be interviewed about the article, when Gayle King walked in and pointed to the TV: "Did you see, Rowanne Brewer Lane just went on *Fox and Friends* to dispute your story?"

Brewer Lane was the first person quoted in the article. A former model who had met Trump at a pool party at Mar-a-Lago in 1990, she had described in an interview how Trump had focused in on her, led her into a room, encouraged her to put on a swimsuit, and then showed her off to the guests. Brewer Lane wasn't disputing her quotes about the interaction. She disagreed with the way it was characterized: as "a debasing face-to-face encounter between Trump and a young woman he hardly knew."

The account made up a handful of paragraphs in a five-thousand-word story, one that had pointed out that Brewer Lane went on to date Trump. But her public criticism provided Trump with a toehold to attack the entire article. He immediately seized on her comments and started punching back in a series of tweets:

> The @nytimes is so dishonest. Their hit piece cover story on me yesterday was just blown up by Rowanne Brewer, who said it was a lie!

With the coming forward today of the woman central to the
failing @nytimes hit piece on me, we have exposed the article as
a fraud!

Soon his supporters were coming out swinging too, taking direct shots
at Megan and Barbaro on social media, in emails, in angry phone calls. The
article had carefully documented the serious allegations of sexual misconduct against Trump. But because of criticism of a far less grave anecdote,
Megan and Barbaro were on the defensive.

The staff of Bill O'Reilly, the bombastic king of right-wing news, called
Megan over and over, asking, "Are you a feminist?," as if that would discredit
her. Suspicious of their motivations, she refused their interview requests,
then watched as the host took to the airwaves to tell millions of viewers not
to trust her work. "The problem is, Megan Twohey is a feminist, or so it
seems," he said. His argument was absurd—as the *Washington Post* asked,
should a chauvinist report the story?—but he used the full force of his influence to blunt the impact of the findings and to try to discredit her.

Those public attacks were unlike anything Megan had ever experienced.
She was grateful when June 2016 arrived, and a previously scheduled
commitment, her own wedding, took her out of the newsroom.

But did other women have allegations of forcible kissing, groping, or
worse? When Megan returned from her honeymoon, she kept reporting
on Trump.

Several months later, on Friday, October 7, Megan was on the phone
with a source when colleagues started rising from their seats and flocking
to TVs throughout the newsroom. The *Washington Post* had obtained a
snippet of an audiotape from the gossip show *Access Hollywood* from 2005, in
which Trump bragged about his aggression toward women.

*I'm automatically attracted to beautiful—I just start kissing them. . . . I
don't even wait. And when you're a star, they let you do it. You can do
anything . . . Grab 'em by the pussy. You can do anything.*

His words were like nothing ever publicly heard from a presidential candidate. This sounded like confirmation of the behavior that Megan had spent months piecing together.

Trump apologized for his words, then doubled down on his denials. The comments on the *Access Hollywood* tape were just locker room talk, he insisted. Two days later, during an October 9 presidential debate, he denied that he had ever kissed women without their permission or grabbed intimate parts of their bodies. Yes, he had boasted about it. But had he ever actually done those things? "No, I have not," the candidate said.

Within a week, Megan and Barbaro had a new article almost ready, with two other women saying that Trump's words on the audio recording matched their experiences. Both Jessica Leeds, a seventy-four-year-old former stockbroker and great-grandmother who lived in a tidy one-bedroom on the Upper East Side of Manhattan, and Rachel Crooks, a thirty-three-year-old PhD candidate in higher education administration from Green Springs, Ohio, had written emails to the *Times* outlining their allegations.

Leeds had been traveling as a sales representative for a newsprint company in the early 1980s when she had lucked into a first-class upgrade on a flight from Dallas to New York City. In the next seat happened to be Donald Trump, tall, blond, and chatty. Forty-five minutes after takeoff, Leeds alleged, he leaned over, grabbed her breasts, and tried to put his hand up her skirt.

"He was all over me, hands everywhere," she wrote in her email, explaining that she had fled to a seat in coach.

Crooks was the daughter of a nurse and a mechanic who didn't talk politics but identified as Republican. In high school, she had been all-state in basketball, track, and volleyball and voted Most Likely to Succeed. In 2005, she had wanted to experience New York for herself. She and her boyfriend rented a cheap apartment on the outskirts of Brooklyn, sleeping on an air mattress until they had enough money for a futon. To make rent, she took a secretarial job at a real-estate development firm on the twenty-fourth floor of Trump Tower that worked on deals with The Trump Organization. *The Apprentice* had gone on the air the year before, the most popular new show of the season.

One day that winter, when she saw Donald Trump waiting for an elevator outside her office, she rose from her desk to introduce herself, offering him a businesslike handshake. He didn't let go, she said. He kissed her on the cheeks. Then he went for her lips and pressed hard. The whole thing lasted only a minute or two. She was twenty-two. Before that, the only man who had ever kissed her was the boyfriend she lived with.

"I was angry that Mr. Trump had viewed me as so insignificant that he could impose himself on me in such a way," she wrote.

Crooks was describing a forced kiss almost exactly like those allegedly planted on the former Miss Utah. Leeds was describing groping similar to the kind endured by the former beauty pageant business partner. And it all matched the behavior that Trump had been recorded boasting about. On the phone, both Leeds and Crooks had told Megan they were prepared to go on the record. Neither woman was inclined to draw attention to herself. But they wanted the world to know that Trump was lying.

Mindful of the stakes, Megan and Barbaro checked and double-checked with friends and family members in whom the women had confided. They scrubbed the two women's backgrounds to make sure there were no ties to Hillary Clinton's campaign. Megan even asked Crooks to send her an old picture of her at her desk in Trump Tower, to confirm that she worked there. The due diligence could have seemed insulting to the women. But it was to protect them, and the *Times*.

The final step was to run the allegations by Trump's team. As the sun went down, Megan sat at her dining table glued to her email, expecting a perfunctory denial from a Trump spokesperson. Instead her cell phone rang.

Trump was on the line.

Megan had barely begun her questions before he started lashing out. Jessica Leeds and Rachel Crooks were lying. He had no idea who they were. If he had done those things to them, why didn't they complain to the police?

Megan explained that the women did not claim to have known him but only to have had chance encounters with him. She reminded him of the allegations by the former Miss Utah and of his onetime beauty pageant business partner.

Seething, Trump switched aim. The *New York Times* had concocted the women's accounts. If it published the story, he would sue.

Megan pressed forward, determined to keep him talking. What about the recently leaked *Access Hollywood* tape? She asked him again if he had ever done the things he had bragged about.

"I don't do it," he insisted, his voice rising. "I don't do it. It was locker-room talk."

He began to erupt at Megan. "You are disgusting!" Trump shouted. "You are a disgusting human being."

When the line went dead, Megan relaxed. As brutal as the conversation had been, she had provided Trump with adequate opportunity to respond to the allegations. They could move forward with publishing the article, complete with his comments.

Minutes later, Trump stepped onstage in Florida for a campaign rally, and he set to work directing his crowd's thundering energy and anger toward journalists.

"The corrupt media is teamed up against you, the American people," he said. "And I'll tell you what, it's libelous, it's slanderous, it's horrible, and it's really unfair. But we're going to beat the system."

It was less than four weeks until Election Day. The Republican Speaker of the House said he was sickened by the *Access Hollywood* tape. Senator John McCain withdrew his endorsement. Governor Mike Pence, the vice-presidential nominee, said that he was praying for the Trump family. Some Republicans were saying he should drop out of the race.

Other women stepped forward to level accusations against Trump. One had been out with friends at a nightclub. Another was a former contestant on *The Apprentice*. A third was a reporter assigned to write a valentine of a story on Trump's first wedding anniversary with Melania, his third wife. Some of their stories were essentially the same as those Megan had reported. Trump had allegedly grabbed, groped, or fondled them, pushed them up against walls and thrust his hips or genitals at them. Who could ignore or dismiss the pattern of predatory behavior now?

But journalists were not able to vet all of the allegations. An explosive civil lawsuit alleged that he had raped a thirteen-year-old girl two decades before, at a party hosted by a well-known financier named Jeffrey Epstein who was later investigated for running an underage-sex ring for powerful men and convicted of soliciting a prostitute. But the alleged victim of Trump, referred to only as Jane Doe, had never been identified or made available to reporters, even confidentially. Without a woman whose existence could be confirmed and whose story could be vetted, Megan had refused to cover the case and discouraged her colleagues from touching it either.

Other claims drew attention but did not feel newsworthy. Megan watched as a woman tearfully recounted in a televised press conference an incident that sounded like Trump had accidentally brushed his hand against her breast and heckled her as she waited for a ride.

As the carefully reported allegations of Crooks and Leeds swirled together with the other accusations, Trump moved from firm denials to sweeping attacks. His accusers were liars. Out for fame. Working for Hillary Clinton. Too ugly and unappealing to have drawn his attention. He would sue them.

His supporters listened to his cues and once again sprang into action. Fox Business anchor Lou Dobbs shared with his nearly one million Twitter followers a link to a post from a conservative news site that listed Jessica Leeds's phone number and address, along with the false claim that she worked for the Clinton Foundation.

Leeds did not scare easily; Rachel Crooks, on the other hand, was extremely rattled. She couldn't go outside because of the reporters who swarmed her lawn in Ohio. She couldn't go online either, because of the Trump trolls and their barrage of messages: *You're so ugly. You're getting paid off. Someone should put a gun to your head and do this country a favor.* A stranger posted a message on Facebook identifying herself as a family friend and claimed to know that Crooks was lying about Trump. The post became the top hit for any search of Crooks's name. Another man that Crooks had never heard of accused her of stealing from a company she had never worked for.

With every attack, Megan felt worse. She had encouraged the two women to go on the record, telling them it was a public service to share vital information about a presidential candidate. She was the one who had painted intimate details of their lives onto a giant wall, big enough for the whole country to read. Now they were under siege. Crooks, her voice shaking over the phone, had asked what the *Times* would do if Trump followed through with his threat to sue her. The answer was very little. Thousands of people were quoted in the *Times* every week: As with other publications, the paper could not assume legal responsibility for them.

Megan was being attacked too. Threats from Trump supporters arrived through both her phone and computer. She alerted *Times* security after repeatedly receiving anonymous messages from a man who said he was going to rape and murder her and dump her body in the Hudson River. She was pregnant, more visibly so each day, and worried strangers would start tweeting threats about the baby or do even worse.

Trump himself was threatening to sue. His lawyer sent a letter to Baquet, which the Trump team then made public, instructing him to retract Leeds's and Crooks's accounts. "Failure to do so will leave my client with no option but to pursue all available actions and remedies," he wrote.

David McCraw, vice president and assistant general counsel of the *New York Times*, beloved in the newsroom for his unflappability and protection of journalists, replied with equal force.

"It would have been a disservice not just to our readers but to democracy itself to silence their voices," the lawyer wrote.

He all but dared Trump to sue the *Times*. "If he believes that American citizens had no right to hear what these women had to say and that the law of this country forces us and those who would dare criticize him to stand silent or be punished, we welcome an opportunity to have a court set him straight."

It was a rousing defense, not just of journalism but of the rights of women to make allegations against powerful men. When the *Times* published the letter on its website, it went immediately viral.

But inside the newsroom, Megan was afraid Trump would follow through with a lawsuit against her, Barbaro, and the paper, as McCraw suspected he would if he wasn't elected. Trump would ultimately lose in court, but it would be a long, arduous legal process. Megan had begun preserving all of her notes, emails, and text messages, in case of future legal discovery.

On November 7, three and a half weeks later, Megan flew to Illinois to observe what many people thought would be the election of the first female president of the United States. For the sake of symbolism, Megan's editors had asked her to help capture the moment at polling places in Park Ridge, a suburb of Chicago and Hillary Clinton's hometown.

Megan wasn't advocating for Clinton, or for any other candidate. That's not what reporters did. A few weeks before, in an article that had drawn fire from the Democratic nominee's supporters, Megan had highlighted the role that Hillary Clinton had played in battling women who alleged sexual impropriety and worse by Bill Clinton. Her allies insisted the role was minimal, but Megan found evidence that she had signed off on hiring a private detective to dig up dirt to smear the women.

As she stood talking to voters, she knew they would make their decisions based on many factors, beyond the sexual misconduct allegations against Trump. But Megan did expect to encounter concern about them. Using hashtags like #WhyWomenDontReport, in the weeks leading up to the election, a chorus of women had begun speaking up online about other men who had done similar things to them. Rose McGowan, with her tweets about the studio head who had violated her, was among them.

But in interview after interview at the polling place, it became clear that very few of the suburban white women appeared to care much about Trump's alleged trespasses or his own words on the *Access Hollywood* tape. That night Megan hardly needed to look at the television: She already knew Trump had been elected.

That April following the election, Megan and Jodi each watched, with astonishment, a series of developments that would lead directly to the beginning of the Weinstein investigation. Bill O'Reilly, the right-wing television host at the peak of his power, lost his position at the Fox News Network after the *Times* exposed how he and the company had covered up repeated allegations of sexual harassment. The article, by Emily Steel and Michael Schmidt, had taken eight months to report, and it proved that O'Reilly had racked up settlements with at least five women who had accused him of verbal abuse, lewd remarks, and unwanted come-ons. O'Reilly and Fox News had handed over what then looked like a total of $13 million to silence the women: an enormous secret payout from one of America's top critics of feminism.

In that story, only a single woman had spoken on the record about her allegations: Wendy Walsh, a former guest who lost a lucrative offer to be an O'Reilly contributor after she declined an invitation back to his hotel suite. Most of the women in the story were barred from speaking because they had settled with O'Reilly or the network. They had accepted large sums of money in exchange for agreeing never to talk about what had happened.

But Steel and Schmidt had realized something important: Transactions that complex can never be truly secret. The agreements involved lawyers, negotiations, and money, and others inevitably found out too—colleagues, agents, family members, and friends. Together the payments formed a legal and financial trail that told the story of the allegations against O'Reilly. The settlements didn't prevent the story; they *were* the story, a tale of cover-up that illuminated the alleged wrongdoing. This was a new way of reporting on sexual harassment.

Within days, advertisers like Mercedes-Benz and Allstate dropped O'Reilly's show. Most important, other women at Fox started lodging complaints about the host's behavior. On April 19, not even three weeks after the publication of the *Times* story, he was fired. Both he and Roger Ailes, the Republican power broker and architect of the network, had lost their jobs, not due to claims of mistreating women—Fox had known about many of those—but rather because of public exposure of those claims. That it had happened a second time made the story more astounding: It was like a momentary reversal in the physics of power.

Times editors quickly took the measure of the moment. Women seemed increasingly fed up. Just as had been the case after Trump's "grab-'em-by-the-pussy" comments, women vented their frustration at the revelations about O'Reilly. Convincing women to go on the record on matters like these was never simple, but this could be a rare window of opportunity for candor.

The O'Reilly story offered a playbook. Almost no one ever came forward completely on their own. But if patterns of bad behavior could be revealed, there might be a way to tell more of these stories. The editors put together a team of reporters to look at a range of industries: Silicon Valley and the tech industry, a utopian field, supposedly unbound by old rules, which nonetheless excluded women. Academia also seemed ripe for investigation because of the power that professors held over graduate students who wanted careers in the same fields. The journalists also planned to focus on low-income workers who had low visibility, overwhelming economic pressure, and less recourse than women higher on the economic ladder.

A few days after O'Reilly was fired, Rebecca Corbett asked Jodi to pursue the answers to two questions. The first was, Were there other powerful men in American life covering up abusive behavior toward women? Jodi had quietly made some calls for advice, and Shaunna Thomas, a feminist activist, had suggested that Jodi look to Hollywood, Rose McGowan's upcoming book, and Harvey Weinstein. But Corbett also gave Jodi a second assignment: to go beyond individual wrongdoers and pin down the elements, the system, that kept sexual harassment so pervasive and hard to address. How common were these settlements, which seemed to pop up in every story, and how had they masked the problem?

When Jodi phoned for advice, Megan still did not know what stories she would pursue once she returned from leave. But they discussed what had motivated women like Jessica Leeds and Rachel Crooks to come forward and how the O'Reilly article had become proof that the *Times* knew how to execute a project this delicate without a hitch. They analyzed what to say in the very first seconds of a phone call with a stranger who might be a victim, and Megan suggested a few new approaches, including one she had used when getting rape victims in Chicago to share their experiences: "I can't change what happened to you in the past, but together we may be able to use your experience to help protect other people."

That sentence clicked like nothing else had. It did not overpromise or suck up. It suggested compelling reasons to risk talking about a painful, messy subject. It was what Jodi had been trying to say to McGowan in that initial email: We mean business.

The pitch was about helping other people. This was always the truest, best reason to talk to a journalist, and one of the only potent answers to "I don't want the attention" or "I don't need the stress."

After that phone call, Jodi had a question for Corbett: How soon would Megan be back from maternity leave?

CHAPTER TWO

HOLLYWOOD SECRETS

Megan's advice was valuable, but as the Weinstein investigation continued in June 2017, the daunting question was how to even get top actresses on the phone. The vocation of these women demanded they keep up appearances, and they lived in a way intended to limit public scrutiny. The typical procedure to reach these stars was to call their publicists. But that was out of the question, as was contacting agents and managers. Those people were paid to build and maintain barriers and were often loyal to power brokers like Weinstein. Besides, the questions were private, too awkward to share with paid intermediaries. Jodi's only hope was to connect directly with actresses. But she wasn't sure she knew a single one: It was a world in which she had virtually no sources or connections.

Jodi clicked through red carpet photos from the recent Cannes Film Festival in France. As usual, there were few shots of men. Nicole Kidman, Jessica Chastain, Salma Hayek, Charlize Theron, and Marion Cotillard posed for the cameras; Uma Thurman stood in a glittering gold skirt at a charity event annually championed by Weinstein, a black-tie party and auction for the American Foundation for AIDS Research, or amfAR. Was it possible that any of them had been Weinstein victims? What did they know about the experiences of others? The women looked flawless, serene, and hopelessly out of reach.

She began seeking private email addresses and phone numbers for women who had appeared in Weinstein's films—especially Ashley Judd, who had given an interview to *Variety* in 2015, in which she had described being sexually harassed by a producer. Some of the searches for contact information practically turned into full investigations themselves: calls to relatives who were listed in public phone records; searches for go-betweens who might make introductions.

The few times Jodi got actresses on the phone, the conversations were mostly short and unproductive. Then came a tip from well-connected friend: call the actress Judith Godrèche. She's a household name in France and has said privately that Weinstein victimized her. Plus she's outspoken by nature. Jodi emailed Godrèche. No reply. She tried again and got a note back. "I am so sorry, my lawyer doesn't want me to be involved," Godrèche wrote. A frustrating response, but also a clue: involved in *what?*

Contacting Weinstein's former employees was a little more fruitful. They were certainly more reachable, on LinkedIn or at their office numbers or homes. Their responses fell into conflicting categories. Many sounded unsurprised to hear from a reporter but still refused to speak. Others were willing to provide bits and pieces: old suspicions that had lingered across the years; guidance on which Hollywood stars to try to reach.

Some of the former employees gave lectures: Harvey Weinstein's sex life was his private business. The "casting couch," or the practice of actresses submitting to producers and directors in exchange for roles, was as old as Hollywood itself, an unpleasant but permanent part of the business, they said. (As if to underscore their point, there was an actual casting couch sculpture in Los Angeles, near the famous old Chinese theaters where movie premieres were often held.) Several used the same phrase to describe how Weinstein had treated actresses: "Oh, he may have chased her around a couch," they said of this or that woman as if they were describing a pantomime. Those former employees spoke to Jodi as if she were a naïve idealist. Weinstein's treatment of women had been an open secret for years, they said. Jodi would never get the story, and even if she did, no one would care.

On Friday, June 30, Jodi walked into a tiny West Hollywood restaurant to meet with the actress Marisa Tomei. A former Miramax employee had said Weinstein harassed Tomei, upsetting her so much that she had cried at work. Jodi had tracked down Tomei through a playwright, and now she was sitting at the other end of the restaurant table.

The tip was wrong. Tomei wasn't a Weinstein victim. But she had decades' worth of frustration with the way women were treated in her business. She had headlined films and television shows from *A Different World* (1987) to *My Cousin Vinny* (1992) to *Empire* (2015). She had struggled with seemingly hopeless pay disparities, and repeatedly found herself reduced to an accessory in scenes revolving around male characters. Often, acting just meant reacting to whatever the men were doing, she said.

Tomei shared a theory: Actresses and the public were stuck in a cycle of mutual misperception. From very young ages, girls were taught to admire and model themselves on the fantasy women onscreen. That made many of them want to become actresses themselves. The lucky ones who made it could never really describe the harassment or the punishing physical standards; that would be self-sabotage. So the cycle continued, with the next generation of girls growing up with Hollywood dreams and little understanding that the industry could mistreat them too.

Tomei was giddy at the thought of an exposé. She had almost never discussed her theory, even with other actresses. Sharing her impressions about a business that was all about appearances would make her too vulnerable, she said. For solidarity, she hung on to a clip from a 2013 *Vogue* magazine profile in which Claire Danes discussed what she had learned from Meryl Streep and Jodie Foster. "You have to ask for money because there's always more money and they won't give it to you because you're a girl!" Danes had said.

"Can you imagine me finding this little part of a paragraph in an article that I actually had to cut out in order to feel connected?" Tomei later asked Jodi. "To feel like it isn't just me."

Slowly, Jodi began to reach a few other well-known actresses, through a mutual friend here, an unusually helpful manager there. Some of their email addresses were pseudonyms, often comical ones, and once they were on the phone, they swore Jodi to secrecy. But they were direct.

Hollywood was plagued by rampant sexual abuse, most of them said. Daryl Hannah, her voice familiar from years of hit movies but filled with anxiety, said that she had been victimized by Weinstein but felt too fearful to go into any detail. Another actress, an Oscar winner, said she had wanted to see him stopped for years, but hadn't really known how to help, because the fellow actresses who had confided in her about their encounters wanted their privacy protected. This woman had tracked the failed reporting efforts years earlier at the *New Yorker* and the stalled *New York Magazine* article and wondered why every story in the works seemed to disappear.

The conversations with these actresses would not be made public, but they were telling, contradicting the lectures about how Weinstein was a non-story. Tomei and the others had global success, important roles, awards. They were insiders, but on this topic, they felt they had little ability to spur change, and they wanted the *Times* investigation to succeed.

When Jodi reached out to a few other women they had suggested, nothing came of it: Everyone said no. Soon even some of the actresses who had been helpful stopped responding to Jodi's emails and texts.

The same week she met with Tomei, Jodi received a promising email. Lisa Bloom, a celebrity feminist lawyer and the daughter of famed women's rights attorney Gloria Allred, wanted to talk. She had represented women in some of the most important and high-profile male misconduct cases, including the ones against Bill O'Reilly and Bill Cosby. Jodi figured that Bloom had clients with allegations against Weinstein, had caught wind of the *Times* project, and was getting in touch to help.

Jodi forwarded the email to her colleague Emily Steel, one of the reporters who had broken the story about Bill O'Reilly's settlements. Steel was about a decade younger than Jodi, petite, with a high voice, and Jodi had quickly learned to listen to everything she said. As soon as she got the email, Steel called with a warning. Bloom was in business with Weinstein, she said. The information was public. Bloom had posted a gushing tweet a few months before: "BIG ANNOUNCEMENT: My book SUSPICION

NATION is being made into a miniseries, produced by Harvey Weinstein and Jay Z!"

Jodi realized the person behind the email wasn't Bloom. Harvey Weinstein knew what the *Times* was working on and he was going on the offensive.

There had been no obligation for Jodi to give Weinstein notice of the investigation—it wasn't even clear that there would be a story yet—and the duty to ask him for an interview or responses would come later. But now that he knew, it would make the reporting even more difficult. Any investigation into serious wrongdoing was a contest with its subject to control information, to get to sources—a race to expose on the reporters' end, a race to hide on the other.

She would have liked a little more running room, but there was nothing to do but to keep reporting. Jodi arranged a call with Bloom and kept it short, saying little.

Nicholas Kristof, the *Times* opinion columnist, made getting in touch with Ashley Judd simple. He had written the foreword for her autobiography. Days after he made an introduction, Jodi was on FaceTime with Judd, who had already figured out the reason for the call. And unlike Tomei, she had a personal story to tell about Weinstein.

In 1996, when Judd was in her late twenties, becoming a star in films including *Heat* and *A Time to Kill*, she had met Weinstein at a Los Angeles event. The producer had asked to get together, and Judd had assumed they would have a business conversation. They planned to meet at the Beverly Hills Hotel—at the Polo Lounge restaurant there, Judd presumed. She suspected nothing. Her father was on the trip, and she had introduced the two older men at the event. "My own dad didn't see it coming," Judd said.

When she arrived at the hotel, she was directed to meet Weinstein in a suite, where he had a bottle of champagne on ice. She took only a few sips. They made small talk, and "I got myself out of there as fast as I could," she remembered, a little suspicious about what he wanted.

Days later, he issued another invitation, this time to a breakfast meeting at the Peninsula Hotel in Beverly Hills. A conversation so early in the morning would surely be safe, Judd reasoned.

She arrived at the hotel exhausted. She had been up all night filming her first big thriller, *Kiss the Girls*, with Morgan Freeman, and had come straight from the set. When the reception staff told her that she would be meeting with the producer in his suite, instead of the restaurant, she was annoyed: She needed sleep and room service would likely take forever to arrive. She figured she would order cereal to save time.

When she arrived at the room, she recalled to Jodi, Weinstein was in a bathrobe, which was not what she expected. He wanted to give her a massage. She refused. He countered by suggesting a shoulder rub. She rejected that too. Next he steered her toward a closet, asking her to help pick out his clothing for the day. Then toward the bathroom. Two decades later, she could still picture the layout of the hotel room, she said.

Weinstein's requests turned even more overtly sexual, she said. She refused each one, but he kept going. "I said no, a lot of ways, a lot of times, and he always came back at me with some slimy ask," she said. His movements were almost like military commands, she told Jodi, with a chop-chop quality, first you go here, and then you go there. Finally, he raised the possibility of her watching him take a shower, as if that was some sort of compromise.

She recalled feeling trapped in the room and fearful of hurting her film prospects. "There's a lot on the line, the cachet that came with Miramax," she said.

She needed an exit strategy, a way of getting away from Weinstein. "I'll make you a deal, Harvey," she recalled saying. "When I win an Academy Award in a Miramax movie, I'll give you a blow job," she said, before exiting.

Judd said she had been in a no-win situation: To rebuff the producer was to risk career consequences. So she had quickly come up with a joke that wouldn't offend him while finding a way to leave safely.

At the time, Judd mentally classified it as a creepy incident. Soon after, she described what happened to her mother, the singer Naomi Judd; her father; her agent; and later on, other confidantes. Judd had sounded serene during the call, and maybe that was why: She had not suppressed her story, so there was little confessional rawness to her telling.

A few years later, she took a Miramax role, in the film *Frida*, at the request of Salma Hayek, the star who was playing the Mexican artist Frida Kahlo. (Judd was cautious about Weinstein but wanted to help Hayek.) During filming in Mexico, they spent a day off at a resort, relaxing with their costar Valeria Golino. The three women were sitting together at an outdoor table when Weinstein walked by. He warmly greeted the others, and barely acknowledged Judd, she recalled.

After he left, she told the other two women what had happened in the Los Angeles hotel room. That's his thing, they said. He was always making those kinds of requests. He had done similar things to them too.

Judd asked the others why the women weren't banding together to stand up to Weinstein. "I didn't understand how any of us could be so scared of him," Judd said. But *Frida* was Hayek's labor of love, it was being made by Weinstein, and he had the power to halt production at any moment.

During the hour-long call with Judd, the investigation shifted a little. Judd had described a group of actresses who, years earlier, had identified Weinstein's troubling behavior. He was a powerful boss who used the pretext of business meetings to try to pressure women into sexual interactions, she said, and no one did anything about it.

Loneliness had defined Ashley Judd's upbringing. Born in 1968 with the name Ashley Ciminella, her parents had split early. Her mother was then an amateur musician who practiced harmonies at home but worked as a waitress and then a secretary to pay the bills, and Ashley attended thirteen schools in four states before graduating from high school, each time losing friends. She yearned for playmates and company so badly that she invented a cast of fairies to keep her company. By third grade, "I made myself meals like Chef Boyardee pizza from a box and baked my own chocolate-chip cookies from scratch and walked myself to the school bus, even on the first day of school, although I wasn't entirely sure where I was supposed to go," she said in her memoir, *All That Is Bitter and Sweet.* The refrain of her childhood, she wrote, was "Where is everybody?"

Growing up, she was molested several times, she wrote. In grade school, an old man offered her a quarter for a pinball machine if she would sit in his lap. "I was shocked when he suddenly cinched his arms around me, squeezing me and smothering my mouth with his, jabbing his tongue deep into my mouth," she wrote. She told the adults who were supposed to be looking after her, but they didn't believe her. One summer in high school, when she worked as a model in Japan, she was sexually assaulted by her boss and raped by an acquaintance, she said.

But at the University of Kentucky, she found female companionship in a sorority and gender studies courses. The lighted pathways and call boxes on campus struck her as a sign of unfairness, she said later. Why did women have to confine themselves in order to stay safe? Driven by a sense that things could be better, she discovered a taste for activism, leading a student walkout to protest a trustee's use of a racial epithet. She thought of becoming a Christian missionary, and she applied and was accepted to the Peace Corps, which she intended to join after graduation.

But she became an actor instead—she wanted to try it while she was young and could take chances—and then a star. Still, in her free time, she used her celebrity for advocacy work, visiting poor villages, slums, and clinics all over the world to draw attention to AIDS, violence against women, and maternal health and family planning. In 2006, she and Salma Hayek visited HIV clinics and brothels in Guatemala, where they met with prostitutes who explained that they needed money and could earn two dollars per client, ten or twelve times a day. Despite the problems Judd had seen in Hollywood, she kept her two lives, in entertainment and public health causes, separate.

In 2009, at the age of forty-one, she enrolled in a midcareer master's program at Harvard's Kennedy School. (Secretary-General Ban Ki-moon of the United Nations had completed the same program—and so had Bill

O'Reilly.) Privately, she was thinking of going into politics. The state of Tennessee had then never had a female governor or U.S. senator.

At Harvard, she felt more at home than she had in show business, and she wasn't sure she would return to acting at all. "I found my people," she said. Her favorite course, called Gender Violence, Law and Social Justice, was taught by a law school professor named Diane Rosenfeld. Judd bonded with the second- and third-year law students, asking to form a study group, baking biscuits for them, and speaking easily in class, but rarely about Hollywood.

In the course, Rosenfeld argued that the legal system had been constructed to protect men more than women. In contrast, she introduced students to research on the egalitarian behavior of bonobo apes, who over the course of evolution have eliminated male sexual coercion in their communities. If a male does get aggressive toward a female bonobo, she lets out a special cry, Rosenfeld explained. The other females come to her aid, descending from the trees and fending off the attacker.

For Judd, the class was a revelation, and, in some sense, a return. Rosenfeld was taking things Judd had known and seen her whole life— from her childhood, in Hollywood, on the trips to the brothels and clinics abroad—and giving her the intellectual framework and theory to understand them in new ways. "She metabolized everything in my class with her whole being," Rosenfeld said. Judd showed up to everything, the professor noticed: visiting lectures, receptions, a research presentation on GPS monitoring for high-risk domestic violence offenders.

She channeled her thoughts into a final paper that called for women to recognize their common experiences and take on sexual coercion. "I propose a model based on female-female alliances," she wrote on the first page. She wanted women to follow the example of the bonobos, becoming less separate and secretive, joining together to chase away overly aggressive men.

It would be hard to convince women that things could change, she wrote in her research paper, which won a Dean's Scholar Award. "Bias is built into the very structures of our formal institutions, economy, and daily life," she said. But "something is waiting on the other side."

What was needed, she wrote, was a "bold step of trust that breaks isolation."

till, in June 2017, Judd was not sure if she wanted to accuse Weinstein publicly. She had already tried to call out his behavior once. In 2015, she had given that account to *Variety* magazine, without naming Weinstein, Hayek, or Golino, hoping it would spark something, maybe a surge of others coming together.

Nothing much happened. The ensuing burst of attention was directed at Judd, not Weinstein, and it was brief and sensationalized. Judd had to scale back publicity for a film, *Big Stone Gap*, to avoid getting too many questions about the incident. To come forward again might repeat that experience.

This was a cautionary tale. Judd's account in *Variety* had been gutsy, but it was a lone account without a perpetrator's name or any supporting information. Impact in journalism came from specificity—names, dates, proof, and patterns. Jodi didn't want Judd to decline to participate in what might be a much stronger story because a weaker one had gone nowhere.

Judd was also wary because just a few months before, she had paid a price for speaking out. Over the years, she'd had a lucrative contract as a spokesperson for Copper Fit, a line of socks, compression sleeves, and braces. In commercials, she cheerfully recited lines like: "I love my hardwood floors, but they can be hard on my feet. That's why I love my Copper Fit Gripper socks." Her relationship with the company was amiable, and she sometimes socialized with the chief executive.

In the weeks before the Women's March in January 2017, she had sent him a protest poem about female rage, written by then nineteen-year-old Nina Donovan of Franklin, Tennessee, which Judd had discovered and planned to read from the main march stage. "I'm a nasty woman," it began. "I'm not as nasty as a man who looks like he bathes in Cheeto dust." The poem wasn't vulgar, but it was confrontational: "We are here to be nasty like bloodstained bedsheets," Ms. Donovan wrote, making the point that menstruation was part of life. Copper Fit raised no objections. But a few weeks after the march, Judd was fired. Customers were complaining about the poem, the company said.

So Judd had reason to be cautious. But on the call, Jodi had used a word she had been waiting to hear: "pattern." An important factor for her, Judd said, would be how many other stories the reporters were able to track down and whether other actresses were going on the record. True to her Harvard paper, she wanted to be one of many women standing up to Weinstein in unison.

The call ended with a plan: Judd was going to reach out to Salma Hayek. For additional advice, Jodi also spoke to Jill Kargman, lately the writer, producer, and star of the television show *Odd Mom Out*, and a contact who had provided guidance in unfamiliar worlds before. Kargman urged Jodi to talk to Jenni Konner, Lena Dunham's producing partner on the television show *Girls*. Konner, in turn, wanted Jodi to speak to Dunham too. Jodi hesitated. From the outside, Dunham seemed like the opposite of a secret keeper. She tweeted constantly and turned even intimate parts of her life into material.

The calls were worth the gamble. Konner and Dunham had heard stories about Weinstein's alleged predatory behavior and had wanted to expose him in *Lenny Letter*, their online newsletter, but they didn't have the investigative or legal resources. Dunham, who had served as a surrogate for Hillary Clinton during the 2016 campaign, told Jodi she had told Clinton's aides to stop relying on Weinstein as a fund-raiser, but her warnings went nowhere. (Later, Tina Brown, the magazine editor who herself had briefly partnered with Weinstein in the late '90s on *Talk* magazine, told Jodi she had delivered a similar warning to the 2008 Clinton campaign. After the revelations became public, Clinton and her team expressed shock and denied the extent of Dunham's warning.)

Konner and Dunham became a two-woman celebrity switchboard, sending Jodi some of the direct contact information she needed, working quickly and discreetly. Another entertainment executive with a feminist bent did the same.

The response rate from the actresses was still low. But by the end of June, Konner had news: Gwyneth Paltrow wanted to talk.

At the outset, Paltrow had barely been on Jodi's list of people to contact. She had been Weinstein's golden girl, one of his top stars, and twenty years later, the memories of her acting career were still tied to him. They had been photographed together many times, a laughing father-daughter pair. In 1999, when Paltrow won the Oscar for Best Actress for her role in *Shakespeare in Love*, Weinstein stood next to her, radiating pride: He had made the movie, molded the star. Back then, Paltrow's nickname had been First Lady of Miramax. She seemed unlikely to help the *Times*. She was hardly a rebel like McGowan or an activist like Judd. She had become a health-and-beauty entrepreneur, and for some people, a love-to-hate figure.

But once their phone call was scheduled, for the final weekend of June 2017, Paltrow cut a different figure: She was a dead-center source who might know more than anyone yet. On the telephone, Paltrow was polite and sounded a little jittery. After the ritual reassurances—yes, this was off the record; yes, Jodi understood the delicacy of the situation—Paltrow shared the unknown side of the story of her relationship with Weinstein.

They had met by an elevator at the Toronto Film Festival in 1994 or '95, when she was around twenty-two, Paltrow recalled. At that point, she barely had a career. Her parents, the actress Blythe Danner and Bruce Paltrow, a director and producer, were successful, and she had gotten encouraging reviews in a film called *Flesh and Bone*, but she was still auditioning for more parts.

Right there at the elevator, Weinstein gave her his vote of confidence. I saw you in that movie; you have to come work for us, she remembered him saying. You're really talented. "I just remember feeling legitimized by his opinion," she said.

Before too long, he offered her two films. If she would do a comedy called *The Pallbearer*, Weinstein said, she could also have the lead in his upcoming adaptation of Jane Austen's *Emma*—a dream job, a star-making role.

Paltrow joined the downtown Miramax fold, which at that time struck her as warm and creative. "I felt like I was home," she said. She was dating Brad Pitt, who was far more famous than she at the time, and flying between New York and Los Angeles. On one of those trips, before shooting started for *Emma*, she got a fax from her representatives at Creative Artists Agency, telling her to meet Weinstein at the Peninsula Hotel in Beverly Hills.

That was the same hotel as in Judd's story. What Paltrow said next also felt familiar. The meeting seemed routine, held in a suite for privacy. "I bounced up there, I'm sort of like a golden retriever, all happy to see Harvey," she said. They talked business. But Weinstein closed by placing his hands on her and asking to go into the bedroom and exchange massages. Paltrow could barely process what was happening, she said. She had thought of Weinstein as an uncle. The thought that he was interested in her sexually shocked her and made her feel queasy. He asked a second time to move into the bedroom, she said.

She excused herself, but "not so he would feel he had done something wrong," she said. As soon as she left, she told Brad Pitt what had happened, then a few friends, family members, and her agent.

The next part of Paltrow's story diverged from Judd's and made it potentially more consequential. Weeks later, when Paltrow and Pitt attended the same theater premiere as Weinstein, Pitt confronted the producer and told him to keep his hands to himself. At the time, Paltrow felt relieved: Her boyfriend was her protector.

But when she returned to New York, Weinstein called and threatened her, berating her for telling Pitt what had happened. "He said some version of I'm going to ruin your career," she said. She remembered standing in her old apartment on Prince Street in SoHo, fearful she would lose the two roles, especially the starring one in *Emma*. "I was nothing, I was a kid, I was signed up. I was petrified, I thought he was going to fire me," she said.

She tried to put the relationship back on professional footing, explaining to Weinstein that telling her boyfriend had been natural, but that she wanted to put the episode behind them and move forward. "I always wanted peace, I never wanted any problem," she said. For a time, their relationship was restored. "In this funny way, I was like, well, that's behind us," she said. The more successful her partnership with Weinstein became, the less she felt she could say about the ugly episode at the start of their collaboration. "I had this incredible career there, so I could never in a way traverse back over what happened," she said. "I was expected to keep the secret."

The ethos of Hollywood, she said, was to swallow complaints and to put up with exactly that kind of behavior. She didn't think about the encounter as part of something larger or more systemic. During her years with Miramax, she heard the occasional disturbing rumor about Weinstein, but never with specifics attached. Weinstein was abusive in other ways that made the moment in the bedroom seem mild in comparison. He threw things. His tirades were beyond anything Paltrow or others had seen from a grown man. The Miramax employees she knew lived in fear of his volatility. "It's the H-bomb, the H-bomb is coming," they would warn before he approached.

After two Miramax movies starring Paltrow tanked—*Bounce* in 2000 and *View from the Top* in 2003—Weinstein's treatment of her changed, she said. "I wasn't the golden girl with the Midas touch," she said. "My worth had diminished in his eyes." By the time Paltrow was pregnant with her first child, she quietly distanced herself from the producer.

That remained the case until 2016, when Miriam Weinstein, the producer's mother and a beloved figure at Miramax, passed away, and Paltrow wrote Weinstein a brief condolence email. To her shock, he read it aloud at the funeral and called her soon afterward—to thank her, Paltrow figured.

But after the niceties, he began to pressure her again. *New York* magazine was working on an exposé of his treatment of women. They have nothing, Weinstein told Paltrow. He wanted her to promise that she wouldn't talk about the incident at the Peninsula all those years before. "I just really want to protect the people who did say yes," he said, meaning women who had succumbed to his overtures. Paltrow declined the magazine's interview request, but she avoided saying whether she would ever speak.

The story needed to come out, she said to Jodi. For a long time, she had assumed she would never disclose what had happened. But twenty years later, everything looked different, and that's why she was on the phone now.

Paltrow made it clear that she was a long way from going on the record. She was not having a good public relations moment, to put it mildly. At the time, her e-commerce business and lifestyle brand, Goop, was selling a sixty-six-dollar jade egg meant to be inserted into the vagina to "help cultivate sexual energy, clear chi pathways in the body, intensify femininity, and invigorate our life force," as the site put it. The eggs had generated months of derisive laughter and accusations that Paltrow was blithely selling products with dubious or no health benefits. "Organically sourced, fair trade urine pH sticks coming soon to GOOP for seventy-seven dollars I presume?" wrote Dr. Jen Gunter, an ob-gyn who made cutting critiques of the product and other practices Goop had championed.

On Instagram, Paltrow looked as untroubled as ever. Privately, she was feeling crushed and unsure if she could handle any more controversy. She was certain that any story involving her, Weinstein, and sex was likely to be sensationalized, turned into the trashy celebrity scandal of the week. "I didn't know if I was going to be dragged through the mud," she said. "That's usually what happens to women if you look, historically." More than a hundred people were working for her, paying mortgages and raising children, and wading into more controversy could hurt them too. "I can't wreck the business," as she put it.

But Paltrow decided that she would use her Hollywood network to help Jodi identify and enlist other Weinstein victims so the women could share the burden of speaking up together. (Jodi couldn't mention Judd to her or vice versa.) Paltrow listed a half dozen other famous names she wanted to call, asking for pointers on the protocols of investigative journalism. Jodi suggested others. Paltrow was on vacation with her children in Europe, and her social media feeds showed wine glasses, a picnic, and an Italian lake. Privately, she also was texting old costars and acquaintances for so-and-so's contact information, asking other women if they would speak.

On July 5, Megan returned to the *Times*, undecided about what to cover. On that first day, Rebecca Corbett spelled out Megan's options. The first was to return to Donald Trump. In the final months of her pregnancy, Megan had started scrutinizing Trump's company and ties to Russia, turning up his pursuit of a Trump Tower Moscow during the presidential race and other questionable dealings. The second was to join the investigation of Harvey Weinstein. Jodi was still eager for Megan to join her. Was she interested?

Megan took a day to deliberate, seeking the advice of a few trusted colleagues. Those who covered Trump were unequivocal: He was the story of a lifetime. Much more important than a sleazy Hollywood producer accused of preying on young actresses. Passing up the chance to report on the president would be a huge mistake. But Megan wasn't so sure; she had watched hard-hitting articles about Trump pile up without much impact.

However, the Weinstein investigation was a question mark. The McGowan accusation was grave, but some of the material Jodi had gathered didn't seem that awful compared to the sex crimes Megan had reported in Chicago. How much demonstrable harm was really involved in the massage stories? She had a hard time conceiving of famous actresses as a category of victims. A prime mission of journalism was to give voice to the voiceless, to those who were often ignored. Movie stars, with their fame and fortune, were far from that.

Did the casting couch even meet the legal definition of sexual harassment? The women were not technically employees of Weinstein, and for some of them, there were no specific roles on the line. How much could this investigation really prove?

But, Jodi insisted, if the accounts were accurate, Weinstein personified the way powerful men could abuse their status to establish dominance over women. When he had invited these women to meetings, they had responded because they wanted to work, because they had ambition, creativity, and hopes and dreams. In return, he put them in no-win positions: Submit to sexual demands or risk repercussions. That was sexual harassment, whether or not it met the legal definition.

In perhaps the most famous harassment allegation of all time, Anita Hill had accused Clarence Thomas of asking her out on dates and making pornographic comments at work. While the status of a future Supreme Court justice and a Hollywood producer were different, the claims against Weinstein also appeared to have a predatory edge. And that his accusers were famous women was part of the point: It proved this was a universal problem.

Megan pulled up a seat at Jodi's cubicle and got to work.

Now both reporters were reaching out to some of the most prominent women in the world. Angelina Jolie had a Weinstein story, they heard from a former Miramax employee. Jodi cadged her email address from the helpful Hollywood executive, sent the star a carefully worded note, spoke to an adviser, and waited to see if she might participate. They also wrote to Uma Thurman: She did not reply, the reporters discovered later, because someone had told her they were not trustworthy. Despite repeated notes, Salma Hayek never responded either.

Ambra Battilana Gutierrez, an Italian model who had allegedly been groped by Weinstein during a meeting at his office in 2015—the incident investigated by the NYPD—appeared to have been the only woman who had reported the producer to law enforcement. In the end, the district attorney's office had declined to prosecute Weinstein, but working with undercover detectives, Battilana had apparently recorded the producer discussing what had happened.

Megan wasn't hearing back from the model, and the New York Police Department was refusing to provide her with a copy of the incident report under a long-standing policy that prohibited the release of such records. So she called around to attorneys and others who might have knowledge of the case. While reporting on DNA evidence in Chicago, Megan had interviewed Linda Fairstein, renowned in the field of sex crimes prosecution. Now Megan reached out to Fairstein again, hoping she might have valuable insight into the same sex crimes division where she had once worked, the one that had declined to press charges. But as soon as she heard the reason for the call, Fairstein's tone turned cool. Ambra Battilana Gutierrez's allegations had been unfounded, she insisted. There was no criminal conduct there. And there wasn't anything irregular about how the case was handled. "I don't think there's a road to go down," she told Megan.

In mid-July, the reporters met in person for the first time with Rose McGowan—over dinner at Jodi's apartment, for privacy. McGowan was anything but relaxed. Her eyes darted around the room. She had no interest in small talk. But she gamely answered question after question, especially about the aftermath of the hotel room encounter and who else might remember it or provide evidence. Jodi and Megan asked her to try to obtain a copy of her settlement agreement, explaining that one of the law firms must have retained a copy.

After the interview with McGowan, the reporters mentioned one particularly confusing question to Matt Purdy, a top editor at the paper who had overseen the O'Reilly story, pulled together the broader sexual harassment team and was keeping a close eye on the investigation. Beyond McGowan, some secondary sources were also suggesting that Weinstein had repeatedly committed criminal offenses: assault, rape. Should the reporters concentrate on finding those claims, prioritizing the most serious kinds of potential violations? Not necessarily, Purdy said: Concentrate first on what you can prove, even if what you can prove are lesser offenses. Get the women's allegations of sexual harassment on the record, the documents, and especially the settlements paid to victims. No one had ever nailed the Weinstein story, so the most important thing was to do it cleanly. Purdy wasn't ignoring the possibility of more severe transgressions; he was saying that if the reporters could break the story, everything was likely to tumble out.

On Saturday, July 15, Jodi checked her phone to find a series of panicked text messages and missed calls from Paltrow. Harvey Weinstein was standing in the living room of Paltrow's Hamptons home. She was hiding in her upstairs bathroom to avoid him.

His timing was the surprise, not his presence. Paltrow had heard from him a week or two before. He had caught wind of a party she was throwing, for potential investors in a musical she was backing, and he asked to come. She felt that he was clearly sending a message—I'm watching you. Paltrow had asked Jodi what to do.

Jodi had not wanted to get in the middle of the action. But they had talked through options. Paltrow could tell him not to come, but that might hint she was talking to a reporter. Maybe it was better to include him. On the other hand, what if he confronted her and demanded an answer about whether she was speaking to the *Times*?

Paltrow had decided it was best to say yes and to hope he got lost in the crowd. But he had shown up early, probably trying to speak to her alone, throwing Paltrow off balance. Jodi was anxious too, especially when she saw the accumulation of texts from Paltrow.

From many miles away, Jodi willed Paltrow to stay the course. After the party, Paltrow called: The party had unfolded without incident. She had kept her assistant close. She sounded undeterred—maybe even a little fascinated by what was unfolding.

On the first Friday in August, Jodi and Megan met Paltrow for the first time at her home in the Hamptons. The hope was to encourage her to go on the record. On a back deck, surrounded by bench swings and lush hedges, the interview began. In person, Paltrow was earthy and funny. She asked Megan empathetic questions about new motherhood before retelling her Weinstein story, and she nodded gamely when Megan carefully pushed for elaboration and told her that the reporters would seek to contact Brad

Pitt for confirmation of her account. That was standard procedure, Megan told the star: To corroborate the accounts of alleged victims, they would reach out to people they had told at the time, checking to make sure they remembered the stories the same way.

Asking Paltrow to go on the record was delicate. She was still dealing with the furor over the jade egg. Jodi and Megan understood the criticism but didn't want it to prevent Paltrow from participating in what might be a more consequential story. Also, for all of Paltrow's outreach, she had not managed to convince other actresses to speak about Weinstein problems. One declined because she was friendly with the producer's wife. Others hadn't gotten back to Paltrow.

In the middle of the interview, Paltrow picked up a call from a famous friend, walked out onto the lawn to ask if she had ever been victimized by Weinstein, then returned to explain that the woman had said nothing ever happened. Paltrow summarized her own thinking: She wanted to go on the record, but she didn't want the story to be about her. The more women who spoke in the article, the better. "I want to make sure that I'm not in any way at the focal point," she said.

In the car on the way back from the Hamptons, Jodi and Megan were encouraged. Paltrow hadn't said yes, but they had connected in person. Then the reporters realized that they might be able to catch someone who had not answered their inquiries: a former Miramax executive who lived nearby. So they took a detour and pulled up to the woman's summer cottage. She came to the door and greeted them with a smile. But as soon as she understood why they were there, she slammed the door in their faces, leaving them alone on the front porch.

Rebecca Corbett immediately wanted to hear every detail about the Hamptons trip. As an editor, she fully inhabited stories, worrying them forward, living through her reporters while also maintaining a critical eye. Weinstein, who liked to boast of his coziness with media power players, had likely never heard of Corbett. She was sixtysomething, skeptical, scrupulous, and allergic to flashiness or exaggeration, the cohead of the *Times* investigation department but so low profile that she barely surfaced in Google search results. Her ambition was journalistic, not personal.

But she was revered in newspaper circles because of one quality she did share with Weinstein: She had exerted outsized influence by championing other people's work. At the *Baltimore Sun*, she had mentored a twenty-two-year-old reporter named David Simon, pushed him to stop writing short news items about rowhouse fires and murders and pursue more ambitious ones about the sociology of crime and class, and edited him until the day he left the *Sun* to create shows like *The Wire*. (In the final season, the character of the city editor, one of the show's few heroes, was a man, but he was based in part on Corbett.) A few years after September 11, 2001, when two *Times* reporters discovered that the National Security Agency was secretly spying on American citizens without warrants, Corbett kept the investigation alive despite internal debate and intense pressure from the White House not to publish, producing one of the biggest scoops of the Bush years.

Like Jodi and Megan, she had come of age in male-dominated newsrooms, raising a daughter in the middle of story sprints. When she was appointed to the *Times* masthead in 2013, it became 50 percent female for the first time, but the milestone went mostly unremarked. Later, people would say that two women had broken the Weinstein story, but it had really been three.

As Corbett tracked the growing body of hotel room stories, she had one chief concern. "What is your strategy for getting these women on the record?" she asked every few days. Jodi and Megan had a sort-of answer: If we find enough of them, we can urge everyone to go public at once, for safety in numbers.

That was too risky an approach for Corbett. The sources were extremely reluctant, for understandable reasons. There was something inherently unfair in this kind of reporting: Why was it their burden to publicly tell uncomfortable stories when they had never done anything wrong? Corbett was worried that Jodi and Megan could end up with a shocking pile of off-the-record hotel room stories but no article. Even if the reporters did manage to persuade one or two women, that could lead to the old "he said, she said" problem.

The journalists were realizing the Weinstein story would have to be broken with evidence: on the record accounts, ideally, but also the overwhelming force of written, legal, and financial proof.

CHAPTER THREE

HOW TO SILENCE A VICTIM

In mid-July, with Jodi focused on Hollywood, Megan turned to a basic investigative question: Were there any public records of abusive behavior by Weinstein?

After all, there were laws to protect victims of sexual harassment, and at least in theory, government agencies enforcing them. If Weinstein had been a serial harasser, some of his victims might have filed complaints with the federal Equal Employment Opportunity Commission (EEOC) or the corresponding state agencies in New York and Los Angeles, the cities where Weinstein had run his companies.

The federal and New York agencies had nothing. But Grace Ashford, a savvy young researcher on her first month at the *Times*, obtained a report from California's Department of Fair Employment and Housing, which showed several workplace complaints for Miramax. The information was shrouded in the ultraobscure language of state bureaucracy: addresses, dates, and numerical codes denoting the nature of the allegation and how it was resolved, but nothing about who the people were or what had happened to them.

On September 12, 2001, the agency had received a complaint of sexual harassment against Miramax. Strangely, it had been closed the same day.

The report noted "complainant elected court action," which normally meant the agency had signed off on the merits of the complaint and steered it into the civil legal system. But there was nothing further, nor was there any record of a court case in California's docket. How could a complaint filed with the government disappear within hours?

Megan kept calling the agency to ask, but it was like ringing a house where no one was home. When she finally reached someone by email, the government official told her the complaint against Miramax and any other related records had been destroyed under an agency policy that prevented the retention of documents after three years. Another policy prohibited the official from providing the name of the person who had filed the allegation.

This was maddening. After some additional prodding, Megan secured the name of the government investigator who had been assigned the case at the time that it was filed. The woman was retired. No one at the agency knew where she lived. Through social media sites and address searches, Megan found her living east of Los Angeles and finally got her on the phone.

The interview was brief. The former investigator had reviewed hundreds of complaints during her time with the California agency. She didn't recall this one.

"What's Miramax?" she asked.

On the afternoon of July 14, the *Times* team that had convened to work on harassment stories after the O'Reilly scoop—including Rebecca Corbett, Matt Purdy, Emily Steel, and others—filed into the empty Page One conference room for an update. The room had no ornamentation, no pictures of presidents or historic events. But twice a day, top editors gathered to debate which stories would lead the print and digital editions of the paper. Reporters almost never attended those meetings, so being there lent this session a heightened quality.

The new harassment stories were promising. Two weeks before, Katie Benner, who covered Silicon Valley, had published a detailed exposé of harassment in the tech industry, about female entrepreneurs who had sought investment from male venture capitalists and instead were subjected to inappropriate texts, gropes, and come-ons ("I was getting confused figuring out whether to hire you or hit on you"). For a long time, women in the male-dominated industry had mostly stayed silent about the problem, viewing discussion as risky and taboo.

Now more of them were speaking out together. Earlier that year, Uber had been turned upside down when Susan Fowler, a former engineer for the company, had written a blog post describing the harassment and retaliation she had experienced there. In Benner's article, more than two dozen women had come forward. Many had gone on the record or named the investors. In photographic portraits, which had run with the story, the women looked composed and strong: innovators starting companies and expecting fair treatment.

The story had impact. One of the men and one of the firms had apologized. The women were praised by peers and readers for sharing their experiences. Benner's in-box swelled with new accounts and tips.

That meant the success of the O'Reilly story was no longer a one-off. Megan and Jodi had texted Benner's article, and the supportive reactions, to their Weinstein sources, as if to say yes, this is tricky, but our team knows how to do it.

The meeting opened with quick updates: Jodi and Megan were making slow but real progress on Weinstein. Emily Steel was hearing alarming accounts of violations at *Vice*. Catrin Einhorn was immersed in conversations with restaurant, retail, hotel, and construction workers. Susan Chira was focusing on formerly male blue-collar workplaces, like shipyards and coal mines.

In each industry, harassment had its own particular sociology. In restaurants, liquor was omnipresent at the workplace, eroding judgment and loosening inhibitions, and managers were often loath to confront customers who got out of line. Silicon Valley was filled with young men who got rich overnight and felt accountable to no one. In shipyards, construction sites, and other traditionally male workplaces, men sometimes tried to drive out women by putting them in physical danger. Chira had heard of one woman who had been left deep in a mine without any communication device, and another had been stranded atop a wind turbine.

The journalists had come to the project knowing the basics about sexual harassment. Since the 1960s, a body of law had emerged to protect people from unwanted advances in the workplace. Sexual harassment was not a criminal offense, unless it involved rape or assault, but it was a violation of federal civil rights laws. Everyone in the room knew the stories of Clarence Thomas and Bill Clinton. But now as the reporters combined what they were learning across industries, they were coming to a deeper realization: Some of the weapons intended to fight sexual harassment were actually enabling it.

Emily Steel had the first lead, from her work on Fox and O'Reilly. It was common knowledge that many sexual harassment cases settled out of court, and she and Michael S. Schmidt had already revealed that O'Reilly and Fox had relied on settlements that imposed confidentiality clauses—essentially paying victims to keep quiet. But the specific terms of the agreements were crying out for further investigation.

From what Steel was learning, the language of the deals made them look less like aboveboard legal transactions and more like cover-ups. The agreements included one restrictive clause after another. The women were obliged to turn over all their evidence—audio recordings, diaries, emails, backup files, any other shred of proof—to O'Reilly and his lawyers. They and in one case their attorneys were prohibited from helping any other women who might have similar claims against the host. If they received subpoenas compelling them to talk, they were required to notify O'Reilly and his team, who could fight their being called to testify.

The lawyer for one of the women agreed to switch sides, to "provide legal advice to O'Reilly regarding sexual harassment matters," according to the language of the agreement. Another of the alleged victims promised never to make disparaging statements about O'Reilly or Fox News, "written or oral, direct or indirect," and not to respond—ever—to any journalists who might contact her about the matter. As part of the deal, she confirmed that she had not filed a complaint with any of the government agencies responsible for fighting sexual harassment, including the EEOC.

In return, one alleged victim received about $9 million, and another got $3.25 million. If either woman violated any of these clauses, she could lose the money. Whatever O'Reilly had or hadn't done to the women was thus dropped down a deep well, never to be recovered. Cash for silence; that was the deal.

That summer, as Steel continued to look into O'Reilly, she also had broader questions: Were these clauses even legal? Were women across the country signing documents like these every day, often unbeknownst to almost anyone? And were sexual harassment lawyers actually tackling the problem they purported to fight or pumping out settlements for profit?

Steel had suggested to editors that the paper delve into those questions, so this was part of the assignment Corbett had given Jodi. In between trying to reach movie stars, she had been calling attorneys and legal experts across the country, from small town employment lawyers to scholars, and now she shared her findings.

The kinds of clauses that Steel described were not aberrations, the lawyers said. This was standard practice for dealing with sexual harassment, and often one of the only ways of dealing with it at all.

Women signed these agreements for good reason, the attorneys had emphasized. They needed the money, craved privacy, didn't see better options, or just wanted to move on. They could avoid being branded tattletales, liars, flirts, or habitual litigators. This was a way to get paid and get on with their lives. The alternative, taking this kind of lawsuit to court, was punishing. Federal sexual harassment laws were weak, leaving out vast categories of people—freelancers, employees at workplaces with fewer than fifteen employees. The federal statute of limitations for filing a complaint could be as short as 180 days, and federal damages were capped at $300,000—not necessarily enough to cover lost earnings or attract a good lawyer. No wonder many viewed settlements as surer propositions.

The deals worked out for the lawyers too, especially financially. They generally worked on contingency, getting paid only if the client did, taking at least one-third of the client's award as a fee. Losing in court could mean getting nothing. So sexual harassment settlements had swelled into a cottage industry. Some attorneys fought back against egregious provisions, but others rubber-stamped them or capitulated in order to win bigger awards.

Even the EEOC, the government agency that was supposed to enforce sexual harassment laws, often kept its settlements confidential. The agency had very little enforcement authority, and, under its founding mandate, was required to settle whenever possible, often disclosing little. "We know internally who the companies are that have the most charges," Chai Feldblum, then the commissioner of the EEOC, had told Jodi. But the agency was prohibited from making that information public. Before taking a job, a woman could not check with the EEOC to see what kind of record the prospective employer had on harassment. No wonder Megan hadn't gotten anywhere with the old Miramax complaints to the California agency. Such agencies would gather crucial information with taxpayer dollars and then, for the most part, were required to lock it away where almost no one could see it.

Jodi cut to the point: The United States had a system for muting sexual harassment claims, which often enabled the harassers instead of stopping them. Women routinely signed away the right to talk about their own experiences. Harassers often continued onward, finding fresh ground on which to commit the same offenses. The settlements and confidentiality agreements were almost never examined in law school classrooms or open court. This was why the public had never really understood that this was happening. Even those in the room with long histories of covering gender issues had never fully registered what was going on.

Leaving the meeting, Jodi and Megan realized how much needed to be investigated. Would the public be interested in these obscure legal instruments or their ramifications? There was some reason to be optimistic: After the publication of Benner's story, Benner heard from activists and legislators in California who wanted to change the state's rules on the legality of secret settlements for sexual abuse.

But if Harvey Weinstein had entered into settlements with women besides Rose McGowan, and if those claims had been hushed up by lawyers, could those women even be found?

In 2005, the Weinstein brothers had relinquished control of Miramax, their first movie company. But many of its former employees remained connected, bound by having together worked through terrible and won-derful moments, sometimes almost simultaneously. For many, working there had been an education, a crucible, a privilege, and a trauma. You could influence the world's moviegoing taste, negotiate a deal on a yacht in Cannes, and lose every shred of your dignity to the boss's lashings all in the same day. When former Miramaxers held informal reunions in New York and Los Angeles, they jokingly referred to the gatherings as "Mir-anon" meetings, as if they were in permanent recovery together.

Every day that July, Megan and Jodi continued to work that old Mir-anon circuit, one member passing them to the next. The former employees who supposedly knew the most did not return calls; many of the people rumored to have assisted the most with Weinstein's abuses had no interest in seeing their complicity in his misdeeds exposed. But the reporters asked other ex-employees for tips: Had anyone heard anything over the years about women accepting settlements?

On the last weekend of July, two weeks after the all-hands-on-deck meeting in the Page One conference room, Megan drove north, away from New York City, through the winding roads of a lush suburb. She was pursuing the mystery of an assistant in Miramax's early years who had abruptly quit.

Megan knew her name. Starting at Miramax, she had impressed others as smart and serious and been quickly promoted. But then, in 1990, she had disappeared, leaving behind only running shoes tucked neatly under her desk. In phone interviews, several former Miramax employees had re-called hearing that Weinstein had done something to her. But no one knew the details.

The most promising clue came from Kathy DeClesis, who had served as an assistant to Bob Weinstein at the time. She said a lawyer for the woman's father had sent a letter to the office shortly after her disappear-ance. The specific language escaped her, but DeClesis had the impression that the letter had threatened legal action. Her recollection was more than Megan and Jodi had gotten from anyone else. What had the young woman complained about, how had the matter been resolved, and what had hap-pened to her?

The former assistant had left little online trace of who she was or where she had been living the past twenty-seven years. She wasn't on LinkedIn. She wasn't on Facebook. But Ashford, the researcher at the *Times*, eventually found her on a far-flung corner of the internet, listed in an employee directory in another city. The photo showed no hint of Hollywood or celebrity. Just a regular fortysomething-year-old woman with shoulder-length hair and a face free of makeup.

Contacting the former assistant was even harder than identifying her had been. Megan left several messages with the front desk of the woman's workplace, explaining that she was a reporter from the *Times* wanting to speak with her, but never heard back. Even talking to the receptionists was tricky, because she wanted to avoid making the woman's colleagues aware of the sensitive nature of her questions. Megan briefly considered flying to the city where she lived but didn't want to scare off the woman.

But there had also been a local address for her mother, in that New York suburb. Megan decided to drive there and explain in person why she wanted to learn about the former assistant's experience. If the mother wasn't home, Megan would leave a handwritten letter with her explanation taped to the door. She arrived at the address to find a grand modern house.

Megan had been knocking on doors uninvited as part of her reporting for more than a decade, but it never got easier. It was often necessary in order to get reluctant sources to talk. Over the years plenty of people had welcomed her into their homes, persuaded by the initiative Megan had shown tracking them down. But she had also encountered people who felt violated by her mere presence. As she rapped on the large wooden door, Megan couldn't help but feel like she was intruding into someone's private life.

The person who appeared in the entrance was not the mother but the woman from the picture on the website. Megan was face-to-face with the former assistant.

A young girl was standing by the woman's side, peering out the doorway. Megan introduced herself as a reporter with the *Times*, and a flash of recognition—or perhaps fear—crossed the woman's face. "I can't believe you found me," she said. She and her daughters were back in New York for summer vacation, she explained. Megan had caught them in the middle of a visit with family friends. Reluctant to say too much in front of the other people in the house, Megan asked if the woman would be willing to join her on the front steps for a minute. She agreed.

As they sat side by side, Megan explained that she and Jodi were hard at work on an investigation of Harvey Weinstein. Their reporting had turned up what appeared to be a pattern of predatory behavior. They had reason to believe that Weinstein may have hurt her when she worked at Miramax. Megan wouldn't have gone to such trouble to find her if it wasn't important.

As she spoke, the corners of the woman's mouth turned up ever so slightly. It wasn't a smile, but it was some hint of recognition. "I've been waiting for this knock on my door for twenty-seven years," she said. "All I can say is that I had a business dispute with Miramax, the dispute was resolved amicably, and we've agreed not to discuss it."

Megan paused, turning over the lines in her head. Technically, the woman was saying nothing. But there was meaning to her nondisclosure, as if she were working in the blank spaces between the words. She seemed like she might be saying: *Something bad did in fact happen to me years ago, but I must feed you this carefully crafted line.*

This was exactly how a woman who had signed a settlement would answer. There are times in journalism when the right thing to do is turn and walk away, to leave a source alone. But this was not one of them. Megan was determined to keep the woman talking, if only about unrelated things. How old were her daughters? Megan's own daughter was only four months old. The woman was close in age to Megan, with so many similar reference points. The conversation was easy.

After another half hour of chatting, Megan made her pitch. She asked the former assistant to consider contributing to the *Times* investigation. Megan appreciated how risky it was to break a settlement, but, she said, there were ways to bring settlements to light while protecting sources. Her colleagues had done it with payoffs made by Bill O'Reilly. The woman nodded along. She didn't say no. She didn't say yes. Instead she agreed to give Megan something always coveted by journalists: her cell phone number.

But on her drive back to Brooklyn, Megan got a phone call that punctured her optimism. The woman said she had just spoken to her lawyer. He had instructed her not to talk to the *Times*. Megan maintained a positive tone even as her heart sank. She told the woman that her attorney's advice was predictable, but she didn't have to make a final decision yet. All Megan asked was that they stay in touch and continue to discuss options. Reluctantly, the woman agreed.

As she drove, Megan's suspicions were growing. The rumors about the producer had involved actresses, but now she and Jodi were glimpsing an entirely new category of possible victims: employees of Weinstein's companies. The woman who had stood next to Megan in the kitchen—perhaps the Patient Zero of the Weinstein investigation—wasn't famous at all. And she had been young and vulnerable when she worked at Miramax. Could the producer have abused women more systemically than she or Jodi had ever contemplated? How many women had he victimized since, and would things have been different if the former assistant had been able to speak freely?

On that final weekend of July, Megan still didn't know exactly what had happened to the woman twenty-seven years earlier. But she wanted desperately to keep their conversation going, and so two days after the house visit, she sent the former assistant a text:

> I know I must have thrown you a curveball into your trip home. But please know it's only because this story is so important. There's a real opportunity to make a difference. My hope is that we can continue to be in touch—that I can keep you abreast of what's happening on our end. I suspect you've had some more conversations about this—with family and perhaps others. Seems to me the most important conversation of all is the one you have with yourself.

She also sent a link to the *New York Times* article on O'Reilly's history of settlements. Even as she typed, Megan suspected she might never hear from the woman again.

A few nights later, Megan took another drive, to the home of John Schmidt, a former Miramax executive who had served as the company's chief financial officer in 1990, the year the young assistant had disappeared. Megan figured that Schmidt, who still worked in the film business, would be aware of any settlement the woman might have signed, but he had been dodging her phone calls. So she was staking out his house in Riverdale, a leafy Bronx neighborhood, slouching down every time the local private security patrol drove by, waiting for the living room lights to flick on to indicate that someone was inside. Soon she was face-to-face with Schmidt, apologizing for showing up unannounced at dinnertime, feeling awkward because his wife was also there, listening to her every word.

These settlements were insidious, making victims feel they couldn't speak, potentially saddling them with substantial financial damages if they did, Megan explained to Schmidt. If other people were aware of the payoffs, they were uniquely positioned to provide crucial help. Megan wasn't asking Schmidt to go on the record. She just wanted his perspective on what might have happened all those years ago.

But Schmidt wasn't prepared to speak with her, at least not yet. He told Megan he needed to think about it and escorted her to the door. The reporter understood that people often needed time to come around, but it was frustrating. Some former Weinstein employees appeared aware of problems, and they still wouldn't talk.

One Friday evening that same July, Jodi spoke on the phone with a Hollywood executive named Matt Brodlie who had worked at Miramax many years ago. He listened with unusual care, and she got the feeling that he was assessing her. Shortly afterward, he called her back to give a name and number. He had a close friend from Miramax who had been holding something inside for years, he said. She was both wary and bursting to talk. Her name was Amy Israel and she was also a respected entertainment executive.

"I want to have a long career, I don't want to be marked by this," Israel said as soon as she got on the phone. "I do not want to be quoted, period, end of story." But a memory had troubled her for almost twenty years and she wanted to share it.

In the autumn of 1998, she had attended the Venice Film Festival with Weinstein, scouting for new films to buy. During a meeting in Weinstein's hotel suite, she saw that something appeared visibly wrong with two female assistants, Zelda Perkins, a fixture of the London office, and Rowena Chiu, a more recent hire.

"The two of them were sitting there trembling," Israel recalled. "They were literally vibrating with fear." Weinstein seemed fine, talking about films as usual. Something had just happened involving the two women, Israel had intuited. Weinstein was refusing to acknowledge it.

Israel knew about Weinstein's offenses from firsthand experience. He had praised her, trusted her with significant responsibility at a young age, and harassed her, she said. One year at the Toronto Film Festival, when she arrived at his hotel to pick him up for a gala screening, a male assistant summoned her up to the boss's hotel room. She had complied, thinking the assistant would be in the room as well. Instead she found a nearly naked Weinstein, wearing only a tiny towel, entreating her for a massage. She blurted out that she needed to call her mother and pretended to dial her on the spot, she said.

A year or two later, after being promoted to the head of her department, she was screening a film for Weinstein in New York when he asked her, out of nowhere: "Why don't you take off your shirt and do some cartwheels?"

"Go fuck yourself, you fat fuck," she shot back, and he turned to a game of tic-tac-toe. (Weinstein denied her account.)

But all these years later, she feared that what had happened in Venice was worse. She knew only bits of the aftermath. Zelda Perkins had left the company and signed some sort of contract that prevented her from speaking about what happened—a settlement, Jodi thought. Israel also recommended she call another former employee of the London office, a woman named Laura Madden: She might have something to say too.

Israel was also asking a bigger question: What had all of them, the whole former Miramax crowd, tolerated? That was what she really wanted to know, and the reason she was on the phone with a reporter. Back in the day, Israel had taken small steps to protect colleagues, like forbidding female subordinates from being alone with Weinstein. Doing more had felt impossible—she had only suspicions about what had happened in Venice, and there were few realistic avenues for complaint. When she had reported her own hotel room encounter with Weinstein to one of her supervisors, she was told that another colleague had been victimized too, but no action was taken.

She and her peers focused on their work. "He counted on my shame to keep me silent," she said. Ever since the news of Bill Cosby's crimes had broken, she had been waiting for mention of Weinstein, willing that story to emerge too.

"Why are we not speaking out?" Israel said on the phone. "Why are people still not talking twenty years later?"

Three weeks later, on Wednesday, August 2, Jodi was in London, sitting across a restaurant table from Zelda Perkins in South Kensington, hearing her account of what had taken place in 1998.

Perkins had the no-nonsense manner of a good producer. She was mostly a theater person, a longtime hand to one of the top stage and screen producers in town, working on prestige plays and occasionally television series like *The Crown*. She spent time in a cottage in the countryside where she tended to a flock of sheep and returned to London frequently for work. Because she was legally prohibited from talking about it, only a small number of people knew the full story of her career.

This meeting was the most Perkins had opened up to any of the journalists who had contacted her over the years about the Weinstein rumors. (The others had all been men, she said pointedly.) With her voice low, she plunged back into the story she had started to tell on the phone, when Jodi had first contacted her.

In 1995, Perkins had ended up working for Weinstein when he was near the peak of his powers. She was only twenty-two years old and had gotten the job through a chance encounter. "I didn't know who he was, and I didn't have a driving ambition to work in the movie industry," she said. "I wasn't sophisticated enough to understand that I had landed myself an incredibly rarefied position."

Weinstein had harassed Perkins from practically the first day, she said. "He was pathologically addicted to conquering women," she said. "That was what got him out of bed in the morning." She wasn't speaking figuratively. Each morning, Perkins, or whichever assistant from the London office was on the early shift, had to rouse the partially or fully nude Weinstein out of bed in his hotel room, and turn on his shower, as if he could not rotate the handle himself. Sometimes Weinstein tried to pull Perkins into bed with him, she recalled. There was no one to complain to about this behavior, no human resources operation in the tiny London office, no pretense of policies or rules.

Perkins never succumbed to Weinstein's come-ons. She was small but tough and she had come to the job prepared. Another female colleague had instructed her to sit in armchairs, not sofas, in his presence, so he couldn't sidle up easily, and to wear her winter parka for protection even if she was warm. "I always managed to say no," she said.

While the hazards of working for Weinstein were beyond anything she had ever seen, so were the perks. On trips to Paris and Rome, "he would just hand out the cash, which was your blood money," she said. "You'd come back from trips with him with a weird comedown of guilt and relief that you'd survived." Each trip felt like a bungee jump, she said, exhilarating but close to the void. Sometimes, he would close the trips on a benevolent note, saying to Perkins: Take the company jet, keep the suite at the Ritz for the weekend, invite your boyfriend to come, have fun. "We all took the gifts," she said.

In 1998, Perkins hired another assistant, Rowena Chiu, an aspiring producer so creative and driven that as the president of the Oxford University Drama Society, she had staged a Brecht play in the round and Euripides in the original Greek. Perkins warned her to be careful around the producer. That September, the two women flew to Italy for the Venice Film Festival and the standard Weinstein festival routine: screenings, a stay in a top hotel, and meetings with colleagues from New York, including Amy Israel.

But before the meeting that Israel had remembered, Chiu had come to Perkins for help. When Chiu confided the disturbing details of what Weinstein had done to her the night before, Perkins teared up, said it was unconscionable, and had set off in pursuit of him.

But she couldn't share the details of what Chiu had told her, Perkins said at lunch. Those were for Chiu to describe or keep forever private.

Much later, Chiu told Jodi that part of the story herself. On the Venice trip, it had been her job to tend to Weinstein in the evenings, putting her alone with him in a hotel room for long hours at night. He made advances on her from the beginning, she said, but on the second or third night of the festival, according to Chiu, his behavior worsened. They were supposed to be going through a stack of scripts, and as they paged through, he flattered her, telling her she had real insight and a feel for the business.

That night she had worn two pairs of tights as protection. But as she tried to work, he interrupted with an escalating series of sexual requests, for massages, a bath. She tried to appease him by taking off one set of tights and letting him massage her, she said. When his hands wandered further, she protested that she wanted to get back to the scripts, that she had a boyfriend. He responded by making grandiose promises of career help for him as well.

"I didn't directly say no, I didn't want to be that confrontational," she said. "He was much bigger than me, and as long as he was being pleasant, I wanted to be pleasant too."

This continued for four hours, she said: She would push back to work, and then he would resume pressuring and touching her, saying that they could have oral sex, that he had never had sex with a Chinese girl before. Weinstein removed her second layer of tights. But when he asked her to remove her underwear, she refused.

"It's exhausting, he tries to whittle you down little by little," Chiu said. "I was on high alert; I was worried about being raped." He managed to get her on the bed—he was holding her down, she said, not forcefully, like it was a game. He parted her legs, and told her that with one single thrust, it would all be over. Before anything further happened, she rolled over, wriggled away, and dutifully continued on her shift, leaving the hotel room around 2:00 a.m., when the work was finally done.

Later, Weinstein denied the whole story. "There is not a bit of truth," he said through a representative, "and any reporting retelling this narrative is just continuing the falsehood."

In London, Perkins continued with her story: She had found Weinstein at a business lunch on the hotel terrace. In front of all the other guests at the table, she commanded him to follow her. He was almost docile, she remembered, trailing her down the hallway as if she were the boss and he the assistant. When she confronted him, he swore on the life of his wife and children he had done nothing wrong, Perkins remembered.

She was twenty-four years old by then, the older of the two women and the employee of longer standing. Chiu, her assistant, had her account of the incident, but Perkins knew about her boss's record of misbehavior. Chiu and Perkins banded together and resigned. "I had to protect her," Perkins said. "She couldn't have done anything on her own; it would have just been her word against his. I was her shield."

Perkins consulted with a more senior figure, Donna Gigliotti, a producer who would go on to win accolades for *Shakespeare in Love*, and, many years later, *Hidden Figures*. She was far better connected than Perkins, the relatively rare female producer with the clout and experience to get major movies made. Gigliotti urged Perkins to get a lawyer, recommending one in New York, participating on a call with her, and offering other forms of quiet support. At the time, Perkins was grateful; now, years later, she questioned whether Gigliotti could have done more. (Later, Gigliotti emphasized that she tried to help Perkins find a lawyer who would take the lead.)

She and Chiu, a part-time law student at the time, found an attorney in London, from the firm Simons Muirhead & Burton, and assumed that the next stop would be criminal proceedings.

The lawyers told the two women otherwise. They had no physical evidence. They had not called the police in Venice. They were two twenty-somethings going up against Weinstein and potentially Disney, which now owned Miramax. Instead they were told that their best course of action was a settlement—maybe a year's salary, around 20,000 pounds. This is how such cases were typically handled, they were informed. Perkins and Chiu protested that they did not want any money: It had to be donated to charity, which they hoped would create a public flag. That wasn't how things worked, they were told. Weinstein's attorneys weren't likely to even enter a negotiation without a financial request.

Indignant, Perkins named an even higher figure and then attempted to craft a settlement that would go some way to stopping Weinstein's behavior. She demanded that Weinstein attend therapy and that she be present for his first session. Miramax would finally have a sexual harassment policy, with training and a group of three people to evaluate complaints, one of whom had to be an attorney. If anyone made a similar allegation in the next two years, with a settlement of at least 35,000 pounds or six months' salary, the matter would be reported to Disney or Weinstein would be dismissed.

Weinstein's lawyers fought back. A London law firm, Allen & Overy, represented him and a Miramax attorney named Steve Hutensky, who generally handled deals and contracts with actors, directors, and writers, disappeared from the New York office and materialized in London to work with them. (Hutensky later said that this was the only sexual assault claim against Weinstein of which he was aware, and that the producer insisted to him that the encounter was consensual, and that he was settling the matter to protect his marriage.) One negotiating session lasted until five in the morning. In the end, each woman would receive 125,000 pounds, but both had to agree to extraordinary restrictions.

As Perkins and Jodi ate lunch and talked in London, written proof of those restrictions was sitting in Perkins's bag. Though Jodi and Megan knew about Rose McGowan's settlement, and suspected that one had been struck with the former assistant Megan had met, the reporters had never actually laid eyes on any of the Weinstein settlement papers. In investigative journalism, knowing about incriminating documents was good; seeing them was excellent; and having copies was best. In the days before Jodi's trip, Megan had given her pep talks and sent her encouragement by emoji: You'll see the papers. I know you will.

Now Perkins hesitated before drawing the battered sheets with the distinctive old Miramax logo out of her bag. She began to read aloud. She was not permitted to speak to anybody about her time working at Miramax. Any "medical professional" she consulted about what happened would need to sign a confidentiality agreement. She could not be truthful with her own accountant about the money she received. In the agreement, she had to list everyone she had already told about the events in Venice—not by name, Perkins had fought off that part. Instead there was an odd, anonymous list of parties who knew: She told three employees and her boyfriend that she left Miramax "because of an act," and for moral reasons; she told her two closest friends the precise nature of what happened, and so on.

The roll call of restrictions went on. She was not to speak to "any other media now or hereafter existing" about what happened. (*God bless Perkins*, Jodi thought, sitting here with a reporter almost twenty years later.) "In the event there is disclosure by the parties," Perkins continued, she would be required to provide "such reasonable assistance as it may request in taking such steps as are prudent to deal with the foregoing to prevent any further disclosure or as the case may be to mitigate such effect." In other words, Perkins was required to help conceal the truth even if it somehow got out.

These restrictions were insults to common sense. Though the settlement shaped Perkins's life, she wasn't even allowed to hold on to a complete copy of the paperwork. Instead she was allowed limited visitation rights—if she wanted to see it, she could view a copy at her lawyer's office. The papers that Perkins had brought to lunch were bits and pieces, cadged together. When she had asked her lawyer how she could possibly abide by an agreement she couldn't consult, she had given her these excerpts. Worst of all, after intense pressure from the Weinstein lawyers, Perkins and Chiu, who had a matching agreement, had assented to confidentiality clauses that implied that the two of them could never discuss the matter again.

The date on the documents was October 23, 1998. The mess in Venice had taken just weeks to erase. Chiu sent Perkins a thank-you gift, a Filofax planner, then disappeared from her view.

Afterward, Perkins felt "broken and disillusioned." Her search for a new job was uncomfortable because she couldn't explain to prospective employers why she had left a top company so abruptly. Her career in film was over, she realized. She went to Guatemala to train horses. She had fought hard in the settlement negotiations for the right to attend therapy with Weinstein and had chosen a therapist for him, but she had trouble making the sessions happen and gave up.

The 1999 Academy Awards, which took place five months after the papers were signed, belonged to *Shakespeare in Love*. The film won seven Oscars, more than any other movie that year. Gwyneth Paltrow won Best Actress. Weinstein and Donna Gigliotti took home Best Picture. (Later, she briefly returned to working with him: in 2010, Gigliotti was Weinstein's president of production.) Perkins's name was in the end credits for the film.

Over the nearly two decades since, Perkins's perspective had expanded. She was no longer driven, she said, by wanting to get Harvey Weinstein. Perkins wanted to publicly question the fairness of the entire settlement system, to prevent other women from being pressured to sign away their rights.

"For me, the bigger trauma was what had happened with lawyers," she said later. "I wanted Harvey to be exposed, but what broke my heart is what happened when I went to the lawyers."

Perkins was tempted to defy her stifling confidentiality agreement and speak out, and Jodi was impressed by her courage. So many other women would barely get on the phone, and here Perkins was thinking of exposing herself to serious financial and legal risk. Before traveling to London, Jodi had phoned a top employment lawyer there for an assessment of how much a woman with a settlement would risk if she broke the agreement and spoke out. The attorney was unequivocal. "They'll sue her, ask for the money back," he said. In all of his years practicing law, he said, no client had ever breached a confidentiality agreement. "They're paying for silence," he finished. Perkins decided, like everyone else, that she wanted company: If Jodi and Megan could get other women to break their settlement agreements, she would too.

A safer, if less satisfying, way to proceed was to document the basic facts of her settlement by speaking with others. Amy Israel knew a chunk of what happened, and she wasn't the only one. But that still left another problem. Chiu, the alleged victim, was not responding to emails or phone messages. She did not want to be found.

The week before the London trip, Jodi had gotten on an airplane to the Bay Area, rented a car, and driven up to Chiu's house in Silicon Valley. Like Megan a few weeks before, she had a note on nice stationery and a mental script.

A man stood in the driveway, fiddling with a car. Jodi introduced herself and asked if Rowena Chiu was home.

No, she was out of the country, he said. But he was her husband, and he was certain that his wife didn't want to speak to any journalists. Could she please leave?

Jodi nodded in assent. Before she went, she asked the husband if they could just speak for a few moments, off the record, right there in the driveway. She wanted to explain why she had come all the way from New York.

He didn't say his name, but she already knew it: Andrew Cheung. She tried to read his face. It must have been strange to be cleaning out the car in the driveway one moment, then finding a reporter there the next.

Cheung nodded tentatively. As soon as Jodi laid out the broad strokes, he started asking questions. You're not the only journalist who has been contacting my wife, he said. Why are all of these reporters trying to reach her?

Surely, he knew the answer, Jodi wondered. It seemed impossible that multiple reporters were approaching his wife and he had no idea why. He was probably testing Jodi to see how much she knew and was employing the same script that Megan had heard from the former assistant in the New York suburbs, not even acknowledging that anything happened.

How to respond? She could not lie. She had shown up in this man's driveway asking to speak. If she wanted this couple to be forthcoming with her, she had to be transparent with them too. But at that point, she did not yet know the specifics of the allegations, and if he really had no idea about whatever had happened in Venice, Jodi should not be the one to inform him.

Jodi gently shared that she thought his wife might have been victimized by Harvey Weinstein, making clear that she could be wrong. When she mentioned a settlement, Cheung laughed and gestured at the ordinary-looking house behind him. "Do I look like a man whose wife got a settlement?" he asked.

He really doesn't know, Jodi realized with dread. This woman had never told her own husband. All these years later, the confidentiality clauses had left all three of them in bizarre positions: a woman barred from sharing her own experiences with her spouse. A husband standing incredulously in his own driveway, learning his wife's secrets from a stranger. He promised to relay a message to her but said he was sure that she wanted to be left alone. If Weinstein had victimized so many women, he asked, can't you just do your article and leave her out?

Before she drove away, hoping she hadn't just made things worse, Jodi answered his question. "If everyone takes that stance, the story will never be written," she said.

After she left, Cheung asked his wife, who was then staying with her parents in her native United Kingdom, about Jodi's visit, but Chiu brushed it away, and Cheung didn't want to inquire further. He knew she had worked at Miramax, but because he had no idea about the alleged assault or the settlement, he was also ignorant of one of the most telling details of her employment: Nine months after the Venice film festival, she had returned to the company.

She hadn't wanted to. But like Perkins, she found interviewing for other film jobs in London hopeless under the unexplainable circumstances. As part of the agreement, Miramax had already given her a reference letter, so she asked Hutensky, the company lawyer, for job leads at other organizations.

The message she got back was: *Harvey really values you and would like you back.*

Chiu caved and returned to Miramax in the summer of 1999, to a job based in Hong Kong, scouting for Asian films that could be made into Hollywood productions. She had no contact with Weinstein, save for one conference call, with Hutensky on the line to supervise, and wondered what other employees knew—but of course she couldn't tell them.

"I did my best to make a fresh start. It was a whole new country," she said. "I tried to see it as, 'I'm building my own empire and I'm far from New York and the abuse of Miramax headquarters.'" At the start, she threw herself into finding Asian films but found that Miramax was not serious about the material. She slowly began to suspect that the job was a concoction designed to keep her under Weinstein's control.

"It was a deal with the devil," she said. She fell into a depression and attempted suicide twice before finally leaving Miramax for good and moving back to London, where she studied for an MBA and began to create a new life for herself.

By the time Jodi showed up in her driveway, she had a résumé full of accomplishment and adventure in the world of business and economics, and four children, including an infant. Chiu told her husband to ignore Jodi's visit. Journalists had turned up from time to time, she assured him, but they never wrote anything, and she didn't think they ever would.

Twenty-four hours after the lunch in London with Zelda Perkins, on Thursday, August 3, Jodi was sitting at a picnic table opposite the other woman Amy Israel had recommended: Laura Madden.

When Jodi had asked if she could come see her, Madden had hesitantly said yes. She lived in Wales, but that week she would be on vacation in Cornwall, in the far southwest of England, and she could only spare an hour or so. Jodi went anyway. The flights from London were sold out, so she took a five-hour train ride. In the final hour, the train broke down, so she took a bus. She absolutely had to see Madden, because her story, which she had already started to share haltingly over the phone, brought together so much of what the reporters had already heard.

In 1992, Madden had been just twenty-one or twenty-two, a girl from rural Ireland with little life experience, who had grown up feeling isolated on an estate her family had owned for generations. There was no great fortune left—her parents kept the place going as a hotel—but her family struck locals as too posh, too British. As a child, her pleasures were books and roaming the family property, which held farms and gardens. Madden did not attend university, and aside from a few months of language study in Spain, she had never really been away from home.

When a film began shooting nearby, she got a job wrangling extras and caught the movie bug. That crew told her to look for work on *Into the West*, a film starring Gabriel Byrne and Ellen Barkin. She was hired, and that was how she found herself dispatched to Weinstein's hotel room in Dublin one day, excited for the chance to answer calls and run errands for the producer, whom she had never met. When she arrived, champagne and sandwiches were waiting. Weinstein complimented Madden, telling her everyone on the production had noticed her talent and hard work.

"He told me that I was guaranteed a permanent job in the Miramax London office, to start immediately," Madden wrote in an email to Jodi later. "I was delighted, as this was literally my dream job."

Weinstein, wearing a bathrobe, told Madden that he was worn out from travel and wanted a massage from her. She resisted. He pushed, telling her that everyone did it, that it wasn't a romantic request, he just needed to relax, she remembered. "I felt completely caught in a situation that I intuitively felt to be wrong but wasn't sure whether I was the problem and it was completely normal," Madden wrote.

When he took off the bathrobe and Madden placed her hands on him, she froze. He suggested that he massage her first, to put her at ease. She took her top off, as he had instructed, then her bra, and he put his hands all over her, she recounted. She felt disgusted and scared she would lose the job in the London office.

It was only months later, after the story had broken, that Madden shared the worst details of her account. Soon her pants were off too. Weinstein stood over her, naked and masturbating. "I was lying on the bed and felt terrified and compromised and out of my depth," she wrote. She asked him to leave her alone. But he kept making sexual requests, the same kind Judd had described—can we do this, can we do that. Weinstein suggested a shower and Madden was so numb she gave in. As the water poured around them, he continued masturbating and Madden cried so hard that the producer eventually seemed annoyed and backed off, she said. That was when she locked herself in the bathroom, still sobbing. She thought she could still hear him masturbating on the other side of the door.

Omitting those details, Madden described how she hurried back into the room to recover her clothes and belongings and ran away. (Later, Weinstein denied her account in its entirety.)

The most painful part was that she had felt so enthusiastic at the start of the assignment, tingling at her opportunity and luck. "The overwhelming feeling I can still remember was shame and disappointment that something so full of promise had become reduced to this," she said. "All the optimism I felt for my future was robbed by him. Any hope that I had been offered a job through my own merit was gone."

Afterward, a female colleague she'd enlisted for support phoned Weinstein to confront him about his behavior and he readily apologized. "I was to take the job and never feel compromised," Madden said. The producer swore that it would never happen again.

Madden did take the London job, and she spent six years working in production for the man who had abused her, she said. It had seemed safe in part because he was based in the States. The work was what she had wanted, after all. Her father, at first livid at the mistreatment, eventually backed the decision.

But Madden was never happy at Miramax. When the producer visited London, she never knew which version of him she would see: the charming or the dangerous one. She had plenty more uncomfortable moments in hotel rooms with Weinstein, she said, even if none were as bad. She spent the whole of her employment feeling "compromised"—her word—by what had happened at the start. "I carried the weight of feeling responsible for the assault and that I should have outright turned him down and never taken the job," she wrote later.

Madden's story was a kind of distillation, bringing together the elements of what Jodi and Megan were starting to call The Pattern: Weinstein's hallmark moves, so similar from account to account. Each of these stories was upsetting unto itself, but even more telling, more chilling, was their uncanny repetition. Actresses and former film company employees, women who did not know one another, who lived in different countries, were telling the reporters variations on the same story, using some of the same words, describing such similar scenes. Eager young women, new recruits to Miramax, hoping to connect with the producer. Hotel suites. Waiting bottles of champagne. Weinstein in a bathrobe. They had been so young, so overpowered. They had all wanted what young Laura Madden had wanted: their own equivalent of that job in the London office, the chance to work, participate, and succeed.

As she and Madden talked, Jodi did not mention the lunch with Perkins the day before, nor had she mentioned Madden to Perkins. She couldn't: The conversations were confidential. Though the two women had worked alongside one another in the London office, they had never shared their painful stories with each other. Both women were isolated; no one could see the whole picture. It was tempting to daydream about bringing all of the alleged Weinstein victims together somehow, to show them that they had each been part of something larger. But that would be perilous, even with their permission, for the reporters as well as the women. One source could not know who the others were. Anxiety was contagious, the reporters knew. One woman could talk the rest out of participating. One leak could compromise everything.

Earlier, on the phone, Madden had said she would never be able to tell the story publicly. Now, as they sat on the beach, Jodi registered a clearer impression of her. There was something quietly impressive about Madden: She was careful about what she did and didn't remember, and judicious in her descriptions, with an eye for nuance and detail. After Miramax she had gone on to experience deep happiness from motherhood. But now she was at a profound point of struggle. Her marriage had just ended. She was figuring out how to be a single mother to her four children, ages eleven to sixteen. She had recently had breast cancer, had lost one breast, and would need a second mastectomy in addition to full reconstructive surgery in coming months. She'd never worked full-time since leaving Miramax, only briefly running a small catering business, and was just trying to finish a landscape design course, but her confidence was low. She didn't say this to Jodi at the time, but between the loss of her marriage and her breasts, she felt like her whole womanhood was in question, and she wondered if she would ever feel attractive or wanted again. As they talked on the beach, Jodi realized that even the vacation was trying for Madden. She wasn't used to spending summers on her own.

Besides, her feeling of having been somehow at fault had never lifted. (That was why she had told Jodi only an abbreviated version of the story.) She could never speak out, she had told Jodi, because she was too afraid of being judged for not running away.

But she was speaking privately to Jodi because of a call she had gotten prior to any of their conversations, from an ex-assistant of Weinstein's named Pamela Lubell, to whom she had not spoken in almost two decades. Lubell had effused about how lucky they had all been to work for Miramax, how kind Weinstein had been. Then she asked if Madden had gotten calls from any journalists—"cockroach journalists," she had said. Lubell had wanted assurances that Madden wouldn't speak to them. Madden had refused to make any promises, so Lubell continued to call and push. "If you ever have a project you want to make, you can bring it to me; I can bring it to Harvey," she remembered Lubell saying. Madden was certain that Weinstein had put her old colleague up to the calls. She was direct with Lubell. Yes, Weinstein had harassed her. No, she could not provide any assurance that she wouldn't speak. In fact, she was outraged by the attempt to silence her. That's why she had taken Jodi's first call.

On the beach, Jodi asked Madden to just imagine going on the record with her story. She sketched out the growing scale of the allegations, without using names; told Madden that her story would mean a great deal to others; and promised to go over everything before publication and do whatever she could to make the experience as dignified as possible. If Weinstein retaliated in any way, that would only seal the case against him, she added.

Madden said, cautiously, that she would think about it. She wanted the story to work. Now that Jodi understood the level of personal difficulty Madden was facing, she worried the timing was just wrong for the former assistant. But privately, Madden was thinking the opposite: "Everything felt like it was imploding," she said. "An added bit of implosion didn't seem like such a bad thing." She was craving something proactive, something positive.

And in her own mind, Madden was formulating an even more potent argument to herself. She realized that she was free. She no longer worked in Hollywood. Even more important, she had neither received money to stay silent nor signed a nondisclosure agreement. She began to wonder if she had a responsibility to speak because others could not.

Back in New York, Megan was making one final effort to track down the mysterious 2001 complaint against Miramax filed at the California Department of Fair Employment and Housing. She needed help from someone who knew the territory, who would understand why Megan didn't want to give up. She sent an email to Gloria Allred.

Megan had become acquainted with the feminist attorney in October 2016 while reporting on Trump's treatment of women. After the release of the *Access Hollywood* tape, Allred represented several women who had come forward with allegations against Trump. She had put on tightly controlled press conferences, comforting her clients when they teared up in front of the cameras. When Trump lashed out at his accusers, Allred fought back.

Some journalists and critics saw her as a shameless self-promoter. But after having read Allred's autobiography, spoken with her at length, and interviewed some of her former clients and coworkers, Megan took her very seriously. She knew that as a young, single parent, Allred had struggled to collect child support, been raped at gunpoint at age twenty-five, and gotten an illegal abortion, which almost killed her. Allred's drive to help protect other women and give voice to victims appeared to be the product of her own suffering.

One thing made Megan cautious about seeking help from Allred on the Weinstein investigation: the strange outreach from Lisa Bloom, Allred's daughter. So when she spoke to Allred, she didn't mention Weinstein's name, only that she needed advice on how to obtain an old sexual harassment complaint from a government agency in her state. Allred was muted, with little advice to give. Megan didn't realize, and would never have suspected, that Allred's firm was sitting on separate records about Weinstein, ones that had never come to the attention of the government or the public.

While the attorney cultivated a reputation for giving female victims a voice, some of her work and revenue was in negotiating secret settlements that silenced them and buried allegations of sexual harassment and assault. In 2011, she and a partner had negotiated a settlement with Bill O'Reilly—one of those so breathtakingly restrictive that it had alarmed Emily Steel. In late 2016, when the public was first starting to learn about abuse of elite gymnasts by former team doctor Larry Nassar, Allred was working on a settlement that muzzled Olympic-medal-winning gymnast McKayla Moroney, one of the top names in the sport.

Megan only learned months later that in 2004, Allred's firm had also negotiated a settlement with Weinstein. His alleged victim—the firm's client—was Ashley Matthau (then Anderson), who had worked as a backup dancer in *Dirty Dancing 2: Havana Nights*, a movie produced that year by Miramax. Matthau was twenty-three years old at the time but felt much younger. She had spent her teenage years in the sheltered world of dance, traveling with the American Ballet Theater. Afterward, she had been swept into a world of music videos, Playboy Mansion parties, and other settings where she was expected to look good and say little.

But what happened during the shooting of the film had triggered a deep anger in Matthau, she said. During a visit to the *Dirty Dancing* set in Puerto Rico, Weinstein had insisted Matthau come to his hotel room for a private meeting to discuss future projects. Once they were alone, she said, he had pushed her onto the bed, fondled her breasts and masturbated on top of her. "I kept telling him, 'Stop, I'm engaged,'" Matthau later told Megan. "But he kept saying: 'It's just a little cuddling. It's not a problem. It's not like we're having sex.'" The next day, Weinstein had kept promising her more work, as if they were doing a business deal. "I didn't want him to get away with it. I wanted to stand up for myself."

At the urging of her fiancé, Matthau had turned to Gloria Allred. The fiancé had seen the lawyer on television and thought she could help. Allred steered Matthau to her partner, John West, who encouraged Matthau to enter a private out-of-court settlement. Fearful of going up against Weinstein, and all his power, in public, Matthau had quickly agreed to accept $125,000 in exchange for a legally binding promise to never speak of the allegations again, she said. "I remember John not negotiating that much because he thought I was an emotional wreck and couldn't handle it," Matthau explained. "He suggested I just take the money and move on and try to heal." The firm's cut was 40 percent, she said.

West and Allred refused to comment on the firm's representation of Matthau. But in a separate interview, Allred made the same case for confidential settlements that the reporters had already heard: They were better for clients, many of whom wanted privacy and feared being shunned by employers; going to court was risky and could take years. "Nobody has forced anyone to sign an NDA," she told Megan. "Nobody is holding a gun to their head."

Allred also acknowledged the harsh truth about confidentiality clauses: They served perpetrators of sexual misconduct too. "A client will say, 'I want to be compensated, this is a significant amount you've been able to achieve for me, I'm very happy with that, but why should I have to keep secret?'" Allred said. "That's because that powerful figure wants peace, wants to end it, and wants to move on in the same way that you want to move on."

By 2017, a group of consumer lawyers in California, Allred's home state, had come to see danger in that line of thinking. They thought victims of sexual harassment deserved financial compensation, but settlements shouldn't be used to cover up—and thus perpetuate—predatory behavior. "If there's a serial perpetrator out there, you can't keep these secrets repeatedly because the actions will continue," Nancy Peverini, a lobbyist for the consumer lawyer group, later told Megan.

That January, Connie Leyva, a state legislator, had considered sponsoring legislation, requested by those lawyers, that would transform settlements for sexual harassment in California by banning confidentiality clauses and ensuring that future victims could speak out and name the perpetrators. This was the push that Katie Benner had mentioned to her *Times* colleagues in the Page One conference room.

Then Allred stepped in. On a tense phone call with lobbyists and an aide from Leyva's office, Allred was adamant: Sexual harassers would never make payments to victims without getting silence in return. If the legislation was proposed, she would travel to the state capitol to oppose it.

No bill to protect victims could possibly survive public attack from Gloria Allred, the consumer lawyers knew. She could deploy the many fans who thought of her as the ultimate advocate. Not surprisingly, Connie Leyva backed away from sponsoring the bill. With Allred's threat, an effort to reform the system and protect victims' voices died before it was ever introduced.

CHAPTER FOUR

"POSITIVE REPUTATION MANAGEMENT"

On July 12, Dean Baquet, the executive editor of the *Times*, gathered Jodi, Megan, Corbett, and Matt Purdy in his office. He wanted to hear about the progress of the Weinstein story. But he also had instructions.

Within the newsroom, Baquet's corner office was a place apart, roomier and quieter, containing mementos from a lifetime in the newspaper business. Baquet had grown up in New Orleans, in an apartment behind his parents' Creole restaurant, which was so modest that a cigar box had served as the original cash register. He was the first black editor of the *Times*, but he rarely opened up to his staff about his personal experience of race. Instead, he liked to talk about holding the powerful to account, when to be aggressive or restrained in dealing with them.

That day, Baquet wanted to communicate one thing in particular: Watch out. In 2014, when an early version of Weinstein's troubled theatrical production *Finding Neverland* opened in Cambridge, Massachusetts, Weinstein had tried to get the paper not to review it, knowing that one bad notice could doom the show. He had complained to Baquet and Arthur Sulzberger, then the publisher, making a not-so-subtle reference to the money he spent on advertising in the paper and citing a tradition of New York publications not reviewing out-of-town tryouts. But one of the culture editors had persuaded Baquet that the rule was outdated: *Finding Neverland* was a big budget production, and in the online era, the show was no secret. When Weinstein heard that answer, he told Baquet to expect a call from none other than Meryl Streep.

The call from the famed actress never came, but Baquet was contacted by David Boies, one of the most distinguished lawyers in the country. Boies had tried the government's antitrust case in the 1990s against Microsoft, represented Al Gore in the 2000 presidential recount, and helped convince the Supreme Court to overturn California's ban on gay marriage. He had been serving as counsel for the producer since 2001. But when he dialed Baquet in 2014 to argue against reviewing the *Finding Neverland* tryout, Boies had opened by saying: "I'm not calling as Harvey's lawyer, I'm calling as Harvey's friend." The attorney was being disingenuous about his relationship with Weinstein, Baquet felt, and he had found Boies's chummy, I-just-want-to-straighten-things-out-for-you tone condescending. Baquet refused to change his stance.

The following year, *Finding Neverland* was about to make its Broadway debut, and the *Times* was preparing a story on the production. Weinstein yelled at an editor in the *Times* Culture department to omit any mention of a glaring development: He had just come under police investigation in New York, for the groping complaint from Ambra Battilana Gutierrez. The producer insisted that the accusation was false, and he argued that the *Times* should ignore it, even though it had already gotten widespread coverage in the paper and elsewhere.

Baquet told his staff to keep the reference, and he instructed Weinstein never to speak to his journalists that way again. "You and I are going to have a pretty rough talk soon about how you talk to my editors," Baquet had written in an email to Weinstein in March 2015. "And it will be very rough, trust me."

An investigation of the producer's treatment of women had far higher stakes than any theater coverage, and Baquet predicted that Weinstein would do just about anything to try and stop it. The editor didn't make a big deal of it, but both Weinstein and Boies had already begun calling him and the publisher, requesting off-the-record conversations.

Baquet wanted Jodi and Megan to follow two rules as they went forward. First, expect Weinstein to turn to increasingly desperate practices: employing investigators to trail them or their sources, digging into their pasts. He leveled his gaze at the reporters. "Assume you're being followed," he told them. "Talk like every call is being taped." Second, Baquet did not want the reporters to speak with Weinstein off the record. That would take discipline. What reporter wouldn't want to engage with a subject directly? But Jodi and Megan needed to be strategic, Baquet said. To allow Weinstein to talk in confidence could mean letting him lie with impunity. If he had something to say, he had to say it out loud, on the record.

But in the first week of August, Megan began to question Baquet's rules of engagement after Jodi got an unexpected phone call. It was from Lanny Davis, a Clinton-era Washington lawyer, who ran a lucrative business working as a crisis counselor, often representing unsavory characters, including African leaders who had been investigated by the paper. He had just been hired by Weinstein and wanted to chat off the record. Jodi told him that all communication had to be on the record, but when he resisted, she took the request to Megan and Corbett. As Jodi waited, Davis kept asking her more questions: Could they meet—immediately? Could David Boies join them? "He is a close friend of the client," Davis emailed, repeating the line that had annoyed Baquet years before.

Jodi and Corbett had dealt with Lanny Davis before. He was old school and outwardly cordial, though he had also been known to yell at reporters he thought were treating him or his clients unfairly.

Despite everything Baquet had said, Megan pushed to meet with Davis. She understood the boss's argument, but in her experience, if you engaged with people who had things to hide, they often hung themselves by accident. Besides, she was curious. How had Weinstein supposedly killed previous investigations by journalists? If the producer was up to something, she wanted to know, sooner rather than later.

Megan proposed that she and Jodi talk with Davis on background, meaning they could further report and write about what he said, as long as they didn't attribute any of it to him by name. A couple days later, Corbett said that Jodi and Megan could move forward with the meeting with Davis. But she and Baquet stipulated that the session couldn't serve as a substitute for an on-the-record conversation with Weinstein. Boies was not welcome. And while the reporters had to be straightforward, they would reveal nothing of the actresses and former employees who had begun to quietly tell their troubling stories.

As soon as Jodi called Davis to iron out the details, the loquacious PR man started spilling information about his client. "He's obviously going through very rocky times," Davis said of Weinstein. "And he's not always that rational."

On August 3, Davis pulled up a seat at a long table in a *Times* conference room, chatting about baseball, being one of Hillary Clinton's closest friends, and his years at Yale Law School. Corbett had joined Jodi and Megan for the meeting, a mark of the seriousness of the moment. Megan took out her iPhone and, with Davis's permission, began audio recording their conversation. As often happened, the click of that button ended the small talk.

"The reason I'm here is not to try to kill anything or not to try to spin or misdirect," Davis said. He had several other goals in mind.

The first was to defend. He mentioned the veiled rape claim Rose McGowan had made against Weinstein on Twitter the year before. His team knew she might include the allegation in the memoir she was writing. If Jodi and Megan were intending to report the charge, Davis wanted a chance to respond to the accusation.

That was easy. Of course, the *Times* would ask Weinstein to address any allegations.

The second was to probe: "I don't expect you to name sources, especially in a story like this one—but if it's possible for you to let me know overall what your story is about, it would help me basically do my job, which is to answer your questions and make sure they're true," Davis said.

Another simple one. Jodi and Megan told Davis they were looking into problematic behavior toward women by Weinstein and left it at that.

His third goal was to pitch. While Weinstein adamantly denied any allegation of rape or assault, he was aware of a growing number of complaints about his treatment of women, Davis explained. Weinstein had started to see his previous behavior in a different light. Powerful men of an older generation were changing their understanding of the meaning of the word *consensual*, Davis said—and "why women don't feel it's consensual even if a man convinces himself it is."

Where was Davis going with this? It wasn't easy to say. They saw that day, and in the following weeks, that he was a challenging professional communicator. He delivered statements that lacked precise meaning. He parceled out some useful information about his high-profile clients, but some of his claims proved wrong.

"I believe that there is a story to be told here about the evolution of men, and in particular Harvey Weinstein on this subject," Davis said.

His words grew even more elliptical: "So the bigger story may well be here that what has been out there for a long time about Harvey and lots of people in Hollywood who are men, powerful men, there may be something that when you're done with your article that is speaking much more broadly to men reaching a different awareness of this issue."

Just what did Davis seem to be tentatively offering? Was Weinstein willing to give Megan and Jodi an interview, in which he would discuss his own questionable behavior toward women?

Davis had just started talking to Weinstein about this possibility, he said, noting that his client had to "deal with his wife and children before anything else." But he thought the producer might be willing to have this discussion with the reporters. "I've been at least a little bit encouraged" that it could happen, he said.

This was only the first meeting with Weinstein's team, and his side seemed to already be acknowledging misconduct. That was a hint that the full extent of the findings could be far worse. If Weinstein was already really willing to talk about wrongs he had committed, the interview could be monumental, and the investigation much easier than any of them had anticipated. But the idea of Weinstein coming into the newsroom and opening up about sexual transgressions was implausible. Almost no one ever admitted to these things without being confronted with evidence.

The journalists told Davis that of course they'd be open to hearing anything the producer had to say—on the record. They left it at that: If Davis was trying to dangle some sort of trade, a halt to their investigation in exchange for an interview, they weren't engaging.

Instead, Megan changed the subject back to Rose McGowan. Davis was adamant that her rape accusation was false, and that a main reason she should not be trusted was the absence of any "contemporaneous outcry" at the time of the alleged attack. "Did she tell anybody right away? Did she show signs of distress?" he asked.

But McGowan had told Megan and Jodi that she had indeed appeared upset immediately after her encounter with Weinstein in a hotel room in 1997. She had told her manager, and then a lawyer, who had helped her obtain the $100,000 payment from Weinstein. McGowan had not yet gone on the record with the reporters, and they were still searching for corroboration that she had gotten a settlement. Maybe by pressing Davis on his characterization of events, Megan could back him into a corner and confirm that a settlement had been paid.

Megan leaned in: Was Davis *sure* McGowan hadn't shown any signs of distress at the time? Was last year's tweet the *first* time Weinstein had learned of any concerns that the actress had about an encounter with him?

Davis's narrative shifted. "Concerns?" he said. "Yes, there—he was aware that there were concerns, but not that she was accusing him of rape. So I'm making a bright line on the word *rape.* Anything below that line, he was aware of feeling, concerns . . ."

Corbett asked, "Of what kind?"

"And if the concerns were not about rape," Jodi asked, "then what were they about?"

Davis had intended to tell the journalists what Weinstein *hadn't* done to McGowan. Now he had to explain what the producer *had* done. "The only way I can answer, Jodi, based on what I now know, is a sense of being exploited because of that disparate power relationship. Taken advantage of, exploited, a wide range of verbs that post facto, or even in the middle of an incident, women are made to feel in an unequal position."

"There's mental coercion that isn't physical coercion," Davis said, adding that Lisa Bloom had been working with Weinstein to help him recognize the difference. "I know that he's mentioned that Lisa has looked at this, looked at him, looked at his past conduct, and has helped him understand that."

Lisa Bloom! The attorney who had emailed Jodi a few weeks before. What else was there to know about her relationship with the producer? But instead of asking that question they needed to press Davis on what Weinstein knew about McGowan and when.

If Weinstein had in fact been made aware of McGowan's concerns at the time, how did he respond?

"I believe he had dealings legally with her about them," Davis said.

"How would you characterize those legal dealings?" Megan asked. They were that close to confirmation of a settlement.

"I think he became aware that she did not regard what happened as okay with her," Davis said. "I'm not talking about rape; I'm talking about the effect that he had on Rose McGowan. She says that it was a severe effect. That rather than fighting . . ."

"Rather than fighting—then what?" Megan asked.

"I think that he has agreed to settlements rather than litigating what he might have litigated," Davis said. As Weinstein saw it, Davis explained, "It's better to settle even if you haven't done anything wrong."

Yes! They had been interacting with Weinstein's side for only minutes, and Davis was already confirming the settlement Weinstein had paid to McGowan and hinting at a larger pattern of payoffs.

Were there other cases of "questionable intimate relations with women in which Weinstein settled?" Megan asked. The reporters didn't say so, but so far they were aware of McGowan, Perkins, and Chiu, and they believed one might have been paid to the assistant who had fled the New York office. Megan had also come to suspect that Ambra Battilana Gutierrez, who made the police complaint in 2015, had been paid off. Did Davis know the truth?

Now Davis was squirming. "So I was trying to be careful because I'm not sure what my legal position is on admitting that there have been settlements and that the settlements involved sexual personal behavior. So let's say for now, even on a background basis, that I need to find out what my limits are legally, even if on background I am confirming settlements. I need to just find out where I stand. But the answer is, yes, there have been, but I just need to find out how I can better define that for you."

Before he departed, Megan wanted to ask one more thing. Baquet's warnings about private detectives, intimidation, and threats lingered in her mind. She asked the lawyer: Aside from hiring Davis, what else had Weinstein done in response to the interviews she and Jodi were conducting? Had he tried to interfere with the reporting in any way?

"Listen, the guy can be a jerk," Davis said. "Depends on the mood he's in and how much food he's eaten."

But, no, he insisted, the producer had no intentions of getting in the way of their reporting. Davis said he had asked Weinstein that question directly during their first meeting: "Do you have any plans to engage people to go on the attack for anyone who's cooperating with the *New York Times*? I need to know."

Davis said Weinstein's answer was unequivocal: "No" and "I don't intend to do that."

Davis left the conference room promising to pursue the potential interview with Weinstein. The journalists were still skeptical but felt encouraged. Perhaps Weinstein recognized that he couldn't halt the *Times* investigation. Just as important, Davis was recorded saying Weinstein wouldn't even try.

But the producer had been ahead of the investigation from the start. His efforts to conceal his alleged offenses had begun all the way back in October 2016, when McGowan had first tweeted, *New York* magazine had tried to pursue the story, and Weinstein had told Paltrow not to speak. He had spent hundreds of thousands of dollars to identify people who might talk, to cover his tracks, and even to have obtained passages from McGowan's memoir as she was drafting it. By the time of Davis's meeting at the *Times*, he had been combating Jodi and Megan's work in ways that went far beyond labeling them "cockroach journalists."

The astounding thing was how much help he had.

On July 10, two days before the meeting in Baquet's office and about a month before the conversation with Lanny Davis, David Boies was preparing to board a private helicopter in East Hampton following a family birthday celebration. Weinstein rang his phone—again. The producer had been calling the lawyer frequently, according to Weinstein's assistants. Cloaked in the secrecy of attorney-client privilege, the two men were plotting how to fight any *Times* story.

Weinstein was calling to share a fresh idea, Boies later recalled. The producer explained that he considered Arthur Sulzberger Jr., the *Times* publisher, to be a friend. Weinstein's companies had been a major advertiser over the years. The two men had shared business lunches and long moved in similar circles. Now Weinstein could use that relationship to lean on Sulzberger Jr. to kill the story, he suggested.

The producer and the lawyer, who had been working together for sixteen years, had contrasting styles. Weinstein was bold but erratic, brutish, and sometimes unsophisticated; Boies was polished and persuasive. The lawyer curbed some of the producer's worst instincts but enabled others to protect a man he knew had been repeatedly accused of predatory behavior.

The son of teachers from Illinois, Boies had grown up with undiagnosed dyslexia that stunted his learning. Yet he had gone on to earn a law degree from Yale and slay corporate giants. Boies was daring. He had been an enthusiastic card player since youth, had been expelled from the first law school he attended for having an affair with a professor's wife (he later married her), and had offended previous law partners with his renegade ways.

He also liked to be at the center of popular culture. When Boies left one law firm to start his own—to avoid a conflict of interest that would have prevented him from representing a new client, New York Yankees owner George Steinbrenner—he quickly attracted other celebrities, including Calvin Klein, Don Imus, and Garry Shandling.

Among those seeking his services were the editors of Miramax Books, a new publishing imprint that Weinstein and his brother, Bob, had launched. It was 2001, and Boies had just lost *Bush v. Gore*, a defeat of immeasurable consequence that the attorney had somehow used to win over legions of new fans. The editors wanted Boies to write a memoir, but the famous lawyer wasn't returning their calls. Then, one day, Weinstein himself phoned, asking for a lunch date, Boies later recalled in a series of interviews with Megan.

Soon, Boies was meeting the Weinstein brothers at Tribeca Grill. The lawyer was clear: He didn't have time to write a book, and he wasn't that self-reflective. Weinstein wouldn't let it go. Boies said Weinstein made the task sound easy: All he had to do was write down the story of some of his cases. By the end of the meal, Boies had agreed.

The next year came and went without him writing a single word. One afternoon his wife looked up from the computer. "Sweetheart, you didn't tell me that you'd finished your book," she said. "What book?" Boies replied. "Well, the book for Harvey," she replied. "I just looked it up and it says it will be published this fall." Boies felt completely boxed in. If he didn't follow through, he would look like he had failed. He wrote every day until the book was on his editor's desk. From the start of the relationship, Weinstein seemed to know just how to conscript him, and Boies did not say no.

Weinstein got more than the book. He had secured new legal representation, and within months of their first lunch in 2001, the lawyer was privately helping the producer fight off a potential article about Rowena Chiu's allegation of sexual assault.

In 2002, the *New Yorker* writer Ken Auletta had heard from a source about the settlements that Weinstein had paid to Zelda Perkins and Chiu—the same ones Jodi and Megan were now piecing together. Auletta had been unable to get Perkins and Chiu to speak with him, but he was still hoping to write about the payoffs and the incident that prompted them.

Auletta, David Remnick, the magazine's editor, another editor, and its lawyer met with Weinstein, his brother, Bob, and David Boies to discuss the matter. At first, Boies appeared to be playing referee. When Weinstein insisted he would file an injunction against the magazine, Boies patted Weinstein's arm, saying that there was something called the First Amendment that he couldn't get around. But then Boies turned his attention to the journalists, saying that running the story would be a grave mistake.

Boies later told Megan that he had believed Weinstein's claim that his encounter with Chiu had been a consensual, extramarital dalliance. He had thought it was plausible that women were lying in order to milk Weinstein for money, a point he emphasized in the meeting at the *New Yorker*. In a follow-up session with the *New Yorker* journalists the next day, Bob Weinstein handed over copies of personal checks that he had written to pay off the two women on behalf of his brother: proof, he claimed, that no company money had been used for Weinstein's personal affairs. Without an on-the-record allegation of assault, or any proof of misuse of company funds, Auletta said he and his editors agreed he could not write about the settlements.

By then, Boies had become counsel to the Weinstein brothers, and he was increasingly enmeshed in their work. The brothers were battling Disney. When the parent company refused to distribute Michael Moore's *Fahrenheit 9/11*, Boies helped the brothers regain control of the film and take it to Lionsgate Films. When the Weinsteins decided to leave Disney altogether and form The Weinstein Company in 2005, Boies helped secure contracts that specified the brothers could be fired only if convicted of a felony.

Weinstein and Boies attended film openings, charity events, and political fund-raisers together, two celebrities among celebrities. Boies admired that "Harvey's always selling something," and in Weinstein he had a valuable link to the film world. His daughter, Mary Regency, was an aspiring actress. Boies invested in the industry himself, forming a pro-

duction company, the Boies/Schiller Film Group, in 2012, with one of his
law partner's sons. Over the years, Boies and the group did business with
The Weinstein Company, and Weinstein provided his lawyer invaluable
favors, including discussing a role for Boies's daughter, who had appeared
in a minor role in a little-seen, hardly reviewed 2011 film called *Son of
Morning.*

Dear David,

I hope you're doing well. Thank you for sending me SON OF
MORNING. I watched it with my team—Mary is wonderful in the film.
The movie is a tough one—I don't think it is commercial or the right fit
for me—but Mary shines through in it.

If you can get me all of her scenes and previous work. I'll have my
team put together a great promo reel for her and get it to the right
casting agents. I'll also put her in touch with my people internally to
get her a small role in my upcoming production I DON'T KNOW HOW
SHE DOES IT with Sarah Jessica Parker. Anything I can do to help.

All my best,
Harvey

That part never materialized, but the next year, Mary Regency got a
part in his film *Silver Linings Playbook*. In October 2011, Jon Gordon, a former Weinstein assistant who was helping produce the film, sent an email
to Weinstein about the actress, asking for instructions on behalf of David
O. Russell, the director:

David read and wants David Boies' daughter, Regency, to play Dr.
Patel's secretary.
DAVID O. DID NOT OFFER HER THE PART YET AS HE
WANTED TO KNOW IF YOU WANTED/NEEDED TO DO
SOMETHING FIRST WITH DAVID BOIES.

Did these film entanglements with Weinstein explain why Boies had worked to conceal mounting allegations of sexual misconduct against the producer? "Well, it could, you know?" Boies said. "If I'm Harvey's lawyer, I'm going to try to keep things under wraps. That's my job, right?"

Boies said that with or without entanglements, "I am very dedicated to my clients."

In the following years, the lawyer continued learning of other accusers. Time and again, he came to Weinstein's defense, and helped him to conceal, spin, and silence. He chose to believe Weinstein's claims that he was guilty only of philandering. "I thought, like a lot of people in Hollywood surrounded by very attractive women who want to make him like them, he ended up in multiple affairs," Boies said.

Even years later, after the scale of Weinstein's alleged offenses were revealed, Boies saw no problem with the lengths he had gone to protect him.

"When I look back I don't have any regret that I represented him the way I did," he said.

On a summer evening in 2017, when Weinstein raised the prospect of leaning on Sulzberger, Boies swatted away the idea as a waste of time. Exerting pressure like that might have worked elsewhere, but it would prove worthless at the *Times*.

Instead, Boies was focused on a stealthier way to try to block a *Times* story, just a variation of something Weinstein was already doing.

The producer had long relied on private detectives to protect his reputation. Those companies were basically professional watchers: They observed journalists, wrote reports, sometimes even picked through reporters' garbage. According to the unwritten rules of journalist-subject interactions, using private detectives was a shady practice, but not a surprising or illegal one. As Baquet had said, it was something Jodi and Megan should expect.

But nine months earlier, Weinstein had begun a secret relationship with an Israeli firm of a whole different order: "The black cube group from israel contacted me thru ehud Barack," Weinstein had written in an email to Boies on Oct. 16, 2016, later obtained by Megan. "They r strategists and say your firm have used them." Black Cube did far more than watch other people. It manipulated them as well, even using an actor who adopted a fake identity in order to dupe unsuspecting targets. Others were former military intelligence experts. At the time of the email, two of its operatives had just been arrested on hacking charges in Romania. Boies's law firm, Boies, Schiller & Flexner, had in fact used Black Cube before, and soon the law firm was executing an agreement between Weinstein and the Israeli company. Under the terms of a contract struck that October, Weinstein agreed to pay the professional manipulators $100,000 a month to shield his behavior from scrutiny.

Soon the relationship was in full swing.

Seth Freedman, a British freelance journalist, fed Black Cube information that he was collecting from women whom Weinstein feared would go public with damaging information about him. Freedman told the women he was a reporter who had worked for the *Guardian*, sometimes claiming he was writing about life in Hollywood, other times the film industry. Katherine Kendall, an actress, and other women who fielded phone calls from Freedman, said they spoke freely, never suspecting he was doing anything aside from straightforward journalism.

Black Cube went to work on Benjamin Wallace, the writer investigating Weinstein's treatment of women for *New York* magazine. Freedman had contacted him offering information of interest but never delivering. Wallace had also been approached by a female Black Cube agent posing as a potential source. When they met, Wallace didn't say much to the woman, who called herself Anna, suspecting she might be working for Weinstein. Eventually, he and his editors decided to suspend the investigation. No one was talking, Wallace later explained; the Weinstein story felt like a dead end.

By May 2017, the same agent was targeting McGowan. This time, the woman called herself Diana Filip, and said she was the head of sustainable and responsible investments for the wealth-management firm Reuben Capital Partners in London. She spoke with a German accent, used a UK cell phone number, and offered McGowan $60,000 for a speaking event.

Over the next months, they met at least three times in whichever city was convenient to McGowan, conversing for hours about women's issues and the woman's stated desire to invest in McGowan's production company. McGowan read her a passage of her memoir.

"She presented as someone who really cared about women," McGowan later told Megan.

Now, in July 2017, Boies helped renegotiate Weinstein's contract with Black Cube with the goal of solving two problems. The first was Jodi and Megan's reporting. The second was that Weinstein and Black Cube were in a billing dispute. The Israeli firm expected a bonus for procuring information about McGowan's memoir, but Weinstein refused to pay, arguing that the pages mostly reiterated her tweet, Boies said.

Under the contract that Boies helped revise, Black Cube's mission became much more explicit: to halt Jodi and Megan's investigation.

Black Cube would "provide intelligence which will help the Client's efforts to completely stop the publication of a new negative article in a leading NY newspaper," along with gathering more information from McGowan's book. The agent "Anna," aka Diana Filip, the woman who had approached McGowan and Wallace, would be on the case full time. So would a so-called freelance journalist. The contract also promised continued "avatar operators" to create fake identities on social media, linguists, and "operations experts" to concentrate on "social engineering," all of whom would be advised by former heads of the Israeli intelligence services. If Black Cube was able to stop publication of the article, it would earn a $300,000 bonus. Boies signed the new contract on July 11, weeks before Lanny Davis met with Jodi, Megan, and Corbett at the *Times*.

In genially dangling the prospect of an interview to the journalists, Davis had never mentioned that at his first meeting with Weinstein a Black Cube agent had been present. He only told Megan that much later, saying that he had not known exactly what the agent was doing for his client.

The same week as the meeting with Davis, Jodi received a series of emails and texts from the same Diana Filip. Jodi had never heard of her, but she said she was from an organization called Reuben Capital Partners in London and that she was staging a series of events devoted to advancing women in the workplace and wanted her to contribute. Jodi had already brushed off the requests, but in an email the woman was persistent:

Hi Jodi,

Thanks for clarifying.

We are planning a series of round table discussions about gender inequality and discrimination in the workplace. Our aim is to get policymakers, different industries executives, journalists and other stakeholders to discuss these issues from different perspectives.

Some prominent individuals have already expressed their willingness to take part in this initiative, and we are now in the process of finalising the schedule and agenda.

At some point along the way I would love to get your input (in any way possible, even if not as a speaker), given your work in the field.

I want these events to have real impact and value and be much more than just empty talk, so I want to make sure that all the right questions are asked. As you can probably tell, I am very passionate about this project—in fact, this is very much my own initiative.

I understand the difficulties in you having a direct role, but, nevertheless, I would love to have a quick chat with you and hear your thoughts.

Thanks so much for your time,
Diana.

Something about the email seemed slightly off—Jodi couldn't say exactly what. She sent the message to the paper's online security expert, who said the URL looked fine. The website, showing a smiling picture of a woman in a business suit, was a call for gender equality in the corporate sphere. "Women earn less, get promoted less, and are underappreciated in the workplace," the site said. "This initiative will not only focus on combating all forms of discrimination against women in the workplace, but also work towards promoting the inclusion of women in business—actively and at all levels." By the standards of corporate feminism, the language was tougher than usual, calling for "progressive activism" and "full transparency" from companies.

Instead of beckoning to Jodi, this warned her off. Her job was to gather information and uncover secrets, not participate in activism. And because *Times* ethics rules prohibited journalists from accepting corporate speaking gigs, to protect the paper against attempts at buying influence, she couldn't have accepted the money. Nor did she have time for nice-to-meet-you coffee dates.

A few days later, Filip emailed again. Jodi wrote back tersely to convey her lack of interest: "I am tied up, but good luck w your project."

Later Ronan Farrow would uncover some of Black Cube's work for Weinstein. Boies said he believed the best way for Weinstein to beat back critical stories about his treatment of women was to provide facts that reinforced his defense, and that he thought Black Cube would gather that information. He said he was unaware of the underhanded tactics the firm used against journalists and regretted not paying closer attention. Remarkably, Boies's firm had helped execute a contract to undermine the *Times* investigation even as it was representing the newspaper in legal cases. Boies insisted this did not constitute a conflict of interest, but the paper fired his firm, calling its actions "reprehensible."

But in the summer of 2017, Jodi never guessed that the rah-rah feminist messages she was getting were from an actor-agent hired to sabotage their investigation and undercut victims' stories. Nor did she suspect they were connected in any way to Boies. At Baquet's instructions, she and Megan had rejected the attorney's requests to meet with him. He seemed like a distant suit relegated to the sidelines.

Just as Megan and Jodi were sizing up Weinstein's team, Emily Steel sent over a glowing, newly published profile of Gloria Allred and Lisa Bloom in *W* magazine. "Gloria Allred and Lisa Bloom Are the Defenders of Women in 2017," read the headline.

The article described Allred's daughter as her heir and equal, the two standing together at the forefront of civil rights issues, especially "the sexual harassment and assault of women by powerful men." The lawyers posed against the beachscape of Allred's Malibu home, looking more like sisters than parent and child.

As with her mother, Bloom's métier was public attention. Over the course of her career, she had appeared as a legal analyst on many networks and even hosted her own show on *Court TV.* She had her own Los Angeles firm, and she appeared to more or less replicate her mother's model: She cultivated high-profile clients and then often scored big settlements for them in private.

Her public relations skills were on display in the *W* profile. Bloom boasted about the confidential settlement she had just reached: "Women who were sexually harassed became millionaires," she said. For the interview, Bloom had shown up wearing a "Notorious R.B.G." T-shirt, as if to claim a link with the most supreme feminist lawyer of all, Ruth Bader Ginsburg.

So why had Bloom signed on to work with a rumored sexual predator? Was it related to the movie deal, the one Bloom had tweeted about triumphantly a few months before? What motivated her, and how did she operate?

Megan told Jodi and Steel that she had first become suspicious of Bloom in 2016 when the lawyer got involved in the lawsuit alleging that Donald J. Trump had raped a thirteen-year-old girl at a party hosted by Jeffrey Epstein in the 1990s, the one that Megan had refused to cover because it had been impossible to vet the anonymous victim's claims. One week before Election Day, with debate raging about the *Access Hollywood* tape, and the mounting allegations against Trump, Bloom had announced that she was representing the Jane Doe victim. Megan had never spoken to Bloom, but she quickly sent her an email.

I've long viewed this as a dubious case and have doubted the existence of a real plaintiff/victim.

Have you met with the actual plaintiff and concluded this is
legitimate?
I'd really value your perspective.

Megan never got a response. Instead, she watched as Bloom convened a press conference at her office in Los Angeles, where Jane Doe was to make her first public appearance.

The only person who stepped in front of the cameras that day was Bloom. She announced that the victim, who she said was there at her office, had gotten death threats and was too terrified to go public. Perhaps that was true; maybe Bloom's client had in fact been raped by Trump and was genuinely fearful to speak out. But to Megan the whole thing looked like an elaborate effort to draw media attention to unsubstantiated allegations against the presidential candidate.

Later, Bloom acknowledged that she solicited money from a pro-Clinton political advocacy organization, saying that she needed the money to vet Jane Doe's claim, and that after the lawsuit was dropped, she had accepted $700,000 from pro-Clinton donors for security, relocation, and a possible "safe house" for other potential Trump accusers. When the other women chose not to come forward, Bloom reportedly gave back $500,000 of the donations, but kept the other $200,000, later telling the *Times* that she needed "some funds to pay for her out-of-pocket expenses." When the financial arrangements were later revealed, Republicans accused Bloom of offering money to women to make up lies about Trump. Others saw it as the lawyer manipulating shaky Trump accusations for her own financial gain.

Bloom said later that she had spent months vetting Jane Doe and that, in the end, the woman was too afraid to go public, so she had instructed her team to drop the case and not discuss it further. She said she did not take any fees for her work with Trump accusers.

Around the same time, some of Bloom's own clients came to criticize her. In 2016, Steel had quietly begun interviewing Tamara Holder, a politically progressive lawyer and former Fox contributor, who had filed a complaint with the network, alleging that she had been sexually assaulted. According to legal documents that Steel had seen, Holder claimed that in February 2015, when she was working as host of a show called *Sports Court*, a Fox executive named Francisco Cortes had trapped her in his office and tried to force her to perform oral sex.

As Steel was conducting her reporting, Bloom helped Holder secure a settlement worth more than $2.5 million. Holder said she had not understood the terms of the agreement, which were especially ironclad. If the *Times* or the *Wall Street Journal* published articles about her experience, Holder would lose much of the money. "I never signed this with the understanding that if Steel"—or a *Wall Street Journal* reporter—"wrote a story, I would lose the 2nd payment," she later wrote to Bloom.

Holder was outraged. As she saw it, Bloom had pressured her to accept an agreement without disclosing the extent to which it placed Holder at financial risk. Even worse, she feared she had lost the option to go public with her story, something she had made clear to Bloom was more valuable to her than any payout. When she voiced her concerns shortly after the settlement was struck, she said, Bloom fired her as a client, walking away with $1 million.

"She did not care about me," Holder later told Megan. "She cared about the money."

Bloom denied ever pressuring her to settle, said she goes over settlement agreements line by line with her clients, and that it's standard for representation to end once a settlement is complete. Bloom also pointed out that Holder, herself, is an experienced civil rights attorney.

On Saturday night, August 26, Megan unexpectedly heard a story about Lisa Bloom that began to illustrate the work she was doing for Weinstein.

Megan was meeting someone who she hoped would explain an unusual financial transaction involving *Finding Neverland*, the Weinstein Broadway production that Baquet had mentioned, and amfAR, the AIDS charity for which he helped throw splashy gala auctions in Cannes. As the show struggled to get off the ground, Weinstein had arranged for $600,000 raised at a 2015 amfAR auction to flow into the pockets of the *Finding Neverland* investors, without disclosing that to the charity. Some of the charity's leaders felt duped and feared that something illegal had happened.

Megan was meeting Tom Ajamie, a lawyer who had been hired by amfAR's board to look into the matter. He told Megan how investigating Weinstein was like nothing he had ever been through. The producer had blocked his review of the financial transaction at every turn. David Boies had muzzled members of the board with NDAs. Meanwhile, the more Ajamie asked around about Weinstein, the more he heard about allegations of sexual harassment and abuse.

Ajamie was so troubled by the claims that he raised them with Bloom when he met her for a drink in Los Angeles in October 2016. Ajamie had met Bloom once before, was impressed by her feminist credentials, and hoped to forge more of a professional relationship. If she was willing to go after powerful men like Donald Trump, surely she wouldn't be afraid to take on Harvey Weinstein, he reasoned. Maybe she was already working with some of his victims?

Bloom told Ajamie that she had never heard any complaints about Weinstein's treatment of women and asked him to keep her posted, he said. But several months later, things got weird. Bloom accepted Ajamie's offer to stay with him and some friends at a condo he rented in Park City, Utah, during the January 2017 Sundance Film Festival. After attending a party hosted by Weinstein and Jay-Z, Bloom had returned saying that Weinstein wanted to meet with Ajamie. Reluctantly, he allowed Bloom to bring him to Weinstein's suite at the Main and SKY hotel for breakfast. One minute, Weinstein was lashing out at Ajamie for digging into his past. Moments later, he was pleading that they work out a deal of some kind. All Ajamie had to do was sign an NDA drawn up by Boies agreeing to keep anything he had learned about Weinstein secret. "Let's just be friends," Ajamie recalled Weinstein telling him. "We can do business together."

Ajamie rejected any deal in exchange for his silence, and he left the room convinced that the $600,000 amfAR transaction was the least of what the producer had to hide.

Afterward, he recalled, as he and Bloom were leaving, she turned to him. During the meeting, Bloom had presented herself as a neutral party and mostly kept quiet. Now she had some advice.

"You know, I think you really should reconsider your position toward him," she said.

"What do you mean?" Ajamie asked.

"He can really help your career," she replied.

By the time of the Park City trip, Bloom had already been working with the producer for six weeks, at a rate of $895 per hour.

Much later, Bloom said that representing Weinstein in 2017 was a "colossal mistake" which she "deeply regretted." "I was naïve to believe he had only used inappropriate language with women, and to think that I could get to the root of the problem in a different way, by encouraging him to apologize, which he did when the story broke," she wrote in an email to Jodi and Megan. "Clearly my approach did not go over at all and I should have known better. Should I have assumed that it could have been a lot worse than what I knew at the time? Yes. That's on me."

But contrary to what she wrote in that email, when Bloom was retained by Weinstein in December 2016, she appeared to know a lot about what she was getting into—and proposed a role for herself that was far darker than just encouraging him to apologize. She laid out that vision in a memo, later obtained by Megan, that she sent to Weinstein, along with private investigators named Jack Palladino and Sara Ness:

Harvey,

It was a treat to speak with you today, though yes, we'd all prefer better circumstances. I've spent the rest of the day reading Jack and Sara's thorough reports about Rose, who truly comes across as a disturbed pathological liar, and also your former assistant . . . who seems to be less of a concern. I also read through a lot of Rose's

Twitter feed, to get a sense of her, and watched her short film, *Dawn*. (I'm no film critic, but I found it dreadful, but telling as to who Rose is: boy meets girl. Girl trusts boy. Boy murders girl. All men suck. The end.)

I feel equipped to help you against the Roses of the world, because I have represented so many of them. They start out as impressive, bold women, but the more one presses for evidence, the weaknesses and lies are revealed. She doesn't seem to have much going on these days except her rapidly escalating identity as a feminist warrior, which seems to be entirely based on her online rants. For her to keep her "RoseArmy" following she must continue ramping up the outrageousness of her diatribes.

Clearly she must be stopped in her ridiculous, defamatory attacks on you. She is dangerous. You are right to be concerned.

Options after my initial read, which I can flesh out on our next call:

1. Initiating friendly contact with her through me or other good intermediary, and after establishing a relationship work out a "win-win." Key question: **what does she want?** To direct, it appears?

2. Counterops online campaign to push back and call her out as a pathological liar. A few well placed articles now will go a long way if things blow up for us down the line. We can place an article re her becoming increasingly unglued, so that when someone Googles her this is what pops up and she is discredited. We have all the facts based on publicly available information. This can begin simultaneous with #1.

3. Cease and desist letter from me, warning her of the violation of agreement with you and putting her on notice of causes of action

for CA claims of false light, invasion of privacy, defamation etc. Risk: she posts the letter online, generating heat and backlash. (Sara: I need to see the agreement, please.)

4. You and I come out publicly in a pre-emptive interview where you talk about evolving on women's issues, prompted by death of your mother, Trump pussy grab tape, and maybe, nasty unfounded hurtful rumors about you. This will be headline grabbing if you express genuine contrition for anyone who you hurt, while emphasizing it was always adult consensual behavior. You thought that was enough at the time but now realize it's more nuanced, that a power imbalance means something, etc. You reached out to me to help understand rapidly evolving social mores around sexual misconduct because you are a good and decent person (as evidenced by your life's work making films on important social issues and extremely generous philanthropy). Example: Charlie Sheen, as women were set to come out against him re HIV status, did a Today Show interview recently where he came out with it himself, receiving massive praise. I represented a few of the women and their stories were largely drowned out by his interview and the love he got for it. It is so key from a reputation management standpoint to be the first to tell the story. I strongly recommend this. If you agree, I'd like to come out and meet with you to go over the story in some detail, so this is done for maximum effectiveness. You should be the hero of the story, not the villain. This is very doable.

5. Start the Weinstein Foundation, focusing on gender equality in film, etc. Or establish the Weinstein Standards, which seek to have one-third of films directed by women, or written by women,

or passing the Bechdel test (two named female characters talk to each other about something besides a man), whatever. Announce you will immediately raise standards re gender parity in very specific ways on all films under your control. Announce partnership with Geena Davis' group that works for gender equality in film, for example by mandating that half of all extras in crowd scenes will be female. You get the idea. These details can be worked out, but the point is you decide to be a leader and raise the bar in a concrete, headline-grabbing way.

6. Positive reputation management. I Googled your name, and a few obnoxious articles pop up. I work with the leading reputation management company that can backlink to the positive articles to make a "firewall" which prevents negative pieces from ranking well on Google. Your first page of Google is key as 95% never go beyond the first Google page. Let's improve this. Easy to do. This should happen simultaneously with other option.

A reminder: would you please connect me with David Boies so that I can get retained?

Also, given that your emails with the Clinton campaign were hacked recently, I recommend you set up a secure new email account for emails with this team. We shouldn't be emailing on these sensitive matters to your company email as your IT people and others may have access.

Thanks and really honored to be brought into this team.

Talk tomorrow?

Best,

Lisa Bloom

Weinstein paid her an initial retainer of $50,000. The billing records that followed provided her own private accounting of what she did to help Weinstein.

She collaborated with the Black Cube agent "Anna," aka Diana Filip. She huddled with Weinstein and Boies. She helped orchestrate the collection of information on Rose McGowan, Ambra Battilana Gutierrez, Ashley Judd, and other women who might accuse Weinstein. Bloom worked hand in hand with Sara Ness, the private investigator who was compiling dossiers on journalists investigating Weinstein, tracking their social media accounts for clues on who their sources were. Just as Baquet had predicted: Weinstein and his team were watching the reporters, using their every click on social media to try to figure out with whom they were talking.

"Based on social media activity and comments made by HW, so far the following names appear to be among the more relevant/important potential sources for Kantor and Farrow," Ness said in the dossier, which Jodi and Megan only saw months later. It went on for pages, listing who they followed on Twitter and when they had started following them. Several of Jodi and Megan's most important sources were on the list.

Some assessments turned out to be off-kilter. "It is difficult to predict whether McGowan would grant either Farrow or Kantor an interview," the investigator wrote, after Jodi and Megan had already been in conversation with McGowan for weeks. "It seems unlikely Judd would want to go on the record and rehash the 2015 *Variety* article," she noted. And Weinstein, "does not believe Paltrow is a threat."

But other notes were scarily on point. Several of the women were described as potential "adverse sources," including the assistant who had fled Miramax in 1990, the one Megan had found at her mother's home.

"Adverse sources" sounded a lot like another word: adversaries. With the help of a large team, Weinstein was waging war.

CHAPTER FIVE

A COMPANY'S COMPLICITY

Throughout August and into September 2017, Jodi and Megan had a growing problem: For all they had learned about Weinstein's alleged mistreatment of women, there was little that could be said in print.

One night, Rebecca Corbett took the reporters to a quiet Midtown Manhattan bar and asked for an update. Jodi and Megan listed what they knew, so far. The stars who had told them Weinstein stories. The former employees. The settlements.

Corbett knew exactly what material they had. She was making a point. How many women were on the record? How many settlements had been confirmed? Of the women with firsthand accounts of abuse, only Laura Madden had said yes to going on the record, and her answer was not final. Their evidence of the payoffs was incomplete.

"You do not have a publishable story," Corbett said.

Persuading former Weinstein employees to speak was not getting any easier, particularly when it came to the innermost circle of executives who had served with the producer over the years. Talking was not in their self-interest. Why would they want the world to know that they had risen in their careers by enabling a man who seemed to be a predator? The best shot was to convince them that the *Times* investigation was a way to mitigate past wrongs, a safe way to address behavior that had, perhaps, eaten away at them.

At the end of a not particularly revelatory conversation with one executive, Jodi heard something intriguing. The subject was one of Weinstein's top lieutenants, Irwin Reiter, The Weinstein Company's executive vice president for accounting and financial reporting. Former colleagues had described him as the company's institutional memory: He had done the books for the brothers since 1989. He had also been described as a loyalist, gruff, and unlikely to be concerned about his boss's treatment of women. But this executive also said something no one else had mentioned. "Irwin Reiter *hates* Harvey Weinstein," the source said.

Jodi had been holding on to Reiter's phone number, waiting to call until she had some insight into him. Now that moment had come. When she rang him, he said he didn't want to speak—but before he hung up, he gave her his private email address. Jodi tapped out a note.

Friday, Sep. 15, 2017, 4:46 PM

To: Irwin Reiter

From: Jodi Kantor

Dear Irwin,

Thanks for the email address. We're documenting allegations that have to do with a pattern of mistreatment of women over the years. Our reporting is turning up evidence of numerous settlements. I've been told that this is something you may have been concerned about over time. Helping us get this story right could provide an opportunity to do something about the situation, without anyone else knowing. I'd value the chance to have a confidential conversation with you, and run our information by you to see if it's right.

My sister lives near you, and I was planning on being in New Jersey soon. Can I buy you a cup of coffee, just so you can suss this out more?

Friday, Sep. 15, 2017, 8:27 PM

To: Jodi Kantor

From: Irwin Reiter

Your background is impressive. In 2017, things being what they are,
I have a healthy respect for reporters. Have a great weekend.

Jodi immediately forwarded Irwin's note.

Friday, Sep. 15, 2017, 8:37 PM

To: Megan Twohey

From: Jodi Kantor

What's my line?

Friday, Sep. 15, 2017, 9:11 PM

To: Irwin Reiter

From: Jodi Kantor

Thank you, that means a lot to me. Carefully documenting the truth
seems more important than ever. I can swing by your place around
11 a.m. on Monday to introduce myself. (The phone book says
3 Hebron Drive in East Windsor.) Let me know if there's a better
day or time.

Friday, Sep. 15, 2017, 9:46 PM

To: Jodi Kantor

From: Irwin Reiter

You're a great reporter but you really stink at addresses. I've never in
my life lived in New Jersey. I'm thinking about all of this. I will let you
know on Monday what I've decided.

To keep the dialogue over email going, Jodi made small talk, with Megan invisibly reading his responses and advising on Jodi's replies.

Soon Reiter sent instructions: Meet me at 9:30 p.m. at the bar behind the restaurant Little Park in Tribeca. He set rules for the meeting: He would ask the questions; he reserved the right to leave after five minutes; he would pay the check. That was fine, but Jodi was surprised at his choice of location. Tribeca was Weinstein's world. When he had moved the Miramax offices there decades ago, the company's rise had helped transform the formerly gritty neighborhood to a place of wealth, prestige, and power, home to multimillion-dollar lofts, expensive restaurants, and a famous film festival. Little Park, pricey and stylish, seemed like the kind of spot the movie producer might frequent. His office at The Weinstein Company, cofounded with his brother in 2005, was six blocks away. But she didn't question the choice. If Reiter wanted to meet under Weinstein's nose, that's what they would do.

On Monday night, September 18, Jodi walked into the bustling restaurant, glancing around: Even if Weinstein wasn't there, she wanted to make sure she didn't know anyone, lest an acquaintance come over and interrupt. She continued to an almost hidden space in the back that was sparsely populated: a dim bar that looked like a clubby living room, ideal for private conversations, with plenty of room between one cluster of couches and wing chairs and the next. Where was Reiter? And was he a spy, positioned to find out what the reporter knew?

But the short, fiftysomething man in an armchair in the back seemed too nervous to be a plant, glancing over his shoulders and making dark jokes about evading the goons he was sure Weinstein was employing. He had an avuncular manner, with a bridge-and-tunnel cadence to his speech.

A few minutes into the conversation, Reiter was still jumpy, but he didn't ask Jodi many questions, and he didn't seem inclined to leave, so she ventured a few of her own: She wanted to know if he had any of the financial details of some of the long-ago settlements. As she probed him about the past, he looked a little puzzled, or maybe even disappointed. Finally he asked: Why are you asking about ancient history when Weinstein had committed so many more recent offenses against his own employees?

Recent offenses.

Jodi and Megan didn't know about many of those; aside from the 2015 police investigation of Weinstein's behavior, they only had a few unconfirmed tips. When Jodi asked Reiter to say more, he tensed, then started speaking elliptically. He mentioned a young development executive who read scripts and another who had worked at The Weinstein Company while in business school. He used initials: EN, LO, and a scramble of others. He was unwilling to offer more. What he really cared about, he said, was stopping Weinstein from what he had been doing in recent years to young women who worked at the company.

For the next two weeks, Jodi and Reiter met every few nights, always late, almost always at the bar behind Little Park. Jodi and Megan told no one beyond the editors. In emails and texts to one another, the journalists just referred to him as "the source" or "Jodi's guy." The accountant swore that each meeting would be the last. His job was on the line. He spoke in a nervous rush, willing to reveal some things but not others, sometimes refusing to attach names, zigzagging between episodes that sounded central and others that seemed irrelevant or hard to prove. He did not claim to understand everything that had happened at the company, and he wasn't telling the story in order.

In between those interviews, Jodi and Megan worked to decipher, track down, and back up what he was saying, by speaking with other former employees, obtaining records, and contacting the women Reiter alluded to. They were focused on the fundamentals: What had Weinstein done to these young women and what evidence could they find?

But it was also dawning on them that Reiter was providing glimpses of a story that would take much longer to report. During two harrowing years inside The Weinstein Company, 2014 and 2015, the producer's danger to women had become much more visible within the company's top ranks, with problems surfacing with disturbing regularity.

Harvey Weinstein had long conscripted some of the people and practices of his illustrious companies—from lawyers to assistants, contracts to work expenses—to further his predation or hide it. Some employees knew little or nothing as they worked on movie marketing posters and release dates. But over that two-year period, Reiter, the company's most active board member, and Weinstein's own brother and business partner all became increasingly aware and worried about allegations of sexual harassment and abuse against Weinstein. One by one, they all failed to address the problem, and the producer showed a remarkable ability to create his own reality, to make a series of problems simply disappear.

How could a company become so deeply complicit in abuse?

For a long time, Reiter looked away from his boss's treatment of women. He had started at Miramax on July 15, 1989, thirty years old, a Brooklyn College–trained accountant awed by the daring films Weinstein was releasing, so different from the movies shown at most multiplexes. The next year, he noticed the sudden, mysterious departure of the assistant from the tiny New York office—the same woman Megan later approached at her mother's house. He was told that Weinstein had acted inappropriately with her, she had negotiated some sort of settlement, and that was that.

Almost a decade later, Reiter heard Zelda Perkins had a problem in the London office and knew a company lawyer was dispatched to England to help dispose of it. And like many colleagues, Reiter heard rumors of "affairs" between the producer and actresses but felt unsure about who was taking advantage of whom: Weren't actresses known for doing anything for a part? Besides, he was the back-office numbers guy, paid to do the books, without the authority to question Weinstein. He didn't inquire further.

Until 2014, when he became more alarmed. Over the summer, Reiter picked up some worrisome office chatter about Weinstein's behavior toward women. That October, women of all different backgrounds and ages were publicly accusing Bill Cosby of sexual assault. As the news broke, Cosby's TV projects and tour dates evaporated. When he did perform, protestors and hecklers began expressing disgust.

In light of the Cosby news, Reiter felt he had to intervene. He wasn't yet grappling with whether women had been hurt or how. He was anxious about the state of The Weinstein Company, which projected an image of success—it made prestige hits like *The King's Speech*, and the television show *Project Runway*—but was more precarious than outsiders knew, with many failed projects and hundreds of millions of dollars in losses. A sex abuse scandal could send it on a path to destruction.

In November 2014, he composed an accusatory email to Weinstein, naming some of the women he had heard about through the office grapevine. "Stop doing bad shit," he wrote to his boss, according to a draft of the email. He didn't care about what Weinstein was doing with the women "unless and until it costs the company. Has it?" he asked. The next day, Weinstein confronted Reiter, admitting nothing. Afterward, the producer turned cold to him and began referring to him as "the sex police" around the office. (Weinstein denied this.)

Weeks later, in December 2014, just as the company was supposed to go dark for the holidays, Reiter arrived at work one morning to find some other executives astir with concern. A twenty-five-year-old woman named Emily Nestor, a graduate student, had taken a temporary job as a receptionist in the Los Angeles office, filling in during the holiday period. By her second day of work, Weinstein had badgered her into breakfast at the Peninsula Hotel in Beverly Hills and had offered to exchange sex for mentorship, boasting of all the actresses who had supposedly accepted and gone on to fame and fortune. Nestor kept saying no. He kept offering. When she finally extricated herself and returned to the office, she told other employees about what had happened, and they alerted their counterparts in New York.

Reiter was worried: The company was facing what sounded like an episode of sexual harassment. Nestor didn't want to file a complaint with human resources. So Reiter and several other executives persuaded the employees in Los Angeles who had heard her account firsthand to write everything down. One record noted how long it had taken her to fend off Weinstein: "She said he was very persistent and focused though she kept saying no for over an hour."

In early 2015, Reiter sat in a midtown restaurant arguing with his daughter Shari, who was twenty-six, about the same age as Nestor, a psychology student, and a firm feminist. When her father told her what was happening in his workplace, even passing his phone across the dinner

table to show her and a law student friend some of the emails and documents, she was appalled. Shari urged her father to act, both recalled later,
and he told him he had to find a way to stop Harvey Weinstein's behavior.

Reiter wanted to. He was no longer just afraid for the company: He was
starting to fear for the safety of female employees and was troubled by the
idea of the boss hurting women in his own employ. But he didn't see what
could be done. The company's outside counsel had advised the executives
that because Nestor did not want to file an official complaint, sharing her
account with the company's board might not make sense. Pushing further
felt futile. Besides, he added to his daughter, they both knew what happened in these situations: Victims often ended up being blamed, as if they
had done something wrong.

Shari pressed forward anyway. The conversation grew heated enough
to attract glances from other diners, she remembered later. He had power,
she told her father. He could help create an environment conducive to
women coming forward, and he was obligated to do more.

That winter, Reiter heard concerns from another young female employee. Sandeep Rehal was Weinstein's personal assistant, twenty-eight
years old, working in her first professional job beyond an hourly retail gig.
She began to confide in him and a few other executives about duties she
found uncomfortable. Weinstein had ordered her to rent him a furnished
apartment, using his corporate credit card to stock it with women's linge-
rie, flowers, and two bathrobes. She had to maintain a roster of women,
which she referred to by a phrase Reiter had heard around the office before: "Friends of Harvey." Managing their comings and goings had somehow become part of her job.

Rehal had been too ashamed and scared to tell the male executives
about her worst experiences, she said later. How she had to procure and
organize Weinstein's personal supply of an erectile dysfunction drug called
Caverject, administered through injection into the penis. How she had to
keep a supply of those shots at her desk, hand them off to him in brown
paper bags, and sometimes run the drugs to hotels and elsewhere, just before his meetings with women. And how, after she spent a week finding a
new supplier of the drug, and paid for it with his company card, Weinstein

gave Rehal a $500 bonus, paid for by the company, according to an email she saw him send to human resources. He had implied there would be consequences if she told anyone about these duties, mentioning her student loans and where her younger sister attended school, and saying he could have her kicked out. Staying silent would come with rewards, he suggested. "You are at Harvey Weinstein University, and I decide if you graduate," he told her, she said. Soon Rehal left the company, and Reiter did not hear from her again.

But the accountant began grousing more to colleagues about another issue Rehal had raised—use of company expenses. Weinstein charged massive amounts to his company card, relying on a loose system to classify which personal expenses he would reimburse. On top of his generous salary—$2.5 million in 2015—he sometimes demanded the film company pick up questionable bills, including a $24,000 tip for yacht staff—which he eventually reimbursed—and a private jet stop in Europe to pick up a model. (Weinstein denied that he ever misused company funds.)

After Weinstein requested payments for a new round of women in movie production roles without clear jobs or tasks, Reiter wrote to Tom Prince, the head of physical production at The Weinstein Company:

Tuesday, Feb. 10, 2015
To: Tom Prince
From: Irwin Reiter

How many??????????
How many are enough????
How many are too much???

To: Tom Prince
From: Irwin Reiter

There is no thinking about it . . . it will happen . . . how old is Cosby? How long was he harboring his sexual sickness? Its gonna happen I hope humously not post . . .

To: Irwin Reiter

From: Tom Prince

It truly is mind boggling

In between Jodi's late-night discussions with Reiter, the reporters continued to scramble to confirm what the accountant was saying. Emily Nestor did not wish to comment publicly about what had happened. But soon Megan was on the phone with another young assistant, whose initials Reiter had provided, who had left The Weinstein Company in the summer of 2015. The woman's voice was shaky. But slowly, she started to explain that she had left the company "for moral reasons." Because she had signed a nondisclosure agreement, she was afraid to tell Megan everything she had experienced. Weinstein had preyed on her, bombarding her with solicitations for sex and massages that she repeatedly refused. She hadn't wanted to miss the opportunity to be part of such a highly regarded company, so she had worked her way into a new position that provided more distance from him.

When Weinstein demanded that she resume working for him directly, she complained to a top executive about assignations she was forced to arrange for Weinstein, hoping the executive would help keep her out of the boss's reach, she said. Instead, Weinstein himself called her, pressuring her to deny her allegation, submit a letter saying she had a "positive experience" with the company, and exit.

At the same time, Jodi was having eerily similar conversations with a former assistant named Michelle Franklin, who had worked in the London office in 2012. She was also very anxious about speaking and wanted to talk only off the record. Weinstein had never pressured Franklin for sex. But like the young assistant to whom Megan had spoken, she said she had to arrange hotel room encounters for "Friends of Harvey"—the same term Reiter and others had used. Like Rehal, she was charged with procuring penile injection drugs from the pharmacy, and while tidying his hotel rooms, had even picked up the discarded syringes off hotel room floors. (Weinstein denied their accounts.).

One day, as she had walked a young woman to Mr. Weinstein's hotel room, Franklin confronted him. "It's not my job, and I don't want to do it," she remembered saying. "Your opinion doesn't count," she said he responded. Soon afterward, she was fired.

On the afternoon of September 19, Megan got her own firsthand experience in Weinstein's ability to exert pressure, conscript others, and shamelessly pretend that problems did not exist.

For two weeks, she had been piecing together more details of how the $600,000 raised at the 2015 AIDS charity auction had instead, through a series of complicated transactions, landed in the account of investors in Weinstein's *Finding Neverland* production. Jodi and the editors were worried that she was pursuing a distraction from the larger target of how Weinstein treated women.

But Megan couldn't let go. She had confirmed that the New York Attorney General's office was investigating. She had obtained internal records showing that people inside amfAR had expressed grave concerns. In an email, the chief financial officer had written, "Nothing about this deal feels right to me." Legal experts were telling Megan the arrangement might amount to fraud. Even if he hadn't broken the law, Weinstein appeared to have siphoned off more than half a million for AIDS research to reimburse his own investors.

The story, Megan believed, would show how Weinstein could bend an institution to his will. The producer had maintained a cozy relationship with amfAR for years, helping the organization throw its star-studded fund-raiser in Cannes, France—the one with the splashy red-carpet photos Jodi had studied months earlier. David Boies had helped Weinstein silence amfAR's board when it sought an outside investigation. In a recent interview, Boies had walked Megan in a verbal circle for nearly two hours, with Lanny Davis and Charlie Prince, a Weinstein Company attorney, reinforcing the there's-nothing-to-see-here defense.

Now, Weinstein himself had arrived at the fourth floor of the *Times* building, determined to face off against Megan and beat back the story.

The interview had been approved by Corbett and Baquet under two conditions: first that it was on the record, and second that it focused solely on the financial transaction, not the allegations about mistreatment of women. Megan was eager to push for answers but also to size up the man she and Jodi had been reporting on for months. Corbett would participate in the meeting to help keep it on track.

The producer wore rumpled clothes and walked with a slight limp. He growled hello, his voice low and nasal with an old-school New York accent.

Behind him trailed a posse. Megan wasn't surprised to see Davis and Prince. Another attorney, Jason Lilien, who had apparently just been hired by Weinstein, introduced himself as former head of the Charities Bureau for the New York State Office of the Attorney General. "I know this sounds self-serving, but I quite literally wrote the law in New York on these areas," he told Megan.

The presence of two other members of the contingent was baffling. Megan shook hands with Roberta Kaplan, the litigator who had successfully argued *United States v. Windsor*, the landmark Supreme Court case that had paved the way to federal gay marriage. Then Megan recognized a tall, striking middle-aged woman with dark hair and a strangely familiar face. She was Karen Duffy, aka "Duff," an MTV video jockey of her youth. Why had they chosen to be by Weinstein's side in a matter that they surely knew nothing about?

Corbett wanted to set the expectations clearly: The meeting was to stay tightly focused on the amfAR transaction.

But Weinstein, it became clear, intended to produce his own narrative. About his awakening to the heartbreak of AIDS, his extensive philanthropic giving, and his concern for the suffering of others. The visitors now seated around the conference room were his supporting players.

At first Weinstein's tone was friendly, if condescending. He began with a tutorial of how the world of charitable fund-raising *really* worked. If the journalists dug deeper, he explained, they would see that creative transactions like the one involving amfAR were extremely common. Everyone did them. You had to run charities like a business if you wanted to do good in the world, he said, pointing out that other money that he helped raise at the auction did go to amfAR.

"And legal schmegal," he said, spreading a smile around the room. "Our idea was to get people help."

It was time to discuss how much he had done to battle AIDS. He recalled first seeing the ravages of the disease close-up when the Broadway director Michael Bennett, of *A Chorus Line* fame, became ill decades ago.

"One day I get a phone call from his person saying that Michael's got pneumonia. And I . . ." Weinstein paused, as if to steady himself. "Okay, all right. I'm gonna get through this," he said.

Soon Weinstein was reading from an actual script, a written statement from a former vice president of amfAR who could not attend the meeting. Using the third person, he described his own compassion and generosity:

"Harvey came forward and said: 'Do you need help'?" Weinstein said. "We did, and he literally took over the auction, badgering people."

He appeared to choke up and struggle to get the words out.

"I'm not acting," the producer said.

He started again, stopped, as if he was overcome by emotion, and then slid the script over the table to Duffy, who read the rest. With tears in her eyes, she said that Weinstein had helped save her life when she was diagnosed with a rare disease. Now, she said, it was important "to represent the people who really can't talk right now," AIDS victims who had benefited directly from Weinstein's generosity.

Megan let them finish, then launched into more questions. Shouldn't people bidding on items at a charitable auction know where their money was going? Was it appropriate for charitable contributions to ultimately flow back to Weinstein and other *Finding Neverland* investors?

With each round, Weinstein became visibly annoyed.

Did Megan and Corbett know their own employer was taking money from outside nonprofits to subsidize investigative journalism? "Who gets the write-off? How are they doing it?" he snapped. He quickly swung from attacking the paper to expressing his devotion. "I love the *New York Times*," he said. "My famous story is 1977, I'm in this snowstorm in Buffalo, New

York, as a student, you know, a guy goes out, it's my friend Gary, 'What are you gonna get at the store?' He says, 'I'm gonna get Twinkies.' The other guy is gonna get milk, the girl says 'I want Cheerios,' whatever. And my famous—and this is a longtime quote, you can probably look it up. I said: "Just get me the last copy of the *New York Times*."

If there was anything untoward about the $600,000 transaction, he insisted, Megan should be pressing the lawyers who were responsible for it. And if the bidders of the auction hadn't figured out that their money was serving his business deal, well, that was their problem. "You don't want to make a donation to that, don't," he said.

Kaplan said that she served on the board of another AIDS charity and suggested that if the *Times* followed through with this story, it could hurt AIDS patients around the world. She did not appear to understand the underlying financial transaction that she had come, in effect, to defend.

Megan asked: Would Weinstein do this type of financial arrangement again?

"Not with you around," the producer joked.

"I think we need to wind this up," Corbett said.

But Weinstein had one last point: He wasn't just fighting for good; he was battling villains. The charity board members who had reported him to the attorney general just wanted to take over the organization to serve their own dark interests.

The Weinstein Company attorney tried to cut in, but Weinstein swatted him away.

'I'd rather go down with the truth," Weinstein told the journalists. "That's what I grew up with. I grew up with the truth."

Megan thanked the group for their time. For all of the theatrics, she was still going to write her story about the $600,000 transaction. She watched the producer leave, trailed by his supporters, and was struck by the display of this man forcing his way through the world, expecting everyone to fall in line.

When Jodi saw the group filtering out, she went down to the lobby. She had made a point of introducing herself to Weinstein before the meeting started, and as he left, she wanted to see him once more, to remind him of Lanny Davis's suggestion of a possible interview.

The producer was standing outside the security turnstiles, amid the usual mix of office workers and tourists snapping pictures of the *Times* sign. When she approached him, he leaned in to Jodi with such intensity that she had to remind herself not to show any signs of intimidation. She told him that while that day's meeting had been about amfAR, she and Megan hoped to interview him later about his treatment of women.

Weinstein started mocking that investigation to his retinue, describing the findings even though the reporters had never shared them. "Luring them to hotel rooms," he said dismissively.

Let's sit down and talk about it *now*, he suddenly proposed. "I'll tell you everything. We'll be transparent and there will be no article," he said. "Go ahead, let's do it."

Jodi declined. She and Megan would reach out when they were ready, she said.

He stepped in closer, and Jodi let out a nervous laugh. He hadn't done the terrible things that women were accusing him of, he said. He wasn't that bad.

He smiled sardonically, then said: "I'm worse."

The tactics Weinstein used during the in-person interview over the amfAR transactions were a guide to how he operated. Later, they helped Megan decipher what had happened at his company in March 2015, when the next and most perilous complaint landed, from Ambra Battilana Gutierrez, the Italian model. Emily Nestor and Sandeep Rehal had just left, but this allegation caused far more tumult than the others, because for the first time ever, a woman made an accusation against Weinstein in full public view. After going to Weinstein's office for a work meeting, Gutierrez went to the New York Police department and accused the producer of groping her. The news made headlines. And for the company, the timing could not have been worse: It was poised to sell its TV division to ITV, a British broadcaster, for over $400 million, a deal that would have served as a potential lifeline. Reiter, who said he had been promised a million-dollar bonus from the sale, was appalled—this was just what he had feared, a public mess.

The police helped Gutierrez secretly record Weinstein discussing the incident and later said they had been eager to see him charged with sexual abuse.

But the district attorney's office soon announced through a spokesperson that it would not prosecute, saying only that "after analyzing the available evidence, including multiple interviews with both parties, a criminal charge is not supported." Gutierrez left New York without giving interviews or otherwise publicly discussing her complaint against Weinstein, making Reiter and others wonder what had happened behind the scenes.

What almost no one knew at the time was that Weinstein had conducted an elaborate campaign to make the model's allegation disappear.

The criminal lawyer, Elkan Abramowitz, a former partner of District Attorney Cy Vance, was the public face of Weinstein's legal team.

Privately, Linda Fairstein, the famed former Manhattan sex crimes prosecutor, provided help too. She was in touch with Weinstein's office about the case and helped connect Weinstein's legal team and the lead prosecutor. (During the summer of 2017, when she had insisted to Megan that the model's allegation was unfounded, Fairstein had not disclosed her ties to the case. Fairstein said later that it was Megan's fault for not asking and that there was nothing unusual about her actions.)

Weinstein's private investigators went to work collecting records from two Italian court cases involving Gutierrez. In 2011, she had testified for the prosecution at the trial of Silvio Berlusconi, the former Italian prime minister who was charged with patronizing an underage prostitute. Gutierrez had described a sex party with teenage girls at Berlusconi's house, in which she said she had refused to participate in lewd acts. On the stand, the defense had pressed her about a sexual assault allegation she had made years earlier against a man in his seventies. Prosecutors had declined to pursue that case when Gutierrez refused to cooperate. During her cross-examination, she denied the original facts that she had provided in a sworn affidavit.

The court records weren't proof that Gutierrez was lying about Weinstein. They weren't even proof that she had lied about the older man. But New York prosecutors would later acknowledge they worried about how credible she would come off in a trial given the history that Weinstein had highlighted on her.

Boies and Abramowitz shared the documents from Italy with Ken Auletta, the *New Yorker* writer. Auletta had been contemplating writing about the case. But the lawyers convinced him Gutierrez was not trustworthy, Auletta later explained.

Rudolph Giuliani, the former New York mayor, had fielded one of Weinstein's first phone calls following the police complaint and steered him to Daniel S. Connolly, a partner in his firm.

After prosecutors declined to press charges, Weinstein paid Gutierrez a seven-figure settlement in exchange for her silence, with Connolly's representation. As part of the agreement, he also secured Gutierrez's copy of the audio recording she had made of him at the direction of the police.

To the company's leadership and others, Weinstein insisted the entire episode was an elaborate effort to blackmail him, but never revealed that he had paid Gutierrez a hefty financial settlement.

"She's a shakedown artist, she's done this—she did this to some older guy in Italy, and she went to Berlusconi's bunga-bunga parties," Lance Maerov, a member of the board, recalled Weinstein telling him. "And, if you don't believe me, I'll have Rudy Giuliani sit down with you."

In a final stroke, Weinstein drew on the power and resources of his own company to help seal his secret deal to silence his accuser.

On Saturday evening, April 18, 2015, the producer summoned two prominent female executives to Giuliani's firm. Gutierrez was present, along with her lawyer. At the producer's instruction, the two women walked the model through steps she could take to break into acting and boost her public profile, people who attended the meeting later recalled.

This was part of the deal both sides had struck: Weinstein would quietly arrange for career assistance for Gutierrez. For the model, it was a way of picking herself up and moving on. For the producer, it was a familiar form of leverage: If you stay quiet, my people and I will help you succeed.

That evening, Weinstein wrote the two executives an email of thanks, which Megan later obtained.

> I appreciate you participating in the meeting at Giuliani's offices today at 6:00 pm. I want to assure you that any financial cost to you will be paid for by me. You are totally indemnified by me and I appreciate everything you're doing. . . . there will be a $10,000 bonus for each of you, and my heartfelt appreciation.
>
> All my best,
> Harvey

No one had more incentive to hold Weinstein accountable for his behavior than Bob Weinstein, his brother and long-term business partner.

The brothers had risen in the movie business by relying on a bond that dated back to the childhood bedroom they shared growing up in a modest apartment in Queens. From the age of ten or twelve, Weinstein had been a voracious reader, tracker of talent, and celebrity maven, noting who was on the late-night shows, in the gossip columns and the hot nightclubs. "Do you know Sinatra's in town tonight?" he would ask around the dinner table, the rest of the family incredulous at what the young kid knew. Bob was more inclined toward numbers, later remembering how the family had to stretch when its rent was raised from $86 to $92 a month.

When they launched Miramax, Weinstein commandeered the prestige movies, while Bob ran the financial modeling and built a lucrative business in horror movies and other mass-market franchises. In those early days of the company, the brothers often stayed on the phone with each other all evening, from nine or ten until one or two in the morning. Some people found Bob difficult to work with in his own right. He was socially awkward and volatile: kind one moment, lashing out the next. In his older brother, Bob found inspiration, creativity, and drive, comparing their relationship to a marriage, to the "ultimate friendship," to one long, rolling conversation, he said in a series of interviews with Megan.

But The Weinstein Company, founded in 2005, never reached Miramax's cultural or financial heights, and the brothers soon fought about money, Bob's more disciplined approach versus Weinstein's insatiable appetite to buy and greenlight films, rack up massive expenses, then buy and do more. Bob watched with concern as his brother grew obsessed with personal fame, eventually turning himself into a single name: Harvey.

He had also seen evidence of the threat his brother posed to women. Bob had participated in discussions about the confidential settlement that was paid to the young assistant who fled Miramax in 1990, two people familiar with the agreement would later tell Megan, though he denied any knowledge. When Harvey Weinstein needed money to pay off Zelda Perkins and her colleague, Bob wrote the checks. (He later said his brother told him the money was to cover up extramarital activity.)

But Bob regarded his brother's sexual behavior as just one more form of excess, he told Megan. In his eyes, his brother was "crazy, out of control—out of control with money, out of control with buying, out of control with your anger, out of control with your philandering."

One day in 2010 or 2011, the brothers were arguing about finances in a little antechamber near Weinstein's office. As Bob rose to leave, Weinstein punched him in the face. Several other executives were right there: Reiter, the assistant general counsel, the chief operating officer, and comptroller. Everyone watched as blood gushed down Bob's face. No one, not even Bob, did anything to hold his brother accountable for the violence.

By that time, even though they shared responsibility for their company, their employees, and the huge sums that had been invested in their business, Bob had decided that he was not his brother's keeper.

From then onward, Bob distanced himself from his brother. They technically co-ran the company, and the world still saw them as a team, but they communicated less and less. The bosses had already been working out of separate buildings. Now the distance took on more meaning.

Bob periodically considered splitting the company in two. He would sneak off to discuss the plan, code-named "splitco," with bankers, but the financial challenges were overwhelming, he said. Whenever Bob raised the suggestion, his brother would reply: "Sure we can split the company. I'll get everything, and you'll get nothing." Ultimately, Bob was unwilling to walk away. "I wasn't ready to give it up," he said. "Not so easy to start over."

His attitude was also colored by a private experience he rarely discussed at the office but that had come to define the way he thought about his brother.

During Bob's divorce from his first wife in the early '90s, he began to drink himself to sleep every night, he told Megan. Only with the help of Alcoholics Anonymous and Al-Anon had he been able to recover from alcohol addiction, and now he saw almost all human behavior through the insights he had gained while fighting substance abuse. He believed the bedrock 12-step principles: No one can change anyone else. People have to want to change.

Bob convinced himself that his brother's problem was sex addiction, and that no one could stop Harvey Weinstein other than Harvey Weinstein. It was a convenient, and arguably disastrous, moral choice, by which Bob justified his failure to do more. He stayed in business with his brother but excused himself from intervening in his brother's actions. He refused to take responsibility or even help employees who came to him upset about his brother's belittling language or lacerating tactics.

"People would come into my office and say, 'Your brother's screaming and yelling at me,'" he said. "I said, 'Quit. You're talented.'"

That was what passed for his management credo. "Send a note to HR," he would sometimes say to his employees, even though the human resources operation at the company was weak and offered little recourse. "Write a letter."

But in the weeks after the public accusation from Gutierrez, Bob finally felt compelled to act. The deal to sell the television division was now dead, a major business blow. He feared that without intervention, his brother could do something else even more destructive to the company. Thanks to an accident of timing, he thought he had just the right opening: The contracts for the Weinstein brothers and other top executives were expiring at the end of 2015. Bob would seize the chance to ensure his brother underwent in-depth professional treatment for his sexual behavior.

That summer, Bob sent David Boies an email containing a letter for his brother. In the email, later obtained by Megan, he explained that his hope was that Weinstein and Boies would come back to him with a "responsible plan of action."

Dear Harvey,

First let me acknowledge how pleased I am that you have begun, taking the first steps with Dr. Evans and Dr. Carnes towards addressing problems that have plagued you for many years. That is a huge start toward facing these issues sincerely and with the seriousness that they deserve for the first time.

From my own experience I want you to see in writing how your past actions have affected me. I only speak for me personally and no one else.

Over the past 15 to twenty years I have been personally involved with the repercussions of your behavior. The reason I state that is for u to truly see how long this has been going on and how it has only gotten worse over time.

There have been instances of behavior that I and David Boies have had to assist u with in getting out of trouble. I am referring to a situation in England. In that case and every and I mean every time u have always minimized your behavior, or misbehavior, and always denigrated the other parties involved in some way as to deflect the fact of your own misdeeds. This always made me, sad and angry that u could or would not acknowledge your own part.

Over the years I can if I wanted to list at least one hundred times, I am not exaggerating, that's five times a year, over twenty employees have come to my office complaining that they have been verbally and emotionally abused by you. They have reported to me that you have called them stupid, incompetent, idiots, etc. you were not speaking about their work, but about them personally. You denigrated these people as human beings.

I would defend you to them, saying you didn't mean it, or it would blow over, but I knew and they knew this was the way that you treated employees and it would continue. And it did and it only got worse. On many occasions I would tell these people if they could to find the courage to quit. These people had families to provide for and that was not an easy choice for them.

For my part I started to feel sad and angry. I looked at you, as someone who had completely lost his way and did not value people as separate human beings. That u did not care about their basic right to have dignity.

I knew in my heart you were a typical bully, acting out of your own insecurities on those that were weaker than you.

I also began to look at myself and my relation to you. I saw my own weaknesses and co dependency on you and realized, I too did not have the courage to face you down. And I too continued at my own will to suffer abuse. I have begun to seriously address this problem in my own recovery. I am not waiting for your recovery to guide my decisions anymore. It is a hard and slow process, but I am getting better.

For the record you have physically assaulted me in your office and lied about it and minimized it as recently as a few weeks ago in Your therapists office, when I brought it up, u said u had told me you were sorry!! You said it with no sincerity or one ounce of real care.

See I said I'm sorry, so let's move on. I feel hate and sadness for you when you display that behavior.

Lastly would u ever hit your children as u have me, would u ever call your children idiots, stupid, incompetent etc. or would u tell a movie star or financial equal or chief that. I highly doubt it.

There are other behaviors that I will not describe that u are aware of that need to be addressed.

You recently told me that anger was your real issue as if to minimize the other one. That is classic addict behavior. Creating a smokescreen to give up one behavior so that u can hold on to another "misbehavior."

You have hurt many people with this behavior as well. You have picked on people and used your power over them. You have brought shame to the family and to your company through your misbehavior.

Your reaction was once more to blame the victims, or to minimize the misbehavior in various ways. If u think nothing is wrong with your misbehavior so in this area then announce it to your wife and family. You told me in Bart Mandels office that u were ashamed of this behavior and didn't want anyone to know.

So slowly I have watched you get worse over the years to the point where from my point of view there is no more person or brother Harvey, that I can recognize, but merely an empty soul acting out in any way he can to fill up that space and hurt that will not go away.

The reason I can say everything about without any judgement is because I have gone done this road as well, brother. I speak from experience. I have suffered, I have acted out and in the end I was completely lost and defeated. And after admitting complete defeat, that I realized I needed help.

I asked for it and received it.

Once I got that help I was told that I get better only if I continued to work at this my whole life, and that if I expected an easy fix or I could quit treatment after a while that I would surely fall back on my bad behavior. I have never had to experience that.

So what do I want to happen. First is that I want you to understand that this letter and following request only comes out of love and caring for my brother.

What I am asking is for u to outline the exact nature of the treatment that u will be engaging in with Dr. Evans and Dr. Carnes etc. how many times a week you will see each of them and for how many years you are committing to your on going treatment.

I would like to know if u are going to commit to a group therapy plan. How many times a week or month are u going to do it and for how long a duration

I would like to have one talk or session with each of these Doctors to explain my experience with u.

I would like u to give me, David Boeis and Bert Fields your word that u will follow thru with your agreed upon plan. The three of us know fully that we have no power to make you keep your word, we just want it for ourselves and for you as a record to indicate that u once gave it.

What I will not do, is share this letter or commitment with any member of our mutual families. I will not share this with any business relation past or present. It is between the three of us.

For my own self of self, I am advising you that should you ever strike me again or verbally abuse or denigrate me that I will take the proper action to protect myself and my family and my interests. This is not a threat. It is merely stating that I will exercise my right as a human being.

As regard to other misbehaviors that do not affect our company I have no intention or care to police u or call u out in any way. That's not my job.

Please discuss the above with David Boies and thru him let me know what you decide. You probably won't realize this now, but this is all for your benefit.

More than anything I look forward to the return of that person that was just Harvey. I knew him when and I can assure you he was quite a great guy, all by himself.

Love Brother, Bob

At the same time, another company leader separately felt motivated to act. The Weinstein brothers had packed the company's board with allies. Almost all of them were male—only one woman, the AIDS pioneer Dr. Mathilde Krim, had ever served, and she was not an entertainment or business specialist. Most of the seats were taken by wealthy executives from the finance and entertainment industries who took a hands-off approach.

But Lance Maerov, who had been appointed to one of the three independent seats in 2013, was different: He was supposed to be a watchdog. Maerov's employer, the advertising giant WPP, Goldman Sachs, and other major investors wanted him to make sure the brothers didn't rip off the shareholders. "Just make sure to keep these guys honest," Maerov told Megan later. "That's what my mandate was."

At first he had given little thought to Weinstein's treatment of women. He had heard rumors about the producer putting "friends" in his films, and Weinstein seemed to always have a young woman on his arm at movie screenings and other events, but Maerov believed it was extramarital cheating, nothing more. His focus was ferreting out financial misconduct and trying to address the broader toxicity at the company. "You would walk out of a board meeting and it felt like the most dysfunctional Thanksgiving dinner you've ever sat at," he said of the verbal brawls that erupted between the Weinstein brothers.

But when the groping accusation made headlines, Maerov, like Bob, feared that Weinstein might be engaged in a pattern of sexual behavior that could pose a liability to the company, and wanted to use the contract renewal to force the issue. He and Bob weren't acting in tandem; Bob saw Maerov as a threat to his own power. But Maerov was one of the board members in charge of renewing the contracts. In the process, he could take the routine step of examining Weinstein's personnel file—which would give Maerov a chance to see if it held anything questionable.

Weinstein refused to let Maerov see the file, with David Boies backing him up. Boies countered that he would review the file himself and report to the board about any potential legal problems for the company.

Maerov found the proposal ludicrous and was growing distrustful of Boies. Sometimes Boies said he worked for the company, other times for Weinstein, creating what felt like a conflict of interest when it came to potentially damaging information that Weinstein might want to hide from the board.

On the morning of July 1, 2015, Maerov received a secret peek inside the file anyway, thanks to someone who was trying to aid his efforts: Irwin Reiter. The accountant and two other executives sat him down for breakfast at the Four Seasons Hotel in Beverly Hills, and began to outline complaints of verbal abuse that had been made against Weinstein over the years. Then Reiter slipped Maerov several pieces of paper, Maerov later recalled. It was the memo outlining what Weinstein had done to Emily Nestor. Reiter and the other executives, who were taking a risk, were afraid to let the board member leave with it, so Maerov flipped through the pages at the table, finally seeing some of the information he had sought—and evidence of the exact type of behavior that Maerov suspected.

Maerov, Reiter, and Bob Weinstein all felt the situation could not stand. But four months later, in October 2015, Harvey Weinstein signed a brand-new contract that secured his power for years to come. With David Boies's assistance, Weinstein had misled, placated, and otherwise outmaneuvered Maerov, Reiter, and his own brother.

For Maerov, attempting to scrutinize Weinstein was like nothing that he had experienced in decades of corporate life. Weinstein and Boies worked in concert, alternating the producer's brute pressure with the attorney's artful persuasion. At a movie premiere during the summer of contract negotiations, Weinstein threatened to punch Maerov, according to the latter. When Maerov complained, Boies responded in a tersely worded letter, calling the claims "exaggerated," "a bit hysterical," and proof "that anyone who feels as you do about Harvey should not be in a position of trying to negotiate with him." Boies threw Maerov what looked like a bone on the personnel file: Rodgin Cohen, one of the most prominent corporate lawyers in the country, reviewed the file and reported back that nothing in it "could result in liability to the company." (What Maerov only learned afterward was that Cohen's son was a junior employee of The Weinstein Company, seeking to get his start in the film business.)

Maerov also brushed aside key information. When Boies acknowledged to him that Weinstein had paid settlements to women over the years, emphasizing that no company money had been used, Maerov didn't press for details. He also chose to disregard the memo about Emily Nestor he had seen. He would later downplay its significance, telling Megan that it looked like a bad Xerox copy, or a scan of a scan, and that he had noted that it had come from the woman's colleagues, not Nestor herself.

He considered the matter taken care of, because in the contract negotiations, Weinstein had agreed to a concession. The company would put a
new code of conduct in place. If it ever had to pay settlements as a result of
Weinstein's misconduct, Weinstein would be required to cover the costs
and be hit with a further series of financial penalties—$250,000 for the
first settlement, $500,000 for the second, and so on, up to a million dollars,
a whole fee structure for potential future allegations. The contract specified that Weinstein could also be terminated for misconduct. It almost
read as if the company expected Weinstein to keep accumulating allegations and that the resultant financial penalties could take care of the
problem.

Maerov's main concern was liability: He was trying to make sure that
if anything went wrong, the company wouldn't suffer. That was different
than trying to guarantee that women would not be harassed or hurt. Once
Maerov felt assured that the organization was legally protected, and with
some additional financial controls in place, he decided he had done enough.

Irwin Reiter didn't know what more to do. He had plotted with Bob
Weinstein on ways to separate his brother from the company only to watch
Bob lose his nerve. He had slipped documents to a board member to no
avail. He was only working three days a week, and that summer, the company tried to bring him back full time, at double his salary, for a total
of $650,000 a year. He refused. He was more deeply worried than ever:
"There is almost no deal I wouldn't sign if HW wasn't my boss and there
is no deal I would sign if he is," he wrote to a board member in the summer
of 2015. But he remained at the company, working at essentially the same
job he had held since he was thirty years old.

Bob Weinstein, who held the most responsibility, walked away satisfied, because his brother finally gave him what he wanted: a promise to
stick with intensive therapy for sex addiction. Originally, Bob had wanted
the requirement that his brother get treatment to be solidified in writing,
like the code of conduct, and the series of escalating penalties. Boies talked
him out of it, saying that Maerov would use the information to try to gain
greater control over the company. Instead, Bob accepted a private promise,
one that was impossible to enforce.

"There were many emails where he'd swear that he would do it, and he's going, and he always delayed it, which has led me to go, addict, addict, addict, addict, addict," Bob said.

"You start to hear this, you get worn down—you get worn down. They come at you hard with their lying, just nonstop. I got worn out. I said, 'I surrender,' see?"

Late on the evening of September 28, 2017, five days after Megan's article about the amfAR mess was published, Jodi again met Reiter at the bar behind Little Park. As the employees at The Weinstein Company had read and discussed the article, Reiter had texted Jodi, narrating the reaction from inside the company. He had not been involved in the questionable transactions with the AIDS charity, since Weinstein's theater business was separate. But he and other employees were riveted by the article, he said: They were finally watching someone hold his boss to account. (Weinstein continued to deny wrongdoing, but later, the authorities took action: Federal investigators in Manhattan opened a criminal inquiry into the transactions but have made no public comment about where their examination stands. The New York Attorney General's office wrote a letter to amfAR, saying the transactions raised several concerns, including whether they "resulted in benefits to private interests," and told the charity to strengthen its corporate governance.)

Reiter had already been so helpful, and back at the paper, the editors were already urging Jodi and Megan to start composing a first article about Weinstein. But the reporters wanted more—in particular, more documentation of what had happened at The Weinstein Company during those tumultuous two years, which could be published without anyone fingering the source. Reiter had mentioned a memo written by a well-respected junior executive named Lauren O'Connor, who he said had departed over Weinstein's treatment of women.

Without giving too much away, Jodi wanted to show Reiter that his mounting outrage since 2014 had been justified. A few minutes into the conversation, Jodi reached into her bag, drew out a printout she had prepared a few hours before, and passed it to Reiter. For all his knowledge about what happened inside the company, he knew very little about what had transpired between Weinstein and actresses in hotel rooms. Jodi explained that this was an account she had heard from a well-known actress. The text was just one paragraph, with no names other than Weinstein's, no location or time. It described how the woman had arrived, unsuspecting, to a meeting at a hotel with Weinstein, and to her surprise, been shown upstairs instead. When she got there, he was waiting in a bathrobe and asked for a massage. He tried to pressure her into sex by saying he could help her career. She fled.

As Jodi had guessed, Reiter appeared aghast. She told him that this actress was far from alone, that she and Megan had heard variations on this same narrative again and again, which closely matched the accounts by employees that had already been disturbing him. She and Megan didn't know how many women had these kinds of stories about Weinstein, she said, but based on what they were hearing, the number might be very high.

Jodi asked him again for the O'Connor memo. He had already read her a few quotes, which she had jotted down, but she wanted to understand the document better. Could he pull it up again on his phone? He started to read the memo aloud, then paused.

"I'm going to pay a visit to the little boys' room," he said. He threw Jodi his phone, open to the email with the memo, rose from the table, and left her alone.

After all of his indignation, his fruitless attempts to intervene, and the moments when he had thrown up his hands, the accountant was finally doing something irrevocable to stop his boss.

The first time Reiter had seen the memo had felt like a case of déjà vu. In November 2015, shortly after Weinstein's new contract had been signed, he had arrived at work to find colleagues huddled in an office, once again examining a complaint about Weinstein. This one was from a woman they knew and trusted: O'Connor was an up-and-comer at the company, respected for her taste and work ethic. Unlike Nestor, she had filed a long, detailed complaint, and it went far beyond one incident. Weinstein had said offensive things to her, but she was writing a much larger indictment, a portrait of how he treated women and how that behavior corrupted the company.

Reiter and the others informed Bob Weinstein, who read the document and agreed that the board needed to know about these accusations. Instead of forwarding the document—too risky—Bob dictated a memo inviting the board members to come to the office to read it in person, waiting half an hour before informing his brother what he had done.

After months of frustration, Reiter felt new hope. The next day at the office, he watched with satisfaction as Maerov sat at a table, looking over the memo. Maerov took photos of the first and last pages, noting all the witnesses and other details that O'Connor had included. "It felt very credible," Maerov said later.

But after that, O'Connor's complaint evaporated, just like the Gutierrez accusation. Reiter couldn't explain it. He figured that Bob Weinstein had lost his nerve yet again. He assumed that David Boies had stepped in to cover his client's misdeeds once more. Soon O'Connor was on her way out the door with little explanation.

Except the allegations had not disappeared: Reiter had seen the memo, and so had several other colleagues. Right after he read it, he stashed away a copy for himself. Nearly two years later, Jodi was sitting blocks away from The Weinstein Company offices with the document in her lap and her source on a very deliberate trip to the bathroom. *He's telling me, without telling me, to copy the memo,* Jodi thought.

She worked quickly, not pausing to read the document, willing her fingers not to make a mistake. After a few clicks, the full memo was in her possession.

When Reiter returned to the table, his phone was waiting on his chair, and Jodi thanked him but didn't overdo it.

As soon as he left, a few minutes later, she headed for the bathroom to send the screenshots to Megan and Corbett. She didn't want sole electronic possession for one more second than necessary. In the subject line of the email, Jodi just wrote *Memo.*

Lauren O'Connor had sent the document on Tuesday, November 3, 2015, with an innocuous subject line ("For your records") and introduction: "As requested, I took some time to catalog and summarize . . ." Then she cut to the heart of the matter.

There is a toxic environment for women at this company. I have wanted nothing more than to work hard and succeed here. My reward for my dedication and hard work has been to experience repeated harassment and abuse from the head of this company. I have also been witness to and heard about other verbal and physical assaults Harvey has inflicted on other employees. I am a 28 year old woman trying to make a living and a career. Harvey Weinstein is a 64 year old, world famous man and this is his company. The balance of power is me: 0, Harvey Weinstein: 10.

I am a professional and have tried to be professional. I am not treated that way however. Instead, I am sexualized and diminished.

I am young and just starting out in my career, and have been and remain fearful about speaking up. But remaining silent and continuing to be subject to his outrageous behavior is causing me great distress.

The rest of the memo was a detailed portrait of Weinstein's behavior, including an assistant's confession to O'Connor that she had to give him a compulsory massage:

She told me Harvey made her give him a massage while he was naked. I asked what happened, and she relayed that she was in the other room of the suite, setting up his electronics and when she went into the bedroom, he was on the bed naked and asked her to give him a massage. She told me she offered to have the hotel call a masseuse, to which he told her not to be silly—she could just do it. She said she didn't want to and didn't feel comfortable. My colleague told me she was badgered by Harvey until she agreed to give him a massage. It was horrible to see her so upset. I would have liked to report this but she asked me to keep it confidential as she feared the repercussions of complaining.

During the Gutierrez scandal, O'Connor wrote, she had to sit and wait outside Weinstein's sex therapy office. When a female "personal guest" of Weinstein's had to wait in a hotel lobby for an hour for a room, he blew his top at O'Connor, telling her she'd be better off marrying some "fat rich Jewish fuck" and "fucking making babies." On another trip, he acknowledged to her that he was a "bad boy" but tried to shush her with muddled logic: "We don't talk about it—can I trust you? I mean, I'm a bad boy but what's important is that I'm honest about it."

When O'Connor complained about Weinstein's verbal abuse toward her to a Weinstein Company human resources executive, "the response was basically—let us know if he hits you or crosses a line physically," she wrote.

Her most fundamental complaint was that her job had been turned upside down by Weinstein's upsetting sexual behavior. She had joined The Weinstein Company to turn books into enthralling films, so how had she ended up entangled in her boss's questionable sexual activities?

On other trips with Harvey, I was instructed by him to meet with aspiring actresses after they have had a "personal" appointment in Harvey's hotel room. Harvey instructed me to greet them when they came down to the hotel lobby and facilitate introductions for them to managers, and agents, as well as assisting in casting them in Weinstein Company projects. Notably, only female executives are put in these positions with actresses with whom Harvey has a "personal friendship," which to my understanding means he has either had or wants to have sexual relations with them. Female Weinstein employees are essentially used to facilitate his sexual conquests of vulnerable women who hope he will get them work.

I am a literary scout and production executive. I was hired to find books The Weinstein Company could make into films, and my role expanded to handle production. Clearly, managing Harvey's past and present sexual conquests was never something I imagined being part of my job responsibilities.

Late that night, when Jodi, Megan, and Corbett read the memo in full, the moral stakes of the investigation suddenly transformed and expanded. What had once been a historical corrective suddenly seemed a far more urgent pursuit. No one had ever stopped this man. If the reporters failed to publish their findings, he might go on to hurt someone else.

CHAPTER SIX

"WHO ELSE IS ON THE RECORD?"

Friday, September 29, 2017

By morning, Corbett had already shared the memo with Baquet and Purdy. The secret document, from inside the company, which confirmed and elaborated on the pattern the reporters had been piecing together for months, was invaluable. They were looking at the situation from the outside. O'Connor had seen it from the inside. Her memo was like a key turning in a lock.

Corbett, Purdy, and Baquet gave the same instruction: *Write!*

But the team debated what to write. Baquet and Purdy, with the O'Reilly article fresh on their minds, were pushing for a narrower story, documenting the settlement trail, which they hoped to get into the paper as quickly as possible. They wanted to lay down a marker, because in recent days, Jodi and Megan had begun to hear footsteps from Ronan Farrow, who was contacting their sources and had apparently taken his findings to the *New Yorker*. The *Times* team had little sense of his material or how close he was to publication.

Jodi, Megan, and Corbett shared the desire to break the story, but they also knew the material better than Baquet and Purdy. They believed the first article had to be broader and capture the power of what they had heard and documented. The sickening repetition of the hotel room stories. The apparent targeting of women who were new on the job. The terrible bargain of sex for work, and the long-standing silence of those who knew. Corbett pushed the reporters to write the story that the three women were beginning to see in their heads as fast as possible, while trying to hold back Baquet and Purdy.

That story would need names, dates, legal and financial information, on-the-record interviews, and documents. Jodi and Megan pushed aside the half-verified accounts and rumors they were still chasing and made a list of the material that could potentially be solidified enough to be included in a first article, with allegations of harassment and assault marked in black and settlements in red:

1990—Assistant at Miramax, New York. Settlement.

1992—Laura Madden, Ireland.

1994 or 95—Gwyneth Paltrow, Los Angeles.

1996—Ashley Judd, Los Angeles.

1997—Rose McGowan, Park City, Utah. Settlement.

1998—Zelda Perkins and Rowena Chiu, Venice, Italy. Settlement.

2014—Emily Nestor, Los Angeles.

2015—Ambra Battilana Gutierrez, New York. Settlement.

2015—Lauren O'Connor, New York. Settlement?

2015—Assistant in NY leaves for "moral reasons."

A few days before, Lanny Davis had finally given Megan an answer, on background, about how many payoffs Weinstein had made to women: eight to twelve settlements. Megan paused, somewhat shocked that Weinstein's team would reveal such damning information.

Do you think that's *normal* for men to make so many payoffs? she had asked Davis. "I do," he had replied, in a matter-of-fact tone.

But they still needed a second source to corroborate those figures. They also needed to contact everyone who might go on the record, including former Miramax and Weinstein Company employees who could attest to the findings. Everyone the reporters planned on mentioning—like Steve Hutensky, the Miramax in-house lawyer who helped negotiate the Perkins and Chiu settlements—would have to be offered a chance to comment. Now was also the time for them to let O'Connor know that they had a copy of her memo.

The draft would be a work in progress, nearly every line requiring negotiation, fact checking, adjustment, or deletion.

By Friday afternoon, Corbett, Jodi, and Megan were on a conference call with O'Connor and her attorney, Nicole Page.

Page did most of the talking. O'Connor didn't speak, but it was clear she was distressed that the *Times* had her memo and planned to publish part of it. She had never wanted to go public. She had tried to move on after the debacle of the Weinstein job, with a fresh start at a new company.

She was afraid that Weinstein would retaliate, and Page asked the journalists to reconsider using the memo, or at least to omit O'Connor's name, describing the stress the article would place on her. The journalists exchanged worried glances. The last thing they wanted to do was cause O'Connor trouble. She was young, not yet thirty. And she had spoken up for others who she believed had been victimized, becoming one of the rare figures in the entire Weinstein saga who had dared to raise questions formally about his conduct.

But newsworthy documents are rarely withheld from readers in newspaper reporting. O'Connor wasn't a source who had confided to the reporters with a promise of anonymity; she was the author of a critical indictment of Weinstein that had been circulated at the highest levels of his company and then covered up. Many publications omit the names of sexual assault victims at their request because of the uniquely private nature of that crime. But O'Connor's situation was different: Although she described verbally abusive treatment from Weinstein, the power of her memo came from her role as a witness, documenting sexual misconduct by Weinstein toward other women.

Corbett assumed control of the call, tucking strands of her neat silver bob behind her ear as she spoke. Her style was always to hear people out as neutrally as possible, and like Baquet, Corbett usually left reporters to deal with sources. But now she spoke for the institution in a way the reporters could not. The paper had to publish the memo, she said gently but firmly. No, not the whole thing. Yes, they could point out that O'Connor had declined to comment, to try to make clear that she was not the source of the memo, and to spare her from retaliation. Yes, the paper intended to name her as the author of the memo to establish its credibility. Corbett added that if Page or O'Connor wanted to make a further case for leaving her name out, they should.

Page did not respond, and her client remained silent. Page said later that the paper's decision sounded set in stone. The attorney ended the conversation saying she appreciated what the journalists were trying to do.

Megan had suspected the reason why O'Connor had not talked during the phone discussion, and with a few more calls she confirmed it: O'Connor had accepted a settlement too. She was legally prohibited from speaking.

Much later, Megan learned the backstory. Right after O'Connor had sent the memo, she was told not to come into the office. Within days, Page was negotiating a settlement with Boies and a Weinstein Company attorney. Boies said he helped craft a cover story for O'Connor: She would stay at the company a few more weeks to finish projects, working in locations that allowed her to avoid any contact with Weinstein. But her career there was over. In an interview with Megan, O'Connor later explained that the company's response to her complaint was: "How can we quickly make this go away?"

Six days after she had sent the memo, the exit agreement had been finalized, Boies said. As required, O'Connor had written a letter to Weinstein thanking him for the opportunity to learn about the entertainment industry, as well as this follow-up note to HR:

Monday, Nov. 09, 2015, 3:23 PM

From: O'Connor, Lauren

Subject: For your records

Because this matter has been resolved and no further action is required, I withdraw my complaint. Lauren

———————

Jodi and Megan agreed the next move was to contact Lance Maerov, The Weinstein Company board member. In that first story, they wanted to be able to demonstrate what they had started to learn from Reiter about the company's complicity.

Maerov answered the call to his cell phone as he was walking into his Park Avenue office building with a cup of coffee. Megan introduced herself and explained that the *Times* was preparing to publish a story about allegations against Weinstein stretching back decades. She read an excerpt from the O'Connor memo, then asked: "What did you do about it?" The cup slipped from Maerov's hands, spilling scalding coffee. *How the fuck does she have those records?* he later recalled thinking.

Only hours afterward, Megan was meeting Maerov in Bryant Park in Midtown Manhattan. Maerov, with his carefully parted hair and expensive scarf, looked every bit the polished businessman.

Maerov explained that, yes, he had been concerned about Weinstein's treatment of women, especially after the NYPD investigation. He told Megan about how Weinstein had called it attempted extortion and the board had approved a code of conduct designed to curb misbehavior. When the board was notified later that year about the O'Connor memo, he said, he wanted an outside lawyer to investigate. But within a day or two, Boies had informed him that the matter was resolved. "Boies told me the complaint was withdrawn," Maerov told Megan. So Maerov had let it go.

Megan nodded as he talked, pressing for more details. She suspected he wasn't telling her everything he knew, but what Maerov was saying was already valuable, especially if she could get it on the record. The Weinstein Company board had in fact been aware of claims of sexual misconduct against Weinstein and, aside from a written code of conduct, had basically looked the other way.

Maerov agreed to be quoted, but he told Megan that he had a duty to tell the other board members that the *Times* story was coming and that he had talked to her. She asked him to please keep quiet over the weekend.

Once Weinstein found out they were close to publishing their article, he would intensify his efforts to stop it. She and Jodi needed more time. Maerov agreed to give them two days.

Before they parted, Maerov had a question. "Are you sure this isn't just young women who want to sleep with a famous movie producer to try to get ahead?"

Maerov felt some relief as he walked out of the park, he told Megan later. For years, he had mostly failed to hold Weinstein accountable. No matter what surfaced, Weinstein always wiggled out of trouble. "It was like watching one of those crime movies where someone like Al Capone keeps getting away with it; he's constantly one step ahead of the law," Maerov explained. Finally someone was closing in.

But Maerov, as usual, felt duty bound to protect The Weinstein Company. Back at his desk, he immediately broke his promise to Megan. He called Bob Weinstein and David Glasser, the company's president, and relayed everything she had told him.

Saturday, September 30, 2017

By that morning, Weinstein somehow knew the details too and called Maerov, begging him to help kill the story: "Lance, I know we have had our differences over the years, but can you just circle the wagons once on my behalf?" Maerov found the conversation so offensive that he took notes.

When Maerov balked, Weinstein turned to threats, he said. Years earlier, Maerov had dated the model Stephanie Seymour when she was separated from her husband, a financial executive named Peter Brandt. Weinstein told Maerov he had obtained a letter that Maerov had written to Seymour and would use it against him. The letter to Seymour is "disgusting," Weinstein said.

Maerov refused. His job was to safeguard the company, not the producer. And he felt there was nothing improper in the letter, he said later.

The next day, he emailed Weinstein a single sentence: "We need to discuss a plan to protect TWC in the event that Megan Twohey runs her article."

Meanwhile, Jodi and Megan were at their keyboards, writing. Jodi typed:

> Actors and former assistants told the *NY Times* variations on the same story, in some cases without any knowledge that others had experienced the same.
>
> Because he usually worked out of his [London] hotel room, rarely coming into the office, the women were often alone with him and there was little escape.
>
> Along the way, he enforced a strict code of silence, threatening women who complained, locking employees in nondisclosure agreements.

Megan wove in what they knew of the remarkable events that unfolded in 2015. Gutierrez's police report had never been made public, but a source had read every word to a *Times* colleague over the phone. Now Megan drew on that language to describe how at the work meeting, Weinstein had allegedly "grabbed her breasts after asking if they were real and put his hands up her skirt." It had never been reported before that behind the scenes, Weinstein had quietly "made a payment" to silence Gutierrez. When O'Connor's memo hit, "with page after page of detailed allegations," Maerov wanted to investigate, but then Weinstein reached a settlement with O'Connor as well.

By Saturday night, they had something resembling a draft to show Corbett. She created a secret file in the *Times* editing system, which only the reporters and relevant editors could open. Typically, stories were labeled, or "slugged," by topic along with dates of when they would be published, for example, 16TRUMPSPEECH, 07EARTHQUAKE, 21BEYONCE. Corbett slugged this one with the generic label 00INQUIRY, so that even colleagues who happened to scroll past the slug in the editing system could not know what the story was about.

Even as the reporters wrote, they were verifying—and to trying to expand—exactly what they could say about which alleged offenses, with which sourcing. Jodi and Megan had only one interview with an alleged Weinstein victim on the record: Laura Madden, with her account of her first meeting with him in Dublin in 1992. Because Zelda Perkins was still locked into her confidentiality agreement and Rowena Chiu had not spoken at all, their entire saga shrank down to four short but crucial paragraphs, meant to show that there had been serious allegations and a settlement while still protecting the two women involved.

The assistant from 1990, the one Megan had found at her mother's house, was essential to the story.

In the end, John Schmidt, the former Miramax executive to whom Megan had made an unannounced visit earlier in the summer, confirmed on background that the former assistant had been paid a settlement following a troubling episode with Weinstein. He had agreed to speak with Megan, explaining that he had been impressed by her amfAR article. Megan had not abandoned hope that the woman would go on the record. But when she had reached out to her, this was the response:

Dear Megan,

I'm sorry but please do not try to contact me again, directly or indirectly. I have nothing to say, nor do I give anyone else authority to speak on my behalf. I do not want to be named or cited as an anonymous source in any article and I will take legal action if this happens.

Because her story seemed to involve a sexual assault, Jodi and Megan would not use her name without permission. They decided to simply refer to her as a young woman who left the company abruptly after an encounter with Weinstein, according to several former employees, and who later received a settlement. They quoted her old boss, Kathy DeClesis, who said: "It wasn't a secret to the inner circle."

Later, Megan would learn that the assistant had allegedly been sexually assaulted by Weinstein when she ran an errand at his home, and Schmidt would tell Megan more: that Weinstein had confessed to him shortly after the encounter that he had done "something terrible." "I don't know what got into me. It won't happen again," Schmidt later recalled Weinstein telling him. (Weinstein denied saying this.)

Next, Megan called Rose McGowan, who had appeared determined to expose Weinstein. But McGowan said she was not in a position to go on the record with her allegations against the producer. Weinstein had recently offered McGowan a $1 million payment in exchange for her silence, and her lawyer was encouraging her to take the money, she told Megan. She wasn't planning to accept it. But because of a host of complications, she was going to sit this story out. She said her lawyer had sent a cease-and-desist letter to make sure Ronan Farrow didn't use any of the interview she had done with him. "I'm sorry," McGowan said. "I just can't."

But at Jodi and Megan's urging, McGowan had obtained a copy of the settlement she struck with Weinstein in 1997. Remarkably, the one-page document did not include a confidentiality clause. McGowan was able to share it with the reporters without facing potential legal or financial consequences. McGowan declined to comment for the story, but their article could quote from the document, saying that following an episode in a hotel room during the Sundance Film Festival, Weinstein had paid McGowan $100,000. The payment was "not to be construed as an admission" by Weinstein but intended to "avoid litigation and buy peace."

Most of the former Weinstein employees whom the reporters wanted to quote were scared, fearing retaliation. Jodi and Megan argued that the story would include overwhelming evidence, that even after all these years, it wasn't too late to speak up. Most of them refused. ("I have a *life*!" protested one executive.) Another offered a quote:

"Sexual harassment was often rumored, rarely revealed. Sadly, shamefully, very few of us had the courage or wherewithal to confront it."

But a few hours later, his employer, a major corporation, nixed the quote, saying it didn't want to be even tangentially associated with the article.

One of the few who came through was Mark Gill, the former president of Miramax Los Angeles. "From the outside, it seemed golden—the Oscars, the success, the remarkable cultural impact, but behind the scenes, it was a mess, and this was the biggest mess of all," he said, describing the producer's alleged offenses against women. Jodi and Megan counted his line, and a few others, as victories and inserted them into the draft.

At midday on Monday, Jodi texted Ashley Judd, asking if she could speak. Baquet and Purdy were still urging the reporters not to get hung up on the actresses. The crucial task, they said, was to break the story, and after that, they predicted, everything would spill out. It would be fine to get Judd and Paltrow on the record then.

Jodi and Megan disagreed. The Weinstein story had two strands: the producer's apparent menacing of generations of his own employees as well as of actresses who wanted parts. The reporters had the first strand well documented. Without the second—many actresses, even some top stars, said they had been harassed by Weinstein—the story would be incomplete.

Judd texted right back. Yes, she was in a dentist's waiting room and could talk.

For more than three months, Jodi had been laying the groundwork for this moment. Two weeks before, she had met Judd in person while the actress was in town for the United Nations General Assembly. On a terrace high above Manhattan's East Side, Jodi asked her to imagine what going on the record would look like and stressed that she was working to get testimonies from other actresses as well. Judd had listened carefully and said she wasn't sure.

Now the ask felt wrong. The story would be published just before the season premiere of Judd's television series, *Berlin Station*, a scenario that she had wanted to avoid. Worse, all Judd had wanted from the beginning was the company of other actresses. But even after dozens of conversations, those accounts had not materialized. Salma Hayek, Uma Thurman, and Angelina Jolie had not gotten on the phone. Jodi was still coaxing Gwyneth Paltrow, but she was still a question mark. Rosanna Arquette, who had also described a harrowing hotel room encounter to Jodi, did not feel ready to go public. Other actresses, prominent and unknown, had told the reporters Weinstein stories and sworn them to secrecy. The pattern that had protected Weinstein for decades—no actress wanted to be the one to speak up and name Weinstein—still held.

On the phone with Judd, Jodi didn't plead or tell the actress how badly she yearned for her to go on the record. Instead she tried to show Judd how strong the article would be: twenty-five years of allegations, a clear pattern, names and examples, human resources records, legal and financial information, and quotes from male and female employees characterizing the problem.

Even as Jodi spoke, she braced for rejection. Judd didn't show her hand. She promised to take the request seriously and call back soon.

A few hours later, a text from Laura Madden popped up. Jodi had been worrying about losing Madden. The speeded-up time line for the article had created an uncomfortable conflict: Madden's long-dreaded next round of breast surgery, a second mastectomy plus reconstruction, was scheduled for October 10. Jodi couldn't give Madden a firm publication date, and it looked like the operation and publication could collide. That was too much stress for any one person to take—but for the journalists, losing Madden would be a disaster.

But instead Madden was worried about being the only woman from the London office on the record. If so, she was out. She asked Jodi more questions about the article: How many women, how many women from this place, this office, this year?

Everyone wanted company, and understandably so.

Monday, October 2, 2017

Just after noon, the reporters filed into Dean Baquet's office to discuss the final step of the investigation: when to take the findings to Weinstein and how much time to give him to respond. After protecting the sources for so long, it was time to approach Weinstein and his representatives, describe the story, and share every allegation they planned to make public. Every anecdote, every date, every woman's name. (They would not mention Judd or Paltrow, who were maybes to go on the record.) Then Jodi and Megan would incorporate his answers into the article. If he denied the accusations, they would say so. If he apologized, they would print that, in his own words. If he refused to comment, they'd go with that. And if he could refute any of the allegations, those claims would have to be omitted.

Presenting findings was standard journalistic practice, the right way to treat any story subject, even a completely untrustworthy one. But the group could not settle on how much time to give Weinstein to respond. They would need to provide him with a deadline: Here's how long you have until we publish. But once Weinstein knew what the *Times* planned to publish, he could pressure women into recanting, intimidate others into contradicting their accounts, or try to undermine the accusers. He could leak information to another outlet, to blunt the story's impact, or preempt publication by rushing out some sort of statement of contrition. The journalists had to protect the victims—and the article.

Six people, all with some form of authority and some final responsibility for guiding the Weinstein story safely into the paper, sat in Baquet's office. Baquet was the boss, the journalist charged with supervising the entire, encyclopedic newspaper every day. The ultimate calls were always his. But Corbett had guided the project from the beginning, and Baquet relied on her in part because her instincts were a little different. They were in running conversation with Matt Purdy, who amid the tumult of supervising many stories across the newsroom was still keeping close watch on the investigation.

But Jodi and Megan as reporters had their own form of authority and responsibility. They had gathered the information. They had the relationships with the sources. They were writing the story, their bylines would appear at the top, and they would take a great deal of the blame or credit for whatever happened.

The sixth figure in the room was David McCraw, the *Times* attorney.

He was there to keep the paper out of legal trouble, so no one present wanted to reject his advice.

Corbett felt they needed to give Weinstein forty-eight hours, as much for the journalists' sake as his. They would be able to say they had done things right and avoid giving Weinstein an opening to say they'd been unfair.

To Baquet, that seemed like too much. Nobody in the group trusted Weinstein, but he was the most suspicious. His instincts told him that Weinstein was just going to run out the clock. Besides, the team figured that however long they gave Weinstein, he would take more time. This was a negotiation and the journalists had to start on the short side.

But Baquet also wanted the investigation to be irreproachable. At the start of his newspaper career, he had covered the case of Gerald Hatcher, a small-time actor who was accused of posing as a talent scout to lure aspiring actresses as young as fourteen into private meetings about their future movie careers and then raping them. The way Baquet had written those stories still made him cringe all these years later. The man was guilty, Baquet was sure. But he had been too quick to convict him on the page, he thought, writing in a way that was too sensationalized and melo-dramatic, without enough fair summary of the arguments for the defense. "It was even probably disrespectful to the women," he said later. "I always felt like everyone in the courtroom lost a little respect for me, including the prosecutors." Baquet wanted to expose Weinstein, but correctly.

Everyone, including Jodi and Megan, took turns arguing every side, trying to weigh which risk was greater: compromising an investigation by moving too quickly in the final moments or being too generous to a proven manipulator. When the reporters stepped away to write more, the editors were still deliberating.

By the time darkness started to fall over Times Square, they had made a decision. Megan called Lanny Davis to put him on notice: She and Jodi wanted to speak to Weinstein and his team at 1:00 p.m. the following day to share the allegations.

Suddenly the journalists were as little as a day or two away from launch. All around them, colleagues were taking the small steps that turn a collection of words into a *Times* article. They needed the right picture of Weinstein for the top of the story and the front page, and Beth Flynn, the photo editor, sent a selection. Should he be smiling, not smiling? On a red carpet? With a woman—*which* woman? Was it a problem if his wife, Georgina Chapman, appeared in one of the shots? Come to think of it, should the article mention that he was married, for the second time, and that he had been married when most of the alleged transgressions occurred?

Only one journalist could log in to the story file at a time, so Jodi worked on the article, then Megan, then Rebecca, then Rory Tolan, a second editor taking an especially close look at language. They were trying to find the exact right phrasing and were rewriting based on notes from McCraw, who had offered recommendations to fireproof the story legally.

Shortly after midnight, Megan and Jodi left the office and shared a car back to Brooklyn. For the first time, they allowed themselves to speculate on how readers might react to the story. Megan suspected that the board of Weinstein's company would be forced to act against him, but would the broader world care? Jodi cited Purdy, who in classic skeptical-newspaper-editor fashion had pointed out earlier in the investigation that Harvey Weinstein wasn't *that* famous. Perhaps many people would find sleazy behavior by a Hollywood producer unsurprising.

Tuesday, October 3, 2017

As they prepared for the 1 p.m. call, Corbett received a peculiar message from Lanny Davis:

> Dear Rebecca:
>
> This is a very personal note.
> I just learned about the Lauren email late last night and read it for the first time. Will do my best to do what should have been done a

long time ago. I am not optimistic re. a statement. I am shooting for 1
pm today since that seems to be the absolute deadline. Correct me if
I am wrong.

In any event, I thank you for your consideration and courtesy—
way beyond what is customary or even necessary.

Lanny

To an outsider, the note might have seemed routine: Sorry, I got some
of the documents late; I'm just catching up and will do my best. Translated into the language of journalism and public relations, the note read
this way:

*Can you believe that Weinstein hired me to deal with your article but never even
shared the Lauren O'Connor memo with me? This is embarrassing, and by the way,
that memo is powerful. Bear with me, I'm trying to get Weinstein to give you some sort
of a statement to print in the story, but this client is challenging.*

David Boies would be unavailable to join the call, but he was still trying to intervene on Weinstein's behalf. At 12:19 p.m., Baquet received an
email from the attorney, who was pushing for more time for Weinstein to
respond in order "to make the article fair and balanced (not in the Fox
News sense, but in the *New York Times* sense)." Boies, who reiterated the
claim that he was not Weinstein's lawyer in this matter, insinuated the
Times should follow the lead of other media outlets.

"Three major publishers/broadcasters, including the *Times*, have re-
searched this story over the last several months, and insofar as I can tell
considered the same allegations and evidence," Boies wrote, in reference
to NBC and the *New Yorker.* "One of the other two has said it has decided
not to publish the story; the other has said that before they publish they
will take the time to thoroughly review with Harvey the charges against
him and give him adequate time to prepare a response. I would hope the
Times would at least do the same."

"I'm not responding," Baquet told the reporters.

Just before 1:00 p.m., the reporters and Corbett settled in for the call.
They had written out almost every word they planned to say. Foremost

on their minds were the women whose names they would be mentioning. In the hours beforehand, Jodi and Megan had warned Madden, Perkins, and the others, saying: *We're about to go to Harvey for response, and we need to share every allegation in the article with him, including yours. I know this sounds scary, but it will protect you and us, because we can say this is a fair process that gives him a chance to respond to the charges. We don't think he or his representatives are likely to contact you. But carry around a notebook just in case, and if you get any calls, write down every word. Any threats or intimidation need to go straight into the article. The only way to combat those tactics is to expose them.*

The women had agreed, their final act of trust.

When the call itself began, Weinstein was joined by not just Davis and Bloom but also a new lawyer, Charles Harder.

Harder had made a name attacking publications that criticized his wealthy or famous clients. He had recently helped shut down the gossip website Gawker, suing it into bankruptcy on behalf of Hulk Hogan over a sex tape, in a case secretly bankrolled by the technology investor Peter Thiel. Harder believed that libel laws, which governed who could say what about whom in print, were too loose. The prevailing legal standard had been established in 1964, when the Supreme Court decided in *New York Times v. Sullivan* that a successful libel suit had to prove not only that journalists printed false information but that regarding public figures, they did so with "actual malice," defined as "reckless disregard for the truth." That was a high bar that generally protected journalists—too high a bar, Harder thought.

He had represented Roger Ailes in his efforts to beat back media coverage of Ailes's alleged sexual harassment. After he negotiated a $2.9 million settlement from the *Daily Mail* over its false report in 2016 that Melania Trump had once worked as an escort, President Trump hired him too. *GQ* magazine had recently called Harder "perhaps the greatest threat in the United States to journalists, the First Amendment, and the very notion of a free press."

On the phone, Harder was clipped and courteous, hearing out the reporters as they presented their material and repeating variations on "we'll get back to you."

His client had no such restraint. From the first moment of the call, Weinstein kept interrupting the reporters, intent on figuring out whom they had spoken to, who had betrayed him. Coming through the phone's speaker, his voice was even more of a force than it was in person, low, gravelly, and insistent, and he had a tactic of repeating the same question over and over. As Megan and Jodi went through the allegations, Weinstein tried to seize control with a stream of interjections:

"Who else is on the record?"

"Is there somebody on the record who said that?"

"Why don't you tell me who's on the record and let me respond to that?"

"And this woman's on the record?"

"And do you have somebody on the record who said this?"

He was so busy trying to grill the reporters that he did not seem to absorb the fact that the journalists had not just interviews but also settlement records and other documents, including the O'Connor memo.

Megan raised the crucial question of how many settlements Weinstein had paid out over the years. She had already heard the answer—eight to twelve—from Davis, but she needed a second source, and getting confirmation from Weinstein would be ideal. But when she cited the number Davis had given, Weinstein lashed out at his own adviser. "That's you talking; that's not me talking," he shot at Davis. "If Lanny spoke, he spoke for himself and not on behalf of his client," he said.

Megan tensed. The circle of people who knew about the settlements was tiny. Was that important figure slipping away?

When the journalists finished listing the allegations, Harder asked how much time they could take to respond. "Our expectation is that you can get back to us by the end of the day," Corbett said, as the editors had agreed.

"That's impossible," Harder shot back. "You've giving us three hours to respond to a laundry list of stuff going back to the early 1990s?" He asked for two weeks, which Corbett rejected, then he reduced his request to forty-eight hours. Corbett agreed to get back to him.

Weinstein's voice surged through the speaker again. "If the timing isn't good, then we will cooperate with someone else," he threatened, reading the journalists' fears that he would hang up from the call and go straight to another outlet with a softened, distorted version of the story.

"I'm not a saint," Weinstein said, "but I'm not the sinner you think I am."

He launched into a lecture about journalism.

"Get the facts right," he said. "We'll help you get the facts right. If I wasn't making movies, I would've been a journalist. I read every book on the *New York Times*, every book about journalism, and I read every newspaper and magazine. The journalists that impress me the most are the ones who go out of their way to be fair."

Weinstein went on. "When you were kids you grew up to tell the right story, to tell the truth," he continued. "You weren't about deadlines. You wanted to tell the truth. If you mess up and you don't tell the truth, and you write just to write, how do you look yourself in the eye?"

Finally, after ninety minutes on the phone, it was over. Corbett and the reporters sat in the conference room.

Corbett was thinking about how to shore up some of the allegations to further strengthen the story and that the paper should agree to Harder's request for more time. An expert in Baquet's thinking, after years working with him, she was crafting an argument to share with him about a new deadline.

Megan was mentally reviewing Team Weinstein's reactions for clues about whether it had information that could refute or weaken the findings. Instead of addressing the grave matters at hand, Weinstein was asking questions that would not help his cause. He was fighting with Davis. He had been trying so hard to turn the tables that it was not clear how much of the information he had even processed.

Jodi was bracing for Weinstein's next move, certain he had a plan to use the information they had provided on the call to try to undermine the article. She felt sure what he would do: leak an item to the gossip pages saying, "The *New York Times* is trying to do a Harvey Weinstein story but barely got one woman on the record."

With one phone call, he could make the article seem like a failure before it was even published.

A n hour later, Judd called Jodi.

The actress was as composed as ever. "I'm prepared to be a named source in your investigation," she said. She had thought deeply on the decision, gone for a run in the woods, consulted her lawyers, considered her obligations as a woman and a Christian, and decided this was just the right thing to do, she said.

Standing amid the neat lines of glass wall and gray carpet, Jodi lost it, like a marathoner collapsing at the finish line. She and Megan had spent months living in a state of suspense and responsibility. They would land the story or they would blow it; they would get actresses on the record or they would not. Weeping, Jodi searched for something to say to Judd that was equal to the moment but still professional. The best she could muster was: "This means the world to me as a journalist."

The rest of the team was standing down the hall in a cluster, and Jodi walked toward them, still on the phone with Judd, gesturing to say that she had news. Megan knew what was happening before Jodi could say it.

They celebrated by rewriting the story draft. The lede, or beginning, was Judd's long-ago account from the Peninsula suite, and the first section of the article ended with a quote of Judd's that was also a call to action: "Women have been talking about Harvey amongst ourselves for a long time, and it's simply beyond time to have the conversation publicly." By that evening, they had a new version of the article, with Judd on the record.

Meanwhile, Corbett prevailed: They would give Weinstein until noon the next day, Wednesday, October 4. That became the new target publication date for the article. Internally, the reporters set their clocks and expectations.

At nine o'clock that Tuesday night, the journalists were still at the office, eating takeout and sweating over the story draft. Their hum of anxiety was nothing compared to what was going on at The Weinstein Company, a few miles to the south, where Weinstein was on an emergency conference call with Boies and the board. Maerov had insisted on the meeting, outraged that Weinstein had hired lawyers and Davis's firm to deal with a story that the board knew nothing about.

Boies did most of the talking. After years of minimizing Weinstein's problems to the board, he was suddenly more forthright. The *Times* story was coming, he told them, and "it's going to be bad" for the company, participants in the call later recalled to Megan. He outlined the conclusions, including the eight to twelve settlements, adding that the number could very well be higher. He didn't think Weinstein in fact remembered how many payoffs he had made to women over the years, he said. Defending Weinstein or terminating him were both extreme and inappropriate, Boies argued. The goal was to find a middle ground and present a unified front. "Guys, if we don't stick together, this is going to be like a circular firing squad," he said.

By 11:38 p.m., Lisa Bloom was advising Weinstein to acknowledge that after all their efforts, they would not succeed in killing the *Times* story. "We can nip at it around the edges—and we should—but it is going to run," she wrote in an email to Weinstein, Harder, Davis, and Boies as she prepared to board a flight from Los Angeles to New York to be by her client's side. Bloom's pitch: Weinstein should acknowledge that he had engaged in the core issue of sexual harassment, express remorse, and promise to do better. "I have often thought of Jesse Jackson, caught saying 'Hymietown,' asking for forgiveness, saying "God isn't finished with me,'" Bloom wrote in the email later obtained by Megan, citing the former presidential candidate's apology for an anti-Semitic remark. "Got my vote in '84."

Bloom, comparing the Weinstein allegations to a single comment by Jackson, proposed a statement to give to the *Times* that emphasized her own role and even her movie project:

"As a women's rights advocate, I have been blunt with Harvey and he has listened to me. I have told him that times have changed, it is 2017, and he needs to evolve to a higher standard. I have found Harvey to be refreshingly candid and receptive to my message. He has acknowledged mistakes he has made. And as we work together on a project bringing my book to the screen, he has always been respectful towards me."

Her message: She was the one who had helped Weinstein see the light.

After privately working to help Weinstein foil investigations into his behavior, she wanted to publicly cast herself as the person who forced him to change his ways.

For his own self-protection, Davis had decided to stay in Washington, DC. By then, he could tell that whatever Weinstein did, the producer would not be able to wiggle away from the article's findings. Even Boies was pushing contrition.

But Weinstein was not prepared to give in.

That day, Weinstein had called an IT staff member over to the computer of one of his executive assistants and ordered him to delete a document called "HW friends," according to people who were there. (That was essentially the same term Megan and Jodi's sources had used: "Friends of Harvey.") The document was a list of names and contact information for women categorized by city.

With the help of Bloom, Weinstein also tried to pressure employees into signing written declarations saying they had enjoyed a positive experience at the company.

The next morning, Megan checked in with the young woman who had left the company "for moral reasons." She explained by text message that Weinstein had called her three times that morning, suspecting she was a source.

"I'm scared," she wrote.

CHAPTER SEVEN

"THERE WILL BE A MOVEMENT"

Wednesday, October 4, 2017

The reporters came to work knowing they had to tell Team Weinstein that Judd was on the record but fearing the producer would weaponize the information somehow—use it to delay the response further or, worse, launch some sort of preemptive public smear campaign against Judd in the tabloids. ("Eccentric activist Ashley Judd has been threatening to go public with wild accusations . . .") But it had to be done. At 8:40 a.m., Jodi called Lanny Davis, who took the news stoically.

The phone call with Weinstein and his team the day before had dealt a potential blow to the crucial finding that Weinstein had struck settlements with as many as twelve women over the years. But now that other executives at The Weinstein Company knew the *Times* story was coming, Megan suspected they might be angry that Weinstein had jeopardized the company through his actions. Maybe that anger would translate into an incentive to talk.

Megan called David Glasser, The Weinstein Company president, in California. It wasn't yet dawn in Los Angeles, but Glasser picked up, sounding sleep-deprived and frazzled. Megan told him she was calling because she thought it only fair that other executives be given a chance to respond to the *Times* story.

Sure enough, Glasser acknowledged it had been a rough night. There had been an emergency board meeting by conference call. Boies had spelled out what the *Times* was preparing to publish, Glasser said, adding that he had been shocked by what he heard.

Really? Megan asked. What was most surprising? Did Boies mention the number of settlements Weinstein had paid to women? Yes, Glasser said: eight to twelve. Could she believe it? What's more, Boies had told the board the number might be even higher.

Megan told Glasser she was eager to include his perspective in the *Times* if and when he was ready to go on the record. Meantime, could she use him as a source for the settlement figure if she didn't name him? He agreed. When Megan told Corbett the news, she jumped up from her seat and hugged her.

The journalists kept their eyes on the clock: The noon deadline was approaching. As it passed, Weinstein's team provided little more than a wild phone call, in which they sort of denied some of the allegations, rambled about episodes that weren't even in the article, and again protested that they didn't have enough time.

A few minutes later, Baquet watched as Megan stood outside his office fielding yet another phone call from Davis, who didn't have any answers. For so long, Baquet had refused to speak to Weinstein or any of his representatives. Now he asked Megan to hand him her phone. "Lanny, I'm sick of this shit," Baquet said, his tone harder-edged than usual. "You've got five different lawyers reaching out to us. We're not talking to five different lawyers. Get your people in line and get back to us with your response."

At 1:43 p.m., Team Weinstein's answer landed, in the form of an emailed letter from Charles Harder marked "CONFIDENTIAL / OFF THE RECORD / NOT FOR PUBLICATION." The journalists didn't consider that binding. Keeping material off the record required agreement on their part. But it was a fitting start to the letter, an eighteen-page exercise in intimidation, all of which boiled down to one message: If the journalists proceeded, Weinstein and Harder would sue the *Times*.

The core team reassembled in Baquet's office. David McCraw handed out printed copies so everyone could review what they were facing. "Demand to Cease & Desist and Preserve Documents and Materials," the subject line said. For all those months—and in the previous few days in particular—they had been waiting to see what stance Weinstein would ultimately take: denial or apology. Now they saw the answer on the page:

> All accusations by NYT and its alleged "sources" that my client engaged in sexual harassment, including toward employees and actors, are untrue. My client did not engage in the wrongful conduct that you are accusing him of.
>
> My client would likely incur more than $100 million in damage from your false story. Should you publish it, he would have no alternative but to hold NYT legally responsible for those damages.

Weinstein and Harder had another, more tactical demand:

> Because these accusations will have the effect, as you know, of causing considerable damage, if not total destruction, to the highly successful career and business that my client has built over the past forty years, and because you have been working on this story about him for several months now, and the alleged events go back more than 25 years in time, at the very least it would be appropriate for NYT to afford my client and his counsel with a reasonable amount of time—we request two weeks—to research these issues and make an appropriate presentation of the facts and evidence which *refute* the many false accusations that NYT is prepared to publish about my client. A court of law affords a defendant at least a year to conduct discovery and present their case at trial. We are asking you for two weeks.

Weinstein was going to fight. According to the letter, he was the real victim, pursued by the *Times*. The letter, seething with contempt for journalism, conjured a dark alternative reality in which newspapers that aired incriminating information about the powerful were violating—not upholding—the public trust.

The letter took direct aim at Laura Madden, calling her a liar. "The accusation is false," Harder wrote:

> We expect to be able to provide you with documents and witnesses
> that will refute this allegation, but it will take us time to locate
> documents and witnesses from 25 years ago. You are now on notice
> of the truth. Should you publish this false accusation before my client
> has had a reasonable opportunity to locate and present to you further
> evidence (witnesses and documents) of the falsity of this allegation,
> will easily demonstrate reckless disregard for the truth.

That phrase was how a plaintiff could win a libel suit: by proving that journalists had heard their information was false and maliciously publishing anyway.

Jodi thought of Madden, somewhere in Wales. If Weinstein had any kind of genuine refutation of her story, she needed to know about it immediately. Or was he just gambling, thinking that this was just one woman with no power and little proof, and that his best bet was just to deny?

The former employees helping the reporters were "disgruntled, have ulterior motives, and seek to supply you with false and defamatory statements," the letter said. "You are on notice that your sources are not reliable; they do not have personal information; and they are seeking to use NYT as a vehicle for their wrongful and tortious efforts to defame and harm my client and his company. The publication of any such false accusations about my client by NYT will be with actual malice and constitute defamation." There was the possibility that Team Weinstein would try to publicly cast the gutsy ex-employees as bitter outcasts, losers.

In the final section, Weinstein and Harder took direct aim at Jodi and Megan:

> Please be advised that you are under a legal duty to maintain,
> preserve, protect, and not destroy any and all documents,
> communications, materials and data, in digital, electronic and hard
> copy form, that may be relevant to the dispute including without

limitation all documents, materials and data that refer or relate to
Harvey Weinstein, The Weinstein Company and/or any of its
executives, employees and/or contractors (collectively, "TWC").

That meant everything: every text, instant message, voice mail, calendar entry. Harvey Weinstein was saying he was going to force the *Times* to turn over the entire contents of the investigation, everything the reporters were sworn to protect.

The journalists sat in Baquet's office and came to a unified decision: There was no reason to change a single element of the story. Harder's letter was essentially legalistic bullying. The journalists would stay open to whatever evidence Weinstein wanted to present, but to capitulate based on this letter was unthinkable.

McCraw reassured the group that the law would protect them. The world that Harder had conjured up sounded scary, but it didn't actually exist. "When the facts protect us, and the law protects us, it's hard to argue with our legal position," McCraw said later.

At 3:33 p.m., McCraw forwarded the reporters a copy of the reply he had just sent to Harder, just three paragraphs long. To the eighteen pages of complaints about journalistic technique, McCraw had a simple answer: "Any notion that we have dealt unfairly with Mr. Weinstein is simply false, and you can be sure that any article we do will meet our customary standards for accuracy and fairness."

In the final paragraph, he delivered his real counterpunch:

I note your document preservation demands. In light of that, please
provide me with assurances that you have taken immediate steps to
secure all data and records that may be relevant to this matter,
whether in the possession, custody, and control of Mr. Weinstein or
one of his business entities. In particular, I ask that you immediately
secure all phone, email and text records of Mr. Davis, Mr. Weinstein's
press representative, as well as the personal and business phone,
email and text accounts of Mr. Weinstein; all records pertaining to
any complaints of improper workplace behavior, whether in the

possession, custody and control of Mr. Weinstein or one of his
business entities; and all records relating to settlements with
employees, whether in the possession, custody and control of Mr.
Weinstein or one of his business entities.

Translated from legalese, this meant: Harvey Weinstein, if you want to
drag this story into open court, go right ahead. If you try to come after our
information, we will demand even more of yours, including every single
document related to your treatment of women.

The paper's one concession was to give Weinstein more time. Two
weeks was out of the question. But the journalists felt they had to say yes
to Harder's earlier request of forty-eight hours, even though it was painful
to leave the material hanging with Weinstein for so long. Anything less
could give credence to his argument about unfairness. The new and final
deadline would be 1 p.m. the following day, Thursday, October 5.

Jodi and Megan were exhausted, but McCraw's response buoyed them.
He had invoked generations of journalistic tradition, a court system that still
protected the free press, and a country where, despite everything, the First
Amendment was still sacrosanct. They also realized that Baquet was savor-
ing each moment of the face-off with Weinstein. The rest of the world could
not see Harder's offensive. But standing together against it was thrilling.

That afternoon, Jodi felt she had to try one last time to convince Paltrow
to go on the record. Hearing from his former top star would be so shocking to readers across the world; even many of the reporters' savviest sources
did not expect that Paltrow had a story of being victimized or threatened
by Weinstein. Three paragraphs about her could rewrite the history of the
Miramax years and give cover to so many of the other women who wanted
to come forward. Jodi summoned every last bit of persuasion she had,
pushing so hard that she worried the pressure would backfire, and that the
star was going to tell her to get lost.

The two had been in near-constant dialogue for a week, in phone calls
and texts, and Paltrow seemed to be truly deliberating. She had helped

with the project from their first contact. But everyone close to her was telling her to stay quiet. Of course, going on the record sounded crazy to them: They were not on the inside of the investigation. Jodi could tell that some part of Paltrow wanted to ignore them, so in phone calls and texts, she continued to gently push.

But Paltrow couldn't bear the thought of weeks of tabloid headlines about her, Weinstein, and sex. She was still afraid the news would devolve into a lurid celebrity scandal.

She was also facing a private reckoning very different from Judd's, because Weinstein had played a far greater role in her life: "The most important man of my career," as she put it later. She wanted to finally call him out. But publication was coming sooner than she'd expected, and she wanted a little more time to sort it out in her own head.

> Since I feel underequipped to make this decision under a
> barrel, I'm going to hold.

> I feel sorry to have let you down. I really do. I'm so torn.

Paltrow's dissatisfaction with her own decision meant that if she did not join this article, Jodi wanted her to be ready for the next one; she could watch from the wings and then enter. Jodi let up with the texts for a few hours, and then started again.

From the beginning, Jodi and Megan had stuck to Baquet's rule: All communication with Weinstein had to be on the record. But around 3 p.m., Megan was informed by Davis that Weinstein was already on his way to share some sensitive, crucial information off the record.

The reporters were confused. He was on his way *where*? To the *office*? Should they refuse to let him in? They had to make a choice, fast: Weinstein would be on their doorstep in minutes, no doubt looking to smear his accusers without leaving fingerprints.

Megan decided to take the meeting. She wanted to know what he had, and the dirty trick of the impromptu meeting gave her another chance to square off against him in person.

Weinstein stepped into the lobby of the *Times*, with an unshaven face, bags under his eyes, and high-profile legal help by his side: not just Bloom but also Abramowitz, the former prosecutor turned criminal attorney who had represented Weinstein in the Gutierrez case. Bringing up the rear was Linda Fairstein, the former sex crimes prosecutor who had told Megan there was nothing to Gutierrez's allegations.

Megan led the group to one of the newsroom's small glass-walled meeting rooms along a heavily trafficked corridor, which put Weinstein on display for all of their colleagues to see. Office passersby lingered at the sight of the producer and his representatives stuffed in the equivalent of a fishbowl. Megan told Weinstein and company that they had fifteen minutes to talk, not a minute more.

The information the group sought to supply was nasty, dubious, and thin. Abramowitz and Fairstein painted Gutierrez as an opportunist with a sleazy past. From a folder, Bloom pulled out pictures of McGowan and Judd smiling alongside Weinstein, as if polite red-carpet photos were proof that nothing untoward had happened. Weinstein accused both women of being mentally unstable. At one point, Judd had sought in-patient psychological treatment for issues stemming from her childhood, and now the producer used descriptions from her own memoir to paint her as a nut.

Megan betrayed as little reaction as possible. This off-the-record meeting had clearly been an ambush, but it did nothing to undermine the investigation. With the help of a colleague in Italy, Jodi and Megan had done background checks of Gutierrez. They had also examined Judd's history, asking Grace Ashford, the researcher, to plow through her memoir, just to make sure there were no surprises that could be used against her or the paper. The only thing the meeting had done was reveal more of the tactics Weinstein and his allies were prepared to use.

The day got stranger. That afternoon, Jodi and Megan sat down to read about themselves in *Variety* and the *Hollywood Reporter*.

Is *The New York Times* about to expose damaging information on Harvey Weinstein?

The Weinstein Co. film and television mogul has enlisted an army of attorneys and crisis managers in recent weeks and has unleashed them on the *Times* over a planned story on his personal behavior, multiple sources familiar with the behind-the-scenes battle tell *The Hollywood Reporter.*

The story had few details but did mention the *New Yorker*'s efforts as well. *Variety*'s article was similar, with Weinstein denying that he even knew about an upcoming *Times* story. "I've not been aware of this," Weinstein told *Variety.* "I don't know what you're talking about, honestly."

"The story sounds so good I want to buy the movie rights," he added.

If the reporters had any remaining doubts about Weinstein's integrity, here was a final sign: He had just told another publication a flat-out lie.

The *Variety* and *Hollywood Reporter* stories meant that Jodi and Megan were on public display. The guessing games about who had spoken to them would begin. Sources would get nervous. The project was exposed for everyone to see, including the competition. Right when the reporters needed the tightest possible control, they were losing it.

"This is bad, gang," Baquet wrote in an email.

The reporters' phones and in-boxes began to fill with messages from people who had seen the stories in the Hollywood trade publications. Jodi and Megan barely responded. They were still too deep in the text of the article, reworking the lede again, targeting problem areas, and carrying out McCraw's instructions for further fine tuning.

Sometime after midnight, the reporters realized they were too depleted to be effective anymore. They had gone with little sleep for many nights in a row. The conversations with Rebecca and Tolan were sputtering in circles. Jodi and Megan gave up and shared a taxi home. About an hour later, Tolan left too. Corbett refused to pull away from the keyboard. They had fiddled so much with various parts of the article that Corbett wanted to stop to reread the whole story and measure what could still be gained and strengthened on the page.

Even under more routine circumstances, Corbett's reporters worried that she did not take care of herself. She never seemed to stop working—because many of her projects were secret, it was hard to gauge how much she was really fielding—and at times appeared to survive on black tea and dark-chocolate-covered almonds. Her days were frenzied, with consultations every few minutes.

But in the hush of a newsroom finally drained of activity, she was able to edit stories with real concentration. (Being "in the zone," her husband called it, acknowledging that his wife was temporarily inaccessible.) Corbett often stayed at work so long that the ceiling lights sometimes automatically clicked off, leaving her working in darkness until she got up and waved her arms.

That night, she sat and worked away, slowly making the words in the story tighter, clearer, and stronger. Sometime before dawn, she fell asleep at her desk for forty-five minutes. When she woke, she worked some more.

At 7 a.m., she finally stopped and left the building. She couldn't go home: Corbett lived in Baltimore, spending every Tuesday through Friday in a hotel room down the street from the *Times*. She showered and changed her clothing. Soon afterward, she was back at her desk.

Thursday, October 5, 2017

Just as Corbett was returning to her hotel, Jodi received an email from Laura Madden, who was now five days away from her surgery. The previous evening, she had stood in her kitchen in Wales and told her older two daughters, Gracie and Nell, that she had to share something. The teenagers assumed it was about the operation. Instead Madden told them what Weinstein had done to her all those years before and that the incident was about to be recounted in a newspaper article.

They looked at her in shock, trying to picture her as a twenty-year-old victim. "My mom is just my mom," Gracie said. "She's such a gentle person. The idea that people could be reading what happened to her . . ." They confessed to Madden that similar things had recently happened to some of their girlfriends: drunken boys preying on them, the young women unsure what to do. It was Madden's turn to be shocked. She knew these kids but had never dreamed of what they were facing.

In the email, Madden wrote to Jodi:

> I feel obliged to talk about the events that happened to me at Miramax as I realise that I'm in the fortunate position of not being employed in the film business and so my livelihood won't be affected. I'm also not one of those that have been silenced even though individuals under Harvey Weinstein have tried to persuade me to be silent. I do not have a gagging order against me either. I feel I am speaking out on behalf of women who can't because their livelihoods or marriages may be affected. I am the mother of 3 daughters and I do not want them to have to accept this kind of bullying behaviour in any setting as 'normal.' I have been through life changing health issues and know that time is precious and confronting bullies is important. My family are all supportive of my decision.
>
> I am happy to go on record.

Just as remarkably, Jodi and Megan were starting to hear from women they had never contacted who had their own Weinstein stories they wanted to share. For months the reporters had been pursuing women, aching for them to speak. Now they were coming to Jodi and Megan, finding them through the *Variety* and *Hollywood Reporter* articles, like a river suddenly flowing in the opposite direction. The journalists did not have enough time to do the reporting, corroboration, and response to include their accounts in the first article. They would have to wait for the next story. But the journalists took the messages as a silent rejoinder to Harder's letter.

At 10:30 a.m., Jodi gave Paltrow one final try. She was sitting in a makeup chair in Atlanta, shooting an *Avengers* movie. That day she was supposed to pose for a big *Avengers* class photo, with all the characters from the preceding decade. Instead she was feeling sick and barely able to get through her scenes. She even pulled aside Michelle Pfeiffer, her costar, quickly briefing her on the situation for one final round of counsel.

At 11:22 a.m., she sent Jodi a text.

> I'm on set in Atlanta. I feel intense pressure because of the
> time frame. I can't believe his response to the Hollywood
> Reporter, I can't believe he is taking this tack. I would have
> hoped he could have seen his way to contrition. I feel like
> he's setting himself up for an even steeper fall.
>
> I think it will be best to hold and then do something with you
> as a follow up.

This made the email that arrived from Davis at 12:04 p.m. especially puzzling. Weinstein's team had fifty-six minutes left on the clock until the *Times*'s deadline. But instead of focusing on the many allegations that would be in the article, Weinstein, through Davis, was pelting the reporters with questions about Paltrow, who he seemed convinced was in the story.

Jodi and Megan were dumbfounded. There was no trace of Paltrow in the story. Why was he focusing on an irrelevant matter? Had he never intended to give any response to the allegations at all? One o'clock came and went. Team Weinstein insisted the statements were almost finished, but by 1:33 p.m., nothing had arrived.

Baquet watched as Megan fielded yet another phone call from Davis, who once again had nothing to offer. Baquet instructed Megan to deliver a message. "Tell Lanny the deadline has passed!"

Suddenly, Weinstein himself was on the phone, asking about Paltrow. "Why shouldn't I just do a fucking interview right now with the *Washington Post* and get this over with, based on your lack of transparency?" he asked. "I will do that interview in the next five minutes unless you come clean. If you don't want to come clean, you'd better write this fast."

Megan and Jodi were back in one of the glass-box conference rooms.

Outside, Corbett and Purdy hovered over Tolan's shoulder, reviewing the article.

"You want some sort of list of who we've spoken to for this story?" Jodi asked. "And if we don't disclose it to you, you're threatening us?"

"I'm not threatening you," he said. "If you're using Gwyneth Paltrow, tell me." However scared Paltrow was of going on the record, he seemed much more fearful.

"We're *not* using Gwyneth Paltrow," Megan said. He did not seem to understand: If Paltrow were in the story, they would have told him so and given him time to respond.

He asked twice more, then a third time. "If you're going to lie to me, don't, okay? Just don't. You're going to slaughter me anyhow, that's the idea of it. I get it. And you know what? I respect your journalism and I respect what you're doing. You're dealing with an important subject matter and people like me need to learn and grow. I get that. You'll read that in my statement. I've known when I hear something that's hidden from me, you know what I mean? I am a man who has great resources. Tell me the truth."

He did seem certain that Jodi and Megan had been speaking with Paltrow. Even months later, they never figured out how he knew.

Megan tried again: "Harvey, we have not robbed you of the opportunity to speak to anything that's in our story," she said.

"Are you talking to Gwyneth Paltrow?" Weinstein repeated.

A figure appeared next to Megan. Dean Baquet was leaning over her shoulder. So many times over the prior few months, Weinstein had wanted to reach him directly, influence him, Important Man to Important Man. Now Weinstein was finally getting the audience he wanted.

"Hey, Harvey? This is Dean Baquet," he started. "Here's the deal. You need to give us your statement now. I'm about to push the button."

Weinstein interrupted. "Hey, Dean, let me tell you something about intimidation." The producer repeated the threat to give the *Washington Post* an interview, to undercut the *Times* story. Baquet had been a journalist for nearly four decades, run two of the country's top newspapers, and gone up against the CIA and foreign dictators. Was he about to explode?

Instead his voice eased, the slight New Orleans lilt returning. "Harvey, call them," he said. "That's fine. You can call the *Post*." He sounded like he was reassuring a child. "Harvey, I'm not trying to intimidate you, I'm trying to be fair with you."

"You *are* intimidating me, Dean," Weinstein said.

Now Corbett and Purdy were in the room too. "No, Harvey, here's the deal," Baquet said. "We're trying to get your statement to be fair. Please give it to us now because we're about to publish."

"I *want* to give it to you," Weinstein said.

"Thank you," Baquet said, hoping for finality.

"But while you're on the phone this is my career, my life," Weinstein said. He started asking about Paltrow again.

"*She's not in the story*," Baquet, Megan, and Jodi said nearly in unison.

"Harvey, I'm about to end this part of the conversation," Baquet said. "So here's what we need to do now, Harvey. We want to give you every word that you want to say. So say it. I also have a newspaper to put out. So give them your statement. I'm going to walk out. Talk to the reporters. Take care. Good luck." And with that, he left.

A minute later, at 1:41 p.m., multiple statements from Weinstein's team began arriving—the final elements the journalists needed to be able to publish.

On the phone, Weinstein was still making speeches ("Even if it costs me at the end of the day, investigations like this are important"), and Bloom was complaining that the paper had "a reckless disregard for the truth" and was going to publish "a hit piece" filled with "false accusations," which would soon be discredited. Corbett and Purdy had slipped out of the room without the reporters noticing.

Megan, who was scanning the statements from the Weinstein side, suddenly saw something important in the text in front of her and interjected. "Lisa, you said that Harvey needs time off to focus on this issue?"

Yes, Weinstein said. He was going to take time off.

"From . . . the company?" Megan asked, wanting to make sure this was what she thought it was. Yes, Weinstein said, he wanted to spend some time learning.

"Learning and listening to *me*," Bloom chimed in.

Weinstein was still talking, advising Jodi and Megan that they needed more of a sense of humor, and that he prayed every single day for the *New York Times*.

But Megan and Jodi were looking at one another in wonder. Weinstein was taking a leave of absence from his company. In the parlance of journalism, public relations, and business, that meant one thing: He was conceding wrongdoing. No one took a leave of absence from his own company when he was planning on fighting with full force. Suddenly, the reporters knew he probably wasn't going to sue the paper or even contest the article much.

Megan pushed him for more specifics on his plans, but he promised to call back later. "We have the Chinese newspaper to do the press conference with," Weinstein joked, wisecracking about his threat to take the story to a competing publication.

Megan laughed out loud.

"She laughed!" Weinstein exclaimed. "They laughed for the first time," he said to Bloom. Maybe this was the rough charm others had tried to explain. Or perhaps Weinstein was looking for one moment of dominance and control amid his own ruination.

It didn't matter. Megan and Jodi hung up from the call and fell together, laughing and crying with relief, esprit de corps, and sisterhood.

The reporters came out of the glass conference room ready to go. But Corbett and the other editors were already far ahead of them. They had been editing as the call was taking place, examining the statements of the Weinstein team, lifting out the crucial material to use, and transplanting those lines into the article.

Together, the written statements of Weinstein and his lawyers were baffling. Lisa Bloom's statement denied "many of the accusations as patently false," but she didn't say which. Weinstein's was vaguely contrite ("I realized some time ago that I needed to be a better person ... My journey now will be to learn about myself and conquer my demons ... I so respect all women and regret what happened.") In rambling paragraphs, he talked of working against the National Rifle Association and referenced nonexistent Jay-Z lyrics.

"I'm making a movie about our President, perhaps we can make it a joint retirement party." It was the most inchoate, least professional statement any of the journalists could remember.

"He wasn't intimidating, really, he was just a screamer," Matt Purdy said. "He had a lot of lawyers. He had a lot of words. He had a big voice. But we had all the facts."

Now the two reporters and three editors lined up behind Tolan, who sat at the keyboard, all of their eyes reviewing the article on his computer screen. The old way of publishing newspaper stories was to send them to presses with giant rolls of paper and vats of ink, and then rumbling trucks, then newsstands and lawns. The new way was to push a single button.

Baquet, jumping out of his skin, thought the story was ready to go. Purdy suggested that the six journalists read through it together one last time.

They started at the top, with the headline:

HARVEY WEINSTEIN PAID OFF SEXUAL HARASSMENT ACCUSERS FOR DECADES

The article started by stacking three separate stories from the Peninsula hotel. The reporters had the reference to at least eight settlements, and the string of allegations they had worked to document, starting with the young assistant in New York in 1990, then Madden in Ireland, the terrible pattern continuing until 2015. "Dozens of Mr. Weinstein's former and current employees, from assistants to top executives, said they knew of inappropriate conduct while they worked for him. Only a handful said they ever confronted him," they had written. The article described the way women who had come forward had been shut down or silenced.

The team read every line in silent unison. When they finished, no one had any fixes or suggestions. At 2:05 p.m., only twenty-four minutes after Weinstein sent his statements, Tolan pushed the button.

Weinstein had not grasped that the article would be published right away. At that moment, he was in his office with Bloom, and other defenders, planning their next move, when an assistant popped his head in. "The story's up," he told them. Employees throughout the office became fixed to their computer screens, taking in the news about their boss.

Back at the *Times*, Jodi's phone rang. "I have Harvey Weinstein for you," an assistant said in a routine singsong.

"There was no sexual harassment in the room with Ashley Judd," Weinstein bellowed as soon as he got on the line. "There was no police report. This is a dead issue."

Jodi and Megan asked him if he planned to retaliate against the women whose names appeared in the story. They wanted that answer on the record.

"The retaliation is going to be about your reporting," he said. His joking tone from an hour before had turned more menacing, and then it switched again. "I'm sorry to the women too," he said. "I'm no saint, we all know." On the phone, as in the statements, he was hopping between denial and remorse and back again. How could the *Times* call his actions harassment, he wanted to know, if the girls had come up to his hotel room?

The final notes he played were of self-pity. "I'm already dead. I'm already dead," he said. "I'm going to be a rolling stone."

The thirty-three-hundred-word article triggered an immediate crisis for The Weinstein Company. Within hours, the company's board convened an emergency meeting by conference call to determine how to respond, according to notes made from an audio recording of the meeting later obtained by Megan.

An enraged Bob Weinstein and several other board members insisted his brother follow through with a leave of absence and more mental-health treatment while the company investigated his conduct. But Weinstein pushed back, making it sound like the statement he provided to the *Times* was more show than substance. The board was engaging in a "rush to judgment." In retaliation, he would use his connections with the Murdochs to launch a negative story about Maerov in the *Wall Street Journal*. Weinstein refused to submit to an investigation that would "put me in jail." He would sell the company before being pushed out. "I will not be railroaded," he told the board.

But after so many years of clouded vision and compromise, Bob Weinstein finally had a clear view of his brother and what the story meant for him. "You are finished, Harvey," he told him.

In the following days, most of the directors would resign without making public comment. But in this private meeting, their views were on display. Richard Koenigsberg, a onetime accountant to the Weinstein brothers, proposed that the company's board walk a "fine line: We don't approve of the behavior, but we can't be held responsible for what Harvey Weinstein did twenty years ago." Tim Sarnoff, of the production and distribution company, thought it would be impossible to disconnect Weinstein from the company Technicolor, and, as a result, the directors "need to protect Harvey." Paul Tudor Jones, an investor, sounded at times downright optimistic, convinced "it will be forgotten."

Even at that late hour, they sounded more concerned with the welfare of the company than the welfare of the women, which had been the problem all along. By focusing so narrowly on liability, they had allowed the problem to grow and ultimately destroy what they had sought to protect.

During that board meeting, Weinstein was already touting a comeback narrative, with the help of Lisa Bloom. They would win the support of women's organizations, forty, fifty, sixty of them.

"There will be a movement," Weinstein asserted.

That evening at 9:07 p.m., Bloom wrote a defiant email to the board, her conciliatory tone from her statement to the *Times* gone.

> This is the worst day.
>
> This is the day the *New York Times* came out with a largely false and defamatory piece, in a major violation of journalistic ethics, giving only two days to respond to dozens of allegations, and then refusing to include information about eyewitnesses and documents negating many of the claims.

Tomorrow there will be more and different reporting, highlighting
inaccuracies, including photos of several of the accusers in very
friendly poses with Harvey after his alleged misconduct.

Bloom was right about more reporting. It wasn't the kind she envisioned.

On the next day, Friday, October 6, Jodi and Megan began hearing
from so many women with Weinstein stories that Corbett recruited other
colleagues to help call them all back. Tomi-Ann Roberts, a psychology
professor, said that in 1984, when she was twenty, Weinstein urged her to
audition for a film and invited her to a meeting; when she arrived, he sat
nude in a bathtub and told her she needed to disrobe for a shot at the part.
Hope Exiner d'Amore, sixty-two, described Weinstein raping her in a hotel room in Buffalo in the 1970s. Cynthia Burr, an actress, said Weinstein
forced her to perform oral sex on him during the same period.

Katherine Kendall said that in 1993, Weinstein gave her scripts, invited
her to a screening, and then took her home, removed his clothes and pursued her around his living room. Another former actress, Dawn Dunning,
said that in 2003, Weinstein appointed himself a mentor to her, arranged a
hotel room meeting, laid out contracts for three upcoming films, and told
her she could have the parts if she had three-way sex with him and an assistant on the spot. Judith Godrèche, the French actress who had refused
to speak earlier, opened up about how he had invited her to a Cannes hotel
room to discuss an Oscar campaign, pressed against her and pulled up her
sweater.

Jodi and Megan faced a question they never thought they would con-
template: How many Weinstein victims could they actually write about?

After the *Times* article was published, Ronan Farrow was finishing his
own powerful, detailed account of Weinstein offenses. Lauren Sivan, a
television journalist, told Yashar Ali of the *Huffington Post* that Weinstein
blocked her in a restaurant hallway, exposed himself, masturbated, and
ejaculated into a potted plant.

Angelina Jolie's representatives arranged a time for her and Jodi to
speak. Rosanna Arquette went on the record. And Paltrow was also ready

to join the next *Times* article, about Weinstein's casting couch harassment, and how orchestrated it was—"meetings," business discussions, assistants, the promise of stardom as a means of predation.

"This way of treating women ends now," she said in the new article that Jodi and a colleague were just beginning to write.

Lisa Bloom suffered through an uncomfortable appearance on *Good Morning America,* which appeared even more awkward when Megan later revealed in the paper that she had promised the Weinstein Company board publication of photos of Weinstein's accusers posing with him. By then, Bloom had resigned from Weinstein's team, as had Lanny Davis. Now Megan was pressing forward, determined to learn more about what Weinstein's companies knew about the allegations against him and when.

The only person who did not hear much of the escalating roar of reaction was Ashley Judd. Just before publication, she had left for the Great Smoky Mountains National Park to go camping alone. She had almost no cell reception, had made a vow not to check Twitter, and asked her representatives to deal with whatever inquiries came in. About once a day, when she got a few bars of cell service, she sent Jodi pictures of serene, lush mountain landscapes. Hiking amid the dogwoods and magnolias, she had only hints of how her statements about Weinstein had been received and whether the story had meant something to others as well.

CHAPTER EIGHT

THE BEACHSIDE DILEMMA

The Weinstein story was a solvent for secrecy, pushing women all over the world to speak up about similar experiences. The name *Harvey Weinstein* came to mean an argument for addressing misconduct, lest it go unchecked for decades, an example of how less-severe transgressions could lead to more serious ones. An emerging consensus that speaking up about sexual harassment and abuse was admirable, not shameful or disloyal. A cautionary tale about how that kind of behavior could become a grave risk for employers. Most of all, it marked an emerging agreement that Weinstein-like conduct was unequivocally wrong and should not be tolerated.

The aftermath, starting in October 2017, was like nothing Jodi and Megan had ever imagined. In the weeks after the first article on Weinstein, an overwhelming surge of tips flowed into the *Times* and other news organizations—a messy, unvetted, alarming record of what women in the U.S. and beyond said they had endured. The investigations became a project across journalism.

The *Times* sexual harassment team expanded, digging into the stories of restaurant waitstaff, ballet dancers, domestic and factory workers, Google employees, models, prison guards, and many others. When Jodi got a tip about the comedy megastar Louis C.K., she and two colleagues documented five women's damning accounts of his misbehavior, and he lost the distribution of his about-to-be-released film, the backing of his television network, and his agency, manager, and publicist. The entire process felt concentrated and accelerated: a trip from tip to downfall in less than a month.

That autumn, women from every arena of life posted #MeToo stories on social media, coming forward in new solidarity and of their own volition—without the months of trust building or persuasion required in the Weinstein investigation. Late one night when Megan took a break from working to absorb the declarations on own social media accounts, the sight of such posts from women she knew made her weep.

The key to change was a new sense of accountability: As women gained confidence that telling their stories would lead to action, more of them opened up. The volume and pain of those stories showed the scale of the problem and the way it had upended lives and undermined workplace progress. Businesses and other institutions investigated and fired their own leaders. Those consequences—the promise that telling the truth could lead to action—persuaded yet more women to speak up.

There were revolts in state legislatures over long-buried allegations. Swarms of protestors in the streets of Stockholm. The resignation of the British minister of defense. The instant professional evaporation of men whose power had seemed fixed: the television hosts Charlie Rose and Matt Lauer and the celebrity chef Mario Batali. Growing consensus that all sorts of previously tolerated practices were wrong: sexual overtures from the boss, corporate mandatory arbitration policies that kept harassment and abuse secret, and even smaller-scale behaviors like bra snapping in school hallways and laughing at movie scenes in which girls were taken advantage of by conquering male heroes. So much was suddenly open to question. The reckoning, and the feeling of rapidly shifting social standards, seemed like a sign that progress was still possible, even at a time of partisan fracture and nonstop conflict.

In its first few months, the post-Weinstein reckoning was mostly transcending partisan politics: Republicans had fallen and Democrats too. The offenses were universal and forced many people into self-examination. It felt like a fresh break from the depressing old formula that had dominated the public conversations around the allegations against Clarence Thomas,

Bill Clinton, and Donald Trump, which were characterized by opinion split along partisan lines, and results something more like holy wars than true moral accountings.

However, the conversation was also circling back to President Trump's treatment of women, in an unexpected way. *Times* readers came to Megan wanting to know if he would now be held accountable for the sexual misconduct accusations leveled against him in 2016, and whether additional women would emerge with new ones. There was little evidence of that happening. Instead, she was quietly pursuing a separate path of reporting, which involved attending a porn industry awards show in Los Angeles, in search of a woman named Stormy Daniels. Megan was among the journalists trying to piece together a secret settlement that Trump had paid to Daniels during the presidential race to keep her from going public with her allegation of an affair with him. She marveled that these obscure legal instruments were now at the center of the public conversation; in the case of Trump, they might amount to a criminal violation of campaign finance laws. California was among the states preparing to pass new laws to lift secrecy from sexual harassment settlements.

The Trump and Weinstein stories were converging in other ways too: It was becoming clear that both men had used American Media Inc., the parent company to the *National Enquirer*, to help conceal damaging stories about women. In 2016, American Media Inc. had purchased, then buried, another account of a Trump affair. Around the same time, one of the company's executives had directed a reporter to dig up dirt on Weinstein's accusers.

So much was surfacing so suddenly, and so many people were asking: What had really happened in the past? What had been concealed? Who was responsible?

Seven months after their first piece on Weinstein's alleged misdeeds had been published, Jodi and Megan sat in a Manhattan courtroom. They were waiting for Weinstein, who had spent that morning at a precinct house a few blocks away being booked, fingerprinted, and recorded in a series of mug shots.

The producer had already lost his job and reputation. But that day he would begin to face the ultimate accountability. He was on the defendant docket behind other workaday cases. Outside the courthouse, long lines of cameras were waiting, strangely reminiscent of the red carpets he had walked for so long.

With the bars of a holding cell momentarily visible behind him, Weinstein entered the courtroom in a posture of humiliation. His arms were immobilized behind his back with three sets of handcuffs to accommodate his girth, and he was led by two detectives, one of them female. The judge called the proceeding to order, and the female prosecutor called out the counts, her voice ringing out: "Your honor, the defendant is before the court, charged with two violent B felonies for two separate forcible assaults." In a terse few minutes, Weinstein was charged with raping one woman and forcing another to have oral sex in a criminal sexual act. He surrendered his freedom, in the form of his passport, before posting a million dollars' bail.

There was no way of predicting the outcome of the trial. Weinstein could not be tried for sexual harassment. That was a civil offense, and though many women had filed lawsuits against him, it was unclear how those would be resolved. Some of the most serious criminal allegations against the producer were not represented that day and would never land in court because they were beyond New York's statute of limitations. Other alleged victims had thus far chosen not to cooperate with the authorities, intent on protecting themselves or pessimistic about the prospect of conviction. Jodi and Megan had not vetted the two women behind the day's charges; they were among the dozens who came forward after their story broke, and one woman's name had not even been made public. (Later, prosecutors dropped a set of charges based on one of those accusers, then added another set related to a third alleged victim.) Sex crimes were notoriously difficult to try, and Weinstein's defense attorney was promising vindication.

But after nearly fifty years of alleged misdeeds, prosecutors finally had Weinstein in their sights. "He's now experiencing all the things he's put everybody else through," Cynthia Burr, who had accused Weinstein of forcing her into oral sex in the 1970s, told the *Times.* "Humiliation, worth-lessness, fear, weakness, aloneness, loss, suffering and embarrassment. And it's only the beginning for him."

In the final moments of his day in court, Weinstein was given a bulky electronic ankle bracelet to monitor his whereabouts. He protested, fighting the inevitable, then gave up: What choice did he have? When he exited the courtroom, Weinstein looked dazed, as if he was still absorbing what had happened.

As spring turned to summer, Jodi and Megan began to focus on a new question: how much was truly changing, and whether it was too much or not nearly enough.

The old rules on sex and power had been partly swept away, but it was not clear what the new ones would or should be. There was little agreement, and rancorous debate, over what behaviors were under scrutiny, how to know what to believe, and what accountability should look like. Years before, Tarana Burke had started the #MeToo movement to promote empathy and healing for victims of sexual violence, but now that label was being used as a catchall for a huge range of complaints, from verbal abuse to uncomfortable dates, many of which lacked the clarity of workplace or criminal violations. Earlier that year, babe.net, an online magazine, published an article accusing the comedian Aziz Ansari of behaving badly in a private romantic situation. But it was hard to tell whether his behavior was just overeager and clueless or worse.

That story was based entirely on one incident, recounted by an anonymous accuser, highlighting another dilemma: Though many publications continued to publish exposés based on in-depth investigation and on-the-record evidence, others were running stories that relied on a single source or unnamed accusers, much lower standards. Once published, some of those stories flushed out additional allegations and more evidence of wrongdoing. But other stories appeared thin and one-sided, raising questions of fairness to those facing accusations. So did allegations leveled on social media without any backup or response from the accused.

"Believe Women" grew into one of the catchphrases of the day. Jodi and Megan were sympathetic to the spirit behind that imperative: They had spent their careers getting women's stories into print. But the obligation of journalists was to scrutinize, verify, check, and question information. (A former editor of Megan's displayed a sign on his desk that read: IF YOUR MOTHER TELLS YOU SHE LOVES YOU, CHECK IT OUT.) The Weinstein story had impact in part because it had achieved something that, in 2018, seemed rare and precious: broad consensus on the facts.

Accountability was easy to insist on, but in some cases, much trickier to assign. Democrats were split over the case of Senator Al Franken of Minnesota, who resigned in January over a variety of incidents that mostly dated from before he took office. Some of the allegations involved unwanted kissing, but others seemed like jokey gestures that stemmed from his comedy background. Many companies, mindful of the lessons of The Weinstein Company's failures to act, started boasting of zero tolerance policies, but for what: An unwelcome hand placed on a back? A stray drunken comment at a holiday party? More and more critics were complaining that men were becoming the victims.

Even Weinstein's then attorney, Benjamin Brafman, seized on the criticism. In June, a month after Weinstein was charged, Brafman gave a radio interview in which he articulated the rising sense of grievance. He argued that the charges against Weinstein were just another way in which the #MeToo movement was becoming a witch hunt, a moral panic. Because of women making exaggerated claims, it was "proving to be so over the top" that it had lost "some of its own credibility," becoming so extreme that officemates now feared telling "an attractive associate that they're wearing a nice outfit." Instead of addressing the strength of the overall complaints against Weinstein, he seemed to be using the most strained #MeToo claims to sow doubt.

As the backlash developed, others argued that the changes hadn't gone nearly far enough. Social attitudes were shifting, and there were dramatic accusatory headlines almost daily, but the fundamentals were still largely the same. Sexual harassment laws largely were outdated and spottily enforced, and aside from some revisions in a few states, they did not appear likely to change anytime soon. Secret settlements were still being paid—in fact, some lawyers said the dollar amounts were higher than ever—allowing predators to remain hidden. Race and class often had an outsized influence on how cases were handled.

Jodi reported on low-income workers, whose experiences suggested little had shifted structurally. Most of the employers she called, from Walmart to Subway, said their long-standing policies were just fine. Many of the workers she spoke to were inspired and angry: They had watched the actors speak up and felt connected to the experiences of those distant celebrity figures. But they felt unclear about whether they had any avenue for addressing the problem.

Kim Lawson, a twenty-five-year-old McDonald's employee in Kansas City, Missouri, told Jodi that she had been harassed in two settings, the first time around 2015 at the run-down studio apartment she shared with her young daughter. Her landlord had repeatedly hit on her, and as she turned him down, he had raised the rent four times, until it was beyond what she could pay. With nowhere to live, Lawson had reluctantly decided to send her toddler, Faith, to reside with her mother, who lived four hours away.

A few months before she became homeless, she had managed to get a new job at McDonalds. But soon after Lawson had started, she said, she faced similar predatory treatment: One coworker stood far too close to her, so that every time she turned around, she couldn't help but brush against him. She had asked the general manager to admonish him, but he didn't stop. Soon one of the shift supervisors started bothering her too, making comments like "You are a chocolate drop" and "You should leave your boyfriend." She hadn't known what options or recourse she had in the situation with the landlord, and when she and Jodi spoke, it hadn't been clear to Lawson what more she could do about the work problems either. As far as she could tell, McDonald's had no sexual harassment training. (It did, but company officials later acknowledged that it didn't reach many employees.) She didn't know how to reach anyone at the parent company for help, and had feared that doing so would trigger retaliation.

"I have no idea of any number to call," Lawson told Jodi. "I don't know if there's anyone else I could talk to."

Jodi and Megan were hearing these sorts of questions—Who do I contact? What process do I follow?—from numerous women of all backgrounds. The reporters' mobile numbers and email addresses had been passed around, and every day, they were contacted about experiences of harassment, violence, and quiet suffering. On uncomfortable phone calls, women begged Jodi and Megan to investigate their cases; certain that, if they were to write something, it could create some sort of justice.

But there were too many alleged victims of Weinstein, and many other perpetrators, to ever possibly write about. The reporters stumbled trying to explain that the paper was overwhelmed with stories of abuse, that not all could be told, and that even the nation's most powerful publications could not bear the entire weight of the reckoning. Journalists had stepped in when the system failed, but that wasn't a permanent solution.

In a way, those who felt #MeToo had not gone far enough and those who protested that it was going too far were saying some of the same things: There was a lack of process or clear enough rules. The public did not fully agree on the precise meaning of words like *harassment* or *assault*, let alone how businesses or schools should investigate or punish them. Everyone from corporate boards to friends in bars seemed to be struggling to devise their own new guidelines, which made for fascinating conversation but also a kind of overall chaos. It was not clear how the country would ever agree on effective new standards or resolve the ocean of outstanding complaints.

Instead, the feelings of unfairness on both sides just continued to mount.

On a Saturday afternoon in early August, Jodi received an urgent text. The attorney Debra Katz, who specialized in sexual harassment, employment issues, and whistleblowing, wanted to speak immediately. No, it couldn't wait an hour.

In the course of their reporter-source relationship, Jodi had turned to

Katz for legal analysis, quoted her in articles, and talked to her about Irwin Reiter, who was now one of her clients. This time when Jodi dialed her number, Katz's voice took on a this-is-complicated tone. She wanted to talk about a new client who might be a potential story. But this was all off the record, she said.

Just a few days before, she had started representing a woman who said she had been attacked by Judge Brett Kavanaugh, Trump's Supreme Court nominee. The two had been in high school at the time in suburban Maryland. According to Katz's client, a drunken Kavanaugh had pushed her into a bedroom during a party with the help of a friend, locked the door, pinned her down, grinded against her, and covered her mouth when she tried to yell. The client said she managed to get away, but that encounter had caused her anguish and anxiety ever since, Katz said.

There was not a lot of corroboration of the alleged assault, Katz said. The woman hadn't told anyone at the time. In recent years, she had discussed the matter with her husband and a few friends—they were still sorting out which. She had also told therapists. Some of the particulars had faded: She didn't know precisely when it happened or some other details. She had already passed a lie detector test Katz had arranged, and she seemed to be mentally preparing to tell her story more widely.

This was the most worried the lawyer had ever sounded to Jodi. She described her client as a research scientist who was careful and precise, who had no reason to fabricate something. But, she continued, the woman had none of the armor that came from being in public life. She was so earnest about sharing her story and didn't seem to grasp how utterly torn apart she, her family, and her life could be. Weeks before she had spoken with Katz, the woman had written a letter with her account to an elected official. That document could easily be leaked, Katz said. If that happened, the attorney wasn't sure how the country would react.

Katz was calling for two reasons. She wanted to tip off the *Times* to do more digging on Kavanaugh's treatment of women, to see if there was a pattern of misbehavior.

She also raised the prospect of her client telling her story to Jodi and Megan in the *Times*, getting ahead of any possible leak. Her client had sent a tip to the *Washington Post* and spoken with a reporter there, but it wasn't clear if the *Post* was moving on the story.

Jodi suggested the first step was for her to talk to the client, off the record, to hear the story firsthand. Katz agreed and also warned: Don't try to figure out this woman's identity on your own or show up on her doorstep. She's frightened and surprise tactics will backfire.

As soon as Jodi hung up, she texted Corbett and Megan: "Need to talk to you asap. Kavanaugh, assault."

From that very first, nameless sketch, the scenario that Katz had described summoned some of the most complicated and unresolved issues in the #MeToo conversation: The dilemmas of how to deal with painful incidents from the past. The challenges of coming up with fair processes for accusers to complain and the accused to respond. The debates over accountability: If this woman's story was true, should job candidates be judged based on something they did in high school?

Had a novelist tried to conjure a scenario to capture the swirl of strong feelings around #MeToo, it would have been hard to write one more flammable. The lack of corroborating evidence from the time of the alleged assault meant that the facts were probably going to be in dispute. If Katz's client went public with her allegation, some people would regard it as a serious attack, even criminal, but others were likely to dismiss it as drunken horseplay. At the time of the encounter, Kavanaugh had been a teenager at a private party, so this was very different from the workplace complaints at the heart of the Weinstein investigation. Then again, she was describing behavior that could be relevant as he was considered for one of the most influential jobs in the country, in which he would help make far-reaching decisions, including about the lives of women and girls.

If this allegation went public, it could be a return to the experience of Anita Hill's testimony in 1991 at Clarence Thomas's hearings. All of this would play out in Trump's Washington, with the retirement of the court's swing justice, at a time when Democrats were enraged by Republicans who had denied President Obama his final pick, and via a nomination process that had been fully politicized long before Trump's election. A Justice Kavanaugh could rule on abortion, perhaps still the single most divisive issue in an utterly divided country. Because the midterm elections were approaching, the political consequences of this woman coming forward could be profound.

Corbett quietly shared the tip with several editors at the paper. Reporters had already been checking into Kavanaugh's interactions with women, but she asked a small group to focus even further and to prepare for the likelihood that an accusation could surface at any moment.

Her name was Christine Blasey Ford. At the beginning of the summer of 2018, she was an established scientific researcher, an independent thinker, and a mother of two sons, who had not fully tuned in to #MeToo news and debate. She had expected that the next couple months of her life would be filled with controversy, because of a paper she and her colleagues were about to publish about the antidepressant effects of the drug ketamine.

Washington, DC, figured in her life mainly as a place she had rejected. She had grown up in the same preppy, privileged suburban circles as Kavanaugh. But she had fled that world back in her twenties for California and immersion in the science of the brain. At fifty-one, she was a professor of psychology and a biostatistician at a consortium made up of professors from Palo Alto and Stanford. Twitter was a foreign land to her. She was a casual Democrat who had made a few campaign contributions here and there, including one to Bernie Sanders, but had little affinity for the pinball dynamics of national politics. Like her peers, she wrote her papers in a language of high science that most people would barely understand. Her name had appeared on studies on trauma, depression, and resilience, but her memories of the attack she had described had never been front and center in her life.

She hadn't known much about what happened to Kavanaugh until 2012, when she happened to read on the internet that George W. Bush had attended his wedding. For the first time, she realized how high Kavanaugh had risen in his legal career. It wasn't unusual for people from her high school crowd to ascend to prestigious positions. "That was the moment when I thought, 'I wonder if he'll be nominated to the Supreme Court,'" she later recalled in a series of interviews.

That same year, she and her husband had gone to counseling for help with communication issues, including resolving some fights that lingered from remodeling their Palo Alto house a few years earlier. Ford had insisted that they build a second front door, explaining that she would feel trapped without it, much to her husband's frustration. At the therapist's urging, Ford for the first time told her husband that in high school, she had been trapped in a room and physically restrained by a boy who molested her while another boy watched. This was why she needed multiple exit routes.

"She said she was eventually able to escape before she was raped, but that the experience was very traumatic because she felt like she had no control and was physically dominated," Russell Ford later wrote in a sworn affidavit. "I remember her saying that the attacker's name was Brett Kavanaugh, that he was a successful lawyer who had grown up in Christine's home town, and that he was well-known in the Washington, DC community."

Through counseling, Ford had become more aware of how she had struggled with the fallout from the incident, how confined spaces could trigger severe anxiety in her, and how she often had the urge to flee in the face of conflict. Over the years, she told her story to other therapists, including a PTSD specialist, and several friends.

In the spring of 2016, she and a friend, Keith Koegler, were watching their sons play sports together one day, when Ford turned to him and expressed outrage. Brock Turner, a Stanford student who had been convicted of sexually assaulting an unconscious woman on campus, had just been sentenced to six months in jail and three years' probation, which critics saw as a miscarriage of justice. Ford told Koegler that she had been assaulted as a teenager, by someone who was now a federal judge. "Partly because the kids were running around, partly because her face didn't show an interest in saying more, I didn't push," Koegler said in an interview. "I had no context, no idea who he was."

That autumn, Ford had been appalled by the *Access Hollywood* tape, with

Trump's crude comments, but she hadn't followed the stories of the women who made allegations against the presidential candidate. A few months later, she joined in the women's march in San Jose, where other women wore pink hats, in protest of sexual violence, but she felt more invested in a separate march that year, to protest federal cuts to scientific research. She and friends wore gray knitted hats, for the gray matter in the brain. After the Weinstein story she had written "#metoo" on social media and left it at that.

But in June 2018, when Trump's short list for the Supreme Court circulated with Kavanaugh's name included, she emailed her friend Koegler about her unease:

> The favorite for SCOTUS is the jerk who assaulted me in high school.
> He's my age, so he'll be on the court the rest of my life. ☹

Koegler wrote back:

> I remember you telling me about him, but I don't remember his name,
> Do you mind telling me so I can read about him?

"Brett Kavanaugh," Ford replied.

By the time the July Fourth holiday approached, she felt rising panic. President Trump was running a reality-show-style search, and he had promised to make an announcement by the following Monday, July 9.

If Kavanaugh was to be nominated for a lifetime appointment, she felt she had relevant information to provide. Still, she wanted to protect her privacy and did not want to embarrass her family back East by hurting a hometown hero's candidacy. Their fathers were still members of the same small, private golf club, awkwardly enough. She didn't want to shame Kavanaugh publicly. She just wanted to pass on her account of what had happened in high school, and she wanted to do it *before* he became the nominee. If she intervened early, those in charge could consider the information and perhaps move on to a candidate with no such liability. But who could she

tell discreetly, who would handle the information in a trustworthy but effective way?

Ford realized that her perspective was limited, that she didn't know if
the behavior she remembered from Kavanaugh was a lone incident or part
of a pattern of predation. *Was that an episodic state, or was it part of a personality
trait?* she asked herself.

Ford was trying to figure out whether or how to influence a Supreme
Court nomination in an unlikely setting. A serious surfer, she and her
husband had met through a website that had identified their common interest in riding waves. Their second date had taken place afloat in the
waters off the San Mateo coast. Once, a great white shark had risen up
beside her in the water. The thrill had been so great that she did not sleep
for two days. Ford often used surfing analogies in her classroom and
longed for the wide beaches and free-spirit atmosphere of Santa Cruz, her
summer escape an hour or so to the south of her Palo Alto home.

Now she and her friends huddled on the sand, gazed out at Pacific
vistas, took long swims, watched their kids train in the California State
Parks Junior Lifeguard program, and weighed her options for quietly intervening. Ford did not call any lawyers. But she wondered if she should
call Kavanaugh directly to tell him to withdraw from consideration for the
court post so as to avoid putting his family through the humiliation that
would come from her stepping forward. Or she could call Mark Judge, the
other man who had been in the room during the assault, and ask him to
pass along the message.

"I was just freaking out," she recalled of that time. "What am I going
to do?"

She didn't speak extensively with her husband: He was commuting
back and forth to Palo Alto for work. Russell Ford was an engineer who
built medical devices, and he had the same type of scientific mind as his
wife, with the same type of blinders. He was also an optimist by nature. At
that point, she said, neither understood that quietly passing on decades-
old information could have substantial consequences for their family.

On Friday, July 6, she walked off the Rio del Mar Beach and, from her
parked car, called the office of her congressional representative, Anna

Eshoo, a Democrat. When a young woman answered, Ford blurted out her message:

Someone on the Supreme Court short list sexually assaulted me in high school. I need to talk to someone in the office. It's urgent; Trump is about to make his selection.

She would hear back as soon as possible, she was told.

Ford picked up her iPhone again. Unsure about when Eshoo's office would respond, she would pursue another route. She clicked on the *Washington Post* anonymous tip line and starting typing:

> 10:26 AM
>
> Potential Supreme Court nominee with assistance from his friend assaulted me in mid 1980s in Maryland. Have therapy records talking about It. Feel like I shouldn't be quiet but not willing to put family in DC and CA through a lot of stress.

An hour later, she returned to the tip line to clarify:

> 11:47 AM
>
> Brett Kavanaugh with Mark Judge and a bystander named PJ

"I had thought my phone would ring immediately," Ford said later. But she got no immediate response from the *Post* either.

On July 9, three days later, President Trump announced his nominee: Brett Kavanaugh, distinguished judge, wholesome figure, coach of his daughter's basketball team.

In a text message to friends, she typed out a sad emoji and added:

> Ugh
>
> Double ugh.

Ford was a rabid football fan—she competed in a fantasy league and had even volunteered to house a Stanford player at her home during summer training—and now she turned to a quarterback analogy to explain what had happened. She had tried to pass the football to her member of Congress and the *Washington Post*. But they had let it drop. The play was over.

The next morning, July 10, Ford returned to the *Post* tip line with the equivalent of a journalism threat: She might go to senators or the *Times* with her story. By late morning, she was on the phone with Emma Brown, a *Post* reporter eager to hear her out.

That same afternoon, her phone rang again. Eshoo's district chief of staff was on the line. The aide had called the day before, asking, "Is it the person who was picked?" Now they agreed Ford would come in to Eshoo's office on Wednesday, July 18.

That was a week away. As she waited, Ford read flattering coverage of Kavanaugh that highlighted his support of women and girls. The *Post* published an opinion piece by a mother who raved about what a terrific girls' basketball coach he was. An old friend from high school told Ford how proud the community was to be producing another justice. (Neil Gorsuch also had attended Georgetown Prep, the same high school as Kavanaugh.) *The math is not in my favor*, Ford recalled thinking.

She could live with him being appointed: "I really consciously divested from the outcome," she said. But the prospect of watching Kavanaugh on the court, while knowing she had not shared her memories, seemed intolerable: "Not saying something is what's upsetting," she said.

So she undertook a mission to gather evidence, driving to her doctor's office in Silicon Valley and requesting copies of the notes from the therapy sessions in which she had recalled being assaulted, the ones she had referenced in her tip to the *Post*.

In the meantime, she told her sons the minimum. "A person who the president wants to hire for an important job did something bad to me when I was your age," she said. "I'm trying to figure out a way to get the information to him. He may find it useful."

"Cool," said her older son, who was the same age she had been at the time of the alleged assault.

On July 18, she met with Karen Chapman, Representative Eshoo's district chief of staff. Ford provided an exhaustive account of everything she recalled, even drawing her a map of the suburban house where she remembered being trapped in the bedroom. Chapman took copious notes and expressed support, but Eshoo wasn't there, so two days later, Ford had to return to the office, relaying her account all over again.

Eshoo promised to be back in touch and issued strict instructions: All of this was to remain confidential. Ford had only told a handful of people other than her husband, including Emma Brown, the *Post* reporter; Keith Koegler; several other friends; and two work mentors. "You can't be talking about this," Eshoo told her. "If it does get around, it will be because you told other people." Eshoo said word traveled fast, and it could impact Ford and how she chose to proceed.

Ford, who still had no idea exactly where this was going, thought the meeting felt like progress: She had gotten her message to someone in a position of authority. "I trust her office," Ford emailed one of her mentors, "and we are consistent in the goal of public service." Following Eshoo's advice, Ford ignored texts from the *Post* reporter.

But during that time, Ford began to get high-pressure texts with messages passed along from strangers. One of her friends had told someone, who had told someone, and soon word of her allegations was traveling around Palo Alto feminist circles. These women, some of them high-powered academics, had come together through the Brock Turner case and the Women's March, and the previous few months of #MeToo activity had strengthened their conviction. Now local activists—one Ford knew, but most she did not—were pushing her to come forward. "This is a crucial time in history," one of her friends stressed in a text.

Ford mostly ignored the outreach. Were it not for Kavanaugh, she would not be paying attention to the nomination process at all, she said, and she was not considering whether or how her actions would affect the #MeToo movement.

But the messages were harbingers: that this situation was going to attract intensely strong feelings from others, that she could lose control of her own story, that other people with various agendas might operate without taking her wishes into account. By ignoring the messages, she was missing important clues.

In the last week of July, Ford was pulled back to the Washington area. Her grandmother had suffered a stroke and was about to die. Ford hated to fly, but she and her sons traveled to stay with her parents at their summer home in Rehoboth Beach, Delaware, for a hot, humid ten days.

Her parents had no idea about her secret—they had never had, she said—and she didn't want to trouble them especially while they were tending to her grandmother. When Eshoo's office called, she stepped out to the porch for privacy. The aide was asking her to write a letter detailing what had happened with Kavanaugh for the Senate Judiciary Committee, which held hearings for Supreme Court nominees. The writing was straightforward: By now, Ford was used to repeating the story. But she debated whom to send it to. The aide told Ford to address the letter to Senator Dianne Feinstein, the top Democrat on the committee, as well as Senator Charles Grassley, the Republican chair. Ford worried that would raise the chances of her name and story becoming public. So she addressed the letter to Feinstein only, who she assumed would have to abide by constituent confidentiality, based on what Eshoo's office had said.

July 30, 2018

CONFIDENTIAL

SENATOR DIANNE FEINSTEIN

Dear Senator Feinstein:

I am writing with information relevant in evaluating the current nominee of the Supreme Court. As a constituent, I expect that you will maintain this as confidential until we have further opportunity to speak.

Brett Kavanaugh physically and sexually assaulted me during High School in the early 1980's. He conducted these acts with the assistance of his close friend, Mark G. Judge. Both were 1-2 years older than me and students at a local private school. The assault occurred in a suburban Maryland area home at a gathering that included me and 4 others. Kavanaugh physically pushed me into a bedroom as I was headed for a bathroom up a short stairwell from the living room. They locked the door and played loud music, precluding any successful attempts to yell for help. Kavanaugh was on top of me while laughing with Judge, who periodically jumped onto Kavanaugh. They both laughed as Kavanaugh tried to disrobe me in their highly inebriated state. With Kavanaugh's hand over my mouth, I feared he may inadvertently kill me. From across the room, a very drunken Judge said mixed words to kavanaugh ranging from "go for it" to "stop." At one point when Judge jumped onto the bed, the weight on me was substantial. The pile toppled, and the two scrapped with each other. After a few attempts to get away, I was able to take this opportune moment to get up and run across to a hallway bathroom. I locked the bathroom door behind me. Both loudly stumbled down the stairwell, at which point other persons at the house were talking with them. I exited the bathroom, ran outside of the house and went home.

I have not knowingly seen Kavanaugh since the assault. I did see Mark Judge once at the Potomac Village Safeway, where he was extremely uncomfortable seeing me.

I have received medical treatment regarding the assault. On July 6, I notified my local government representative to ask them how to proceed with sharing this information. It is upsetting to discuss sexual assault and its repercussions, yet I feel guilty and compelled as a citizen about the idea of not saying anything.

I am available to speak further should you wish to discuss. I am currently vacationing in the mid-Atlantic until August 7th and will be in California after August 10th.

In Confidence,

Christine Blasey
PALO ALTO, CALIFORNIA

"Got it!" the aide wrote back. "Will hand deliver to her today."

Soon the aide was on the phone with Ford, describing every move of another Eshoo staff member in Washington who was walking a hard copy of the letter to Senator Feinstein's office. "Now he's handing it over," the staff member narrated, as if they were discussing the nation's nuclear codes.

Next Senator Feinstein herself was on the phone. The eighty-five-year-old legislator seemed to be hard of hearing. She was yelling out questions about the precise nature of the incident, and Ford was yelling back, to make sure the senator could understand what she was saying. Senator Feinstein said she would keep the letter confidential and promised to be back in touch.

As she hung up the phone, Ford began to envision the power her letter would take on under the Capitol dome, in a way that she had not on the beach in California. For weeks, Ford's confidantes had been telling her to get a lawyer, to protect and retain control of her own story, but she had resisted. She and her husband had been saving for a down payment for a condo in Hawaii, where they could surf and retire and didn't want to deplete their funds, she said. Now she realized she definitely needed an attorney.

The first Washington firms that she contacted did not want to touch the case, but she found one attorney, Lawrence Robbins, who had argued multiple cases before the Supreme Court and listened carefully. "She did not try to minimize the gaps in her memory," Robbins said. "She was extremely clear about the things she could recall. She provided forms of corroboration, perhaps not bulletproof, but good enough that I thought they should be taken seriously. My impression was that she was believable and deserved to have someone go to bat for her." But he couldn't represent her publicly: His partners feared it could harm their appellate court cases if it looked like the firm had done something adverse to a Supreme Court justice, so any help he gave would have to be behind the scenes.

On Monday, August 6, just after Ford's grandmother passed away, right before she was scheduled to leave the Washington area, she was talking with two new lawyers, this time face to face. Senator Feinstein's office had flagged a pair of law partners, Debra Katz and Lisa Banks, explaining that these two were among those who worked with these types of allegations. Ford had studied their website and noticed that they had done whistleblower work. But the most valuable thing about them was that they were available to meet immediately. She said she could squeeze in a quick meeting at a hotel near the Baltimore airport.

Katz and Banks quickly agreed, not sure what to expect. A couple days before, Feinstein's office had reached out to them, with general questions—if you have a very old allegation of sexual assault, what can you do to confirm it?—then followed up with the broad outlines of Ford's account without naming her. Ford, for her part, wasn't sure what to make of the two lawyers or all their detailed, personal questions about her story and background.

She didn't grasp that she was dealing with two of the top gender discrimination lawyers in the country. Debra Katz—Debbie to almost everyone—was Ford's temperamental opposite, a take-charge activist who was steeped in Washington and feminist fights. Katz thought in civil rights terms, and saw the law as a means to progress. She had begun her career as a junior member of the legal team that strategized over how to best argue the first sexual harassment case ever heard by the Supreme Court, *Meritor Savings Bank v. Vinson*, about a bank teller who said that the branch manager had repeatedly assaulted her and told her he would fire her if she did not comply. In 1986, the court ruled in Vinson's favor, nine to zero, establishing the precedent that sexual harassment is a form of discrimination.

Three decades later, Katz was still a diehard lefty but had a closet full of pin-striped suits she wore to negotiate on behalf of employees who felt wronged. Her law partner, Lisa Banks, also her best friend outside the office, had a cooler presence, an impassive glare that could be useful with adversaries, and perseverance that stretched back to childhood, when at age seven someone had shattered her dreams, informing her that she would never be able to play for the Boston Red Sox because she was a girl.

Their office above Dupont Circle was decorated with polished furniture, potted plants—and a painting of Rose McGowan holding Harvey Weinstein's severed head that had been made by a friend of Katz's son. When the attorneys met Ford in Baltimore, they had already been in overdrive for months, trying to make the most of what they saw as a rare window of opportunity post-Weinstein. For most of their careers, progress on harassment and abuse had felt stalled, with the same kinds of cases cropping up repeatedly. They had often won awards for individual women, sometimes very large ones, typically in the form of secret settlements, which they regarded as imperfect but necessary tools.

But the Weinstein case had galvanized their practice, they said later, because their client's complaints were suddenly being taken far more seriously. In the ten months since the Weinstein story, Katz had represented staffers on Capitol Hill whose harassment complaints triggered resignations by a member of the House of Representatives and a high-level congressional staffer. After she and Banks filed a lawsuit against a Washington-area celebrity chef, his partners eventually fled and his empire dissolved. They had met with representatives of Congress and state legislatures, pushing for new laws to better protect victims of sexual harassment. All summer, Katz and Banks had been feeling exhilarated but worried: This moment was so valuable, they felt; change was so overdue. They wanted as much progress as possible, as fast as possible, before too much backlash mounted.

After a few hours with Ford, the attorneys walked out of the conference room with their heads spinning. At first, they just kept muttering to one another: *Oh my God. Oh my God.* They had vetted an untold number of witnesses over the years, and Ford struck both attorneys as very credible, they said. They were also moved by what she called her sense of civic duty. But this woman, with her formidable scientific intellect, also seemed so naïve, a quality that could land her in serious trouble. She seemed unaware of the potential gravity of her own case, but that sense of consequence was part of what drew them to it. Unlike Ford, they had immediately understood the charged nature of the letter she had written to Feinstein. If that letter leaked, she would need protection; if not, she would need counsel on whether and how to pursue the matter further. The lawyers knew they wanted to represent Ford and do it pro bono.

To prepare for what might come, the lawyers set Ford to work on some practical tasks. She soon underwent, and passed, a polygraph test administered by a former FBI agent. She also took on the embarrassing task of calling two of her ex-boyfriends, one from high school and one from right after college. No, I'm not calling to get back together, she told them. I need to know, do you recall if when we were together I ever mentioned being assaulted? Neither did, she said. It became increasingly clear that Ford had told no one about the alleged attack for years.

The lawyers pored over Ford's life history, searching through public records to identify any information that could be used to smear her. Katz called Senator Feinstein's staff and told them that she thought the accusation was credible and suggested that they start searching for evidence of any other assaults Kavanaugh might have committed.

That was when Katz first called Jodi, on Saturday, August 11, asking her to pass the tip to the *Times.* Rebecca Corbett had overseen some of the paper's vetting of prospective Supreme Court candidates over the years and was now doing the same for Kavanaugh. As Corbett pressed the expanding team of reporters to look for any problematic treatment of women, she checked in with Jodi every few days, wanting to know if there was anything more on that Katz client with the allegation.

But Ford declined to speak with Jodi, or to return the latest calls from the *Post.* She was focused on another choice, one that came with a pressing deadline.

Kavanaugh's hearings were scheduled to begin September 4. Three things could happen before then: The letter to Feinstein could leak. Ford could remain silent and likely watch Kavanaugh sail through confirmation. Or she could decide to speak up publicly, which might change the course of the hearings. That's what she, in her heart of hearts, was inclined, if frightened, to do.

Katz and Banks understood why. Ford had a right to tell her story, they believed, and a vital point to make. The violations committed against high school girls, against entire generations of women, mattered, even if those women had maintained long silences or didn't have perfect evidence. The two-part question was what price Ford would pay personally and what impact her coming forward would have—on the nomination, and on the entire raging debate about sex and power.

Other lawyers reinforced the idea that Ford had an important story to tell. In addition to retaining Katz and Banks, she had kept Robbins on as an adviser—and at his referral she took on another adviser named Barry Coburn, a tough criminal defense attorney. Coburn told her he saw a clear distinction between high-school sexual horseplay and what Ford described, "unambiguous attempted rape." "It's not sexual harassment," he later recalled telling her. "It's not a boundary violation. It's not like being insensitive. It's a felony." But Robbins and Coburn understood that this was about more than the underlying incident, and they let Katz and Banks take the lead.

At Katz's request, one more person joined the growing council of professional advisers: Ricki Seidman, a deliberative, discreet veteran of three decades' worth of Democratic judicial fights, who had worked as an aide to Bill Clinton's presidential campaign and served in his administration. Katz had never met Seidman, but she knew that the operative came with deep knowledge and experience of Supreme Court nominations that she and Banks did not have. Seidman had been involved in battles ranging from Robert Bork (who Democrats defeated in 1987) to Sonia Sotomayor (who Democrats confirmed in 2009). She had played a direct role in the only historical proxy for Ford's case: Anita Hill's testimony against Clarence Thomas. In 1991, Seidman had been working for the Senate Labor and Resources Committee as chief investigator, watching the Thomas nomination, when she got a call tipping her off about a professor who said she had been harassed by the nominee. She was the first member of the Senate committee staff to speak with Anita Hill about her experiences, and she had encouraged Hill to engage further with the committee.

Republicans later saw Seidman's history and accused her of harboring a political agenda, of weaponizing Ford to derail a nomination. In fact, that August, Seidman's instinct was that Ford should remain silent.

It was a matter of math. Given Republican control of the Senate, Kavanaugh would likely be confirmed even if Ford spoke up. Her first reaction was that the bar for coming forward was very high, because she didn't think it was going to make a difference in the outcome.

In the decades after Anita Hill's testimony, the adviser had struggled with her role in encouraging the professor to come forward. Hill had prevailed in some ways, catalyzing awareness of sexual harassment. But Seidman thought that any social progress had come at a great personal toll to Hill. She felt the attack apparatus of the Republican Party would almost certainly try to destroy Ford, and the prospect of watching history repeat itself filled her with dread.

Ford's advisers suspected that Kavanaugh had victimized other women, that this had not been an isolated incident—it was just a matter of finding them. *If there were two more women, I would feel better,* Katz thought to herself. *With one more woman, it's risky.* They had zero.

Katz and Banks were trying to stay neutral, sketching out the potential consequences for Ford on each side, knowing that she was the one who would have to live with her decision.

But their worries extended beyond their client's own welfare. In that moment, Katz was also fearful that a national discounting of Ford's story could be detrimental for the entire #MeToo movement. Critics would say it had gone too far, raising violations that were ancient, unprovable, and lacked the more demonstrable harm of workplace sexual harassment or rape. Some men would instinctively side with Kavanaugh, afraid of out-of-the-blue accusations. The wheel of progress could slow, or even spin in the opposite direction, a consequence the lawyers saw as too painful to bear.

The public conversation was still tumultuous. That summer, more men were still being accused, suspended, and fired by the week: the personnel chief of the Federal Office of Emergency Management, a UC Berkeley professor, a Goldman Sachs salesman, two dancers from the New York City Ballet. In August, Ronan Farrow published the first sexual harassment allegations against CBS chairman Les Moonves in the *New Yorker*—but Moonves remained defiantly in place, backed by the company's board. Louis C.K. made his first appearance at a comedy club since the *Times* article, to cheers in the room and jeering outside it. Bill O'Reilly, who had continued writing history books since his ouster from Fox, was about to release his latest book: The previous one had sold nearly half a million copies, his fans ever loyal.

By August 10, Ford was back in Palo Alto, weighing her decision as she was completing a pile of student dissertation evaluations. She barely knew these Washington advisers in whom she had placed her fate; the group's deliberations were taking place by phone or text message. They all said they would support Ford no matter what she decided, but from afar, she could feel their hesitation. *Are they trying to push me forward? Or are they trying to shut me down?* she wondered.

Ford was mulling her own personal concerns. She feared that if she were publicly to point a finger at Kavanaugh, others might point fingers back at her. She had done her fair share of drinking in high school, and early in college, her partying had escalated, and her grades tanked. Shortly after, she had stabilized and succeeded in her studies. In a speech at her old high school in 2014, she had offered herself as an example of how to get a life back on track. She had floundered in statistics in college. Now she taught it. Still she worried that critics would focus only on her younger self's shortcomings and mistakes, she said.

But Ford believed that if she did come under attack, she could withstand it. In 2015, she had been diagnosed with cancer and suffered complications from the treatment. It was the first time Ford had been forced to measure her own mortality, and afterward, she felt she had emerged stronger—with a greater capacity to endure, she said. Her husband had been encouraging her to step forward, to get it over with, predicting the whole thing would die down after a single news cycle.

On August 24, Katz shared an update with Ford: No other allegations of sexual misconduct by the judge had surfaced. If she were going to come forward, she would be a lone accuser. If she did not want Senator Feinstein to share her letter with the rest of the committee, including the Republicans, she needed to say so. To help Ford come to a decision, they agreed on an internal deadline: She would make a call by August 29, seven days before Kavanaugh's hearings were set to begin.

By August 26, Ford was still paralyzed with indecision. Two days later, with no progress, Katz and Banks said they would draft and edit three different letters. Because there was no established process for reporting this kind of story about a nominee, the lawyers were trying to show Ford what various paths could look like. Each version led to a different variation on her future, maybe a different composition of the Supreme Court, even a different version of American history.

In one version, addressed to Senators Grassley and Feinstein, the lawyers used Ford's name and explained that she wanted to meet with them privately to report an allegation of assault against the judge. The second version made the same request, but referred to Ford as Dr. Jane Doe, for a little more protection. The third option, addressed only to Senator Feinstein, used Ford's name but said she was declining to pursue the matter. "She has determined that the personal and professional costs of coming forward before the Judiciary Committee are too great," the letter said. The group agreed that Ford would choose one of the letters by the end of the next day.

The first one struck everyone as too risky: Ford's name would immediately reach the White House. Ford seemed to be leaning toward the second letter, which could allow her to negotiate terms of confidentiality. Together, the women tweaked the language of that letter, and then changed it again, no one fully satisfied.

The more they envisioned delivering the letters, the more the discussion shifted to the question, Then what happens? Ford's lawyers and Seidman told her it would likely be impossible to try to move forward in reporting the claim without having her identity revealed. They predicted she would come under the same type of public attack as Anita Hill had, more than once likening it to the equivalent of stepping in front of a train.

As the self-imposed deadline neared, Seidman flew to California and met Ford for the first time. Once again she warned her from following in Hill's footsteps. Telling the story of the alleged assault still caused Ford pain. She was so unversed in public life, a stranger to scrutiny, not even close to fluent in the flow of the news cycle. Seidman still believed Kavanaugh would be confirmed even if Ford came forward, and the only thing she would accomplish would be turning her life upside down.

At the coffee date with Seidman near the San Francisco International Airport, Ford felt overcome with stress. She didn't know the woman sitting across from her. "I just wanted to leave," she recalled feeling at the time.

Ford spent August 29, the appointed decision day, in academic meetings for hours, consulting with graduate students on their dissertations. As the sun set that evening, Ford was still unable to choose.

"Made edits and having some panic symptoms," she wrote in a text to Katz that evening. "I'll send to you edits soon and we can decide in early a.m. whether to go. Anxiety about leaks and Washington Post."

"Just sent you edits," she wrote again an hour later, "no green light yet."

She didn't have one in the morning either. She was beginning to believe what her team had already told her: that the anonymous letter was pointless, her name was likely to leak, and it was all or nothing. Katz and Banks were twisting too, caught between believing their client was in the right and wondering how many others would feel the same way, unsure which was worse, incineration or silence.

It was Thursday, August 30. The next day marked the start of Labor Day weekend. The following Tuesday morning, Kavanaugh's hearings would begin. In Washington, Katz called Ford.

"This is a life-defining decision, and it's yours," she said.

That afternoon, Ford still wanted a few more hours to think, to go for a walk, to speak to a friend one last time.

In the end, Ford did not choose any of the letters—none of them felt right to her, she said. That, in effect, became the choice she made.

Katz called Senator Feinstein's office to notify them that Ford did not want to take her account further. On August 31 Feinstein replied by email:

"I am writing now to confirm that my office will continue to honor the request for confidentiality and will not be taking further action unless we hear from you. Assure that I understand and regret the deep impact this incident had on her life."

Katz forwarded the letter to her client. "It felt like a 'goodbye and good luck,'" Ford said.

That night, at Ford's house in Palo Alto, she sent one of her sons to sleep with her husband and climbed into his Ikea bed for refuge. Her mind turned to surfing. She had paddled out into choppy waters and had been prepared to ride a rough wave. Maybe she would have stayed upright until she reached shore. Maybe she'd have gotten blasted. But she had worked hard to get in position, and she had deserved the chance to try. Why were the advisers so worried about the apparent lack of other victims? Wasn't what happened to her enough?

Curled up all alone in her child's bed, she sobbed.

CHAPTER NINE

"I CAN'T GUARANTEE I'LL GO TO DC"

F ive days later, on Tuesday, September 4, Christine Blasey Ford sat in the Palo Alto office of a PTSD specialist she had seen on and off for a couple years and asked for advice on putting her brush with the Kavanaugh nomination process behind her.

Across the country in Washington, DC, the hearings on his nomination were starting that day, already at top decibel. Democratic senators were trying to halt the proceedings on the grounds that they had been denied access to documents from Kavanaugh's past, and were failing. Protestors lined the Senate halls, some dressed in red robes and white bonnets, a reference to Margaret Atwood's dystopian feminist novel *The Handmaid's Tale*, interrupted the testimony ("More women are going to be subject to back-alley abortions!") and were arrested by the dozens by the Capitol Police. Republicans, unified behind Trump's pick, were lashing back, calling Democrats a disorderly mob.

Ford's failure to further report her allegation nagged at her, but she wanted to mentally store away the whole episode. Repeatedly revisiting the upsetting memory that summer had taken an emotional toll, and now she was trying to get back on track, she said. Her sons had returned to school. She was preparing for the first day of work teaching.

The therapist listened but expressed doubt that he could help just yet. As part of his treatment method, he encouraged patients to stop talking about the underlying cause of their PTSD. What she had described made him cautious. "You're not ready to pack this away," she recalled him telling her. He wasn't sure her involvement in the Kavanaugh story was over yet.

A week later, on Monday, September 10, Ford showed up to teach the opening session of her Introduction to Statistics doctoral course. She began with the same pep talk she used every year, promising her students that they would work through the intimidating material together. Three hours later, someone asking questions stopped her as she departed. Not a graduate student. A reporter, from BuzzFeed. The journalist said she knew about the letter as Ford ordered her to leave.

Outsiders were starting to push and pull more forcefully on Ford's previously private story. Increasing numbers of prominent women and #MeToo activists seemed to know about it, and now journalists were contacting Ford's colleagues and showing up at her home.

Outraged, Debra Katz confronted a leading Palo Alto feminist whom she suspected of trying to out Ford. This is so unprincipled, Katz recalled telling the woman in a heated phone call. My client doesn't want to come forward. In a phone call the previous week, Eshoo's staff had asked whether Ford wanted them to do more, like put her in touch with a second member of the Senate Judiciary Committee. But in the end, Ford reiterated that she had not changed her mind about coming forward. When the journalists came knocking, she refused to talk to them.

On Wednesday, September 12, an article appeared anyway. *The Intercept*, an online publication, revealed that Democrats on the Senate Judiciary Committee were trying to obtain a letter about Kavanaugh that Feinstein had received. According to the story, the letter supposedly described "an incident involving Kavanaugh and a woman while they were in high school" and someone affiliated with Stanford University had authored it. "Kept hidden," the article noted, "the letter is beginning to take on a life of its own."

That made Feinstein look as if she was withholding vital information about a nominee. The following day, the senator announced by press release that she had sent the letter over to law enforcement for review. She was referring the matter to the FBI, which forwarded it to the White House for Kavanaugh's background file, prompting him to issue a denial for an accusation that was still vague. For more than a week, Ford had been reconciling herself with silence. Now it seemed like she was days, maybe hours, from being fully outed.

By then, Ford was determined to regain control over her own account. She had decided that if anyone was going to reveal her identity to the public, it would be her. On Wednesday, she had driven thirty miles outside Palo Alto to one of the Ritz-Carlton restaurants in Half Moon Bay, where Emma Brown, the *Washington Post* reporter who had fielded the anonymous tip that Ford had sent to the paper weeks before, was waiting. In intermittent phone calls and text messages, Ford had stayed in touch with Brown, telling her bits of her story about the high school encounter with Kavanaugh and her initial plan to report it to Congress. Brown had listened attentively, never pushing Ford too hard. The journalist's deference had been a comfort to Ford.

The interview process was more extensive and difficult than Ford had imagined. It began that Wednesday evening, resumed the next morning, and continued by phone in the following days. Ford cringed at the thought of seeing graphic material in the newspaper, especially explicit references to her body. Brown wanted to know whether Kavanaugh had ever penetrated Ford in any way, whether he had raped her. No, Ford explained. She had to provide excerpts of therapy records in which she discussed what had happened. Brown asked to talk to Ford's husband, who confirmed that she had named Kavanaugh as her attacker as early as 2012.

But as she drove back to Palo Alto, Ford felt almost relieved that her hand had been forced. She would finally be out of purgatory. Katz and her other advisers said they thought the article was the right step, to ensure that her allegation was reported correctly. Her husband maintained the same line he had all summer: The sooner she went public, the sooner their lives would go back to normal. She was thinking wishfully as well, telling herself she would be able to cling to some privacy throughout. After she had married, Ford kept her maiden name for professional purposes, in order to maintain a consistent byline on the scientific papers she wrote. Just before the *Post* article was published, she debated using her husband's last name instead, hoping that because Ford was such a common name, it would be more difficult for readers to identify her on the internet. "In my fantasy world, Googling Ford and Blasey are two different things," she said. Instead, she settled on Christine Blasey Ford. Wherever possible, she also removed photos of herself online. But she had not yet succeeded in taking down her LinkedIn profile, which included a photo of her in sunglasses. Ford dropped her sons with friends, booked a hotel for the evening, and hoped for quick, calm passage through the news cycle.

As soon as the *Post* published the story, on Sunday, September 16, Ford's cell phone went into an uninterrupted state of rings and pings. On her LinkedIn page, she had thousands of requests to connect. Her Palo Alto University email account flooded with so many messages, supportive and scathing, that the account crashed.

Around the world, people were absorbing the article paragraph by paragraph:

> Earlier this summer, Christine Blasey Ford wrote a confidential letter to a senior Democratic lawmaker alleging that Supreme Court nominee Brett M. Kavanaugh sexually assaulted her more than three decades ago, when they were high school students in suburban Maryland. Since Wednesday, she has watched as that bare-bones version of her story became public without her name or her consent, drawing a blanket denial from Kavanaugh and roiling a nomination that just days ago seemed all but certain to succeed.
>
> Now, Ford has decided that if her story is going to be told, she wants to be the one to tell it.

Back in Brooklyn, Jodi and Megan read the *Post* article and saw the eruption it was surely going to cause.

Based on the evidence in the story, Ford and Kavanaugh were each going to amass armies of believers. As Katz had indicated earlier, there were blank spaces in Ford's story, extensive ones: holes in the accuser's memory, no corroboration that dated from the time of the alleged event. Kavanaugh's denial, issued the Friday before by the White House, was forceful: "I categorically and unequivocally deny this allegation. I did not do this back in high school or at any time."

But Ford readily admitted the gaps in her memory, which some saw as a mark of a credible victim. She described specific details: the sound of rock music playing at high volume and both boys laughing "maniacally." "Kavanaugh pinned her to a bed on her back and groped her over her clothes, grinding his body against hers and clumsily attempting to pull off her one-piece bathing suit and the clothing she wore over it," Emma Brown had written. "When she tried to scream, she said, he put his hand over her mouth." The reaction to the *Post* story was far more supportive of Ford than her lawyers had anticipated, a testament to the potency of #MeToo. People around the world, already linked and mobilized in support of victims of sexual violence, were rallying to Ford's cause.

She was becoming an instant symbol for women who had been abused, a figure of great hope for justice—but she also seemed likely to become a focal point for the backlash. Megan—who remembered how Trump had yelled at her on the phone almost two years earlier and knew the ferocity with which he fought these kinds of allegations—wondered if Ford was also about to become his target. In Bob Woodward's *Fear*, Trump was described saying to a friend who had admitted problematic behavior toward women: "You've got to deny, deny, deny and push back on these women." Trump said, "If you admit to anything and any culpability, then you're dead."

Trump might do more than attack Ford: He was likely to take aim at the entire #MeToo movement. The reckoning had already posed a danger to Trump, who still faced multiple allegations of sexual misconduct. Now it threatened his Supreme Court nominee. Just two months before, the president had mocked the phrase #MeToo at a political rally and defended a member of Congress accused of ignoring sexual abuse accusers when he worked as an assistant wrestling coach at Ohio State University. "I don't believe *them* at all. I believe *him*," the president had said.

Legal thinkers were split. Old sources, prosecutors and defense attorneys, told Megan that if the details of Ford's allegation were true, if the two boys had blocked her in the room and turned up the music, if Kavanaugh had put his hand over her mouth when she tried to scream, then he had committed a serious crime. In the criminal justice system, a single credible victim's testimony had weight: eyewitnesses, DNA, and other types of corroborating evidence were not necessarily required for a conviction.

However, others were stressing why statutes of limitations existed. "I oppose Kavanaugh's nomination, think senators should vote no based on his judicial record, but am uncomfortable with asserting that his behavior as a teen tells us anything about his 'character' now," Rosa Brooks, a Georgetown law professor who had served in two Democratic administrations, tweeted. She pointed out that "after thirty-five years, it is nearly impossible to conduct a full or fair investigation."

That afternoon, Jodi talked to Katz, who was in a new and more advanced state of anxiety. "I'm scared for my client," the lawyer said. "She is going to be annihilated by the White House." She didn't trust the Democrats either. With the midterm elections two months away, she feared they might try to use Ford as a prop or foil.

Before they hung up, Katz had one more detail to add. This is beyond off the record, she said.

"My client can't testify," she said.

It was out of the question, Katz said. It had taken everything Ford had to go ahead with the *Post* piece, and she had assumed that once it was published, little else would be required of her. She feared cameras and flying and didn't want to come back to Washington. If members of the Senate Judiciary wanted to question her in California, she would oblige. But being grilled by senators, on live television? It just was not going to happen, Katz said.

But the next morning, Monday, September 17, Katz was on morning news shows, assuring the hosts that her client was prepared to testify in front of Congress.

"The answer is yes," Katz told CNN when asked directly.

It was the bluff of Katz's life. Nothing had changed since the day before. Ford was barely aware that her attorney was asserting that on television.

"We had to say she was coming," Katz explained later.

Weeks before, Katz, Banks, and Seidman had urged caution to Ford, mindful of the dangers of exposure. But now they thought that the best course was for her to testify in an open hearing with cameras, convinced that once many Americans saw and heard her for themselves, they would believe her account. Speaking to senators or their staff behind closed doors would only provide them with an opportunity to spin, conceal, or otherwise dismiss Ford's words.

In that moment, they felt their paramount priority was to preserve Ford's options. "If we had been equivocal, we would have looked weak," Katz said. Republicans would have said Ford was not serious enough to show up and articulate her claim. "If you cede that, you're done," Katz said. So they plunged in, deciding to negotiate the form and timing of the testimony, pushing it off as long as possible, buying their client a few more days to warm up to the idea. (And, they thought, possibly for new allegations to surface.) If Ford was unwilling to show up later, fine—better to fold late than to give everything away at the start.

"You need to trust us, to keep your options open," the advisers told Ford. "You will drive this."

Okay, Ford had replied. But I'm never coming, she told her team. The advisers stepped in for Ford, carving a path, hoping she would follow, and becoming yet another escalating force.

By virtue of a Republican Senate, Judiciary Committee chairman Chuck Grassley controlled almost everything about how Kavanaugh's hearings would unfold. Standing just behind him was Senator Mitch McConnell, the Republican majority leader, known for his brass-knuckled tactics, such as blocking former president Barack Obama from filling an empty Supreme Court seat in his final year.

But Grassley and Trump were already promising that they would treat Ford with respect, a sign perhaps of how much had changed over the past year. That summer, the Senate Judiciary Committee had held a hearing in which Grassley and other committee members had come down hard on allegations of sexual harassment within the federal judiciary. The Republicans in power appeared eager to respect Ford. They also seemed mindful of the potentially damaging optics of a showdown, the all-male members of their side of the Judiciary Committee against a vulnerable woman, just like in the Clarence Thomas hearings. Trump's aides were reportedly stressing to him that it would be a political mistake for him to go into attack mode. "She should not be insulted," presidential counselor Kellyanne Conway told reporters in the White House driveway that Monday morning. "She should not be ignored." With the midterm elections approaching, and Republicans already bleeding female voters, they seemed almost deferential to Ford. In that stance, Ford's team saw a toehold.

Their plan was for Seidman to craft the team's terms behind the scenes, while Katz and Banks negotiated directly with Grassley's staff.

But unbeknownst to television viewers, Katz had a second secret, in addition to a reluctant client, that morning. After the television appearances, she took a car to the hospital, donned a patient's gown, handed her phone over to her wife, and was put under anesthesia. On that day of all days, she was having long-anticipated breast surgery.

Years before, Katz had lived through breast cancer and recovered fully. But like many women, she had an implant that needed to be replaced. She had scheduled the surgery weeks before and her insurance provider would not let her change the date.

She had already sworn to Ford that it wouldn't be a problem. Jodi and Megan were reminded of Laura Madden's surgery just after the Weinstein story. But this was an even more precarious situation, though, because Katz would be going unconscious when she had so much work to do. Was the lawyer so dead set on this testimony that she was going to negotiate with Grassley while still groggy from anesthesia?

Seidman, meanwhile, was out of town. Her mother had died the week before, and she was in Atlanta, sorting out her family's affairs.

At the law office on Connecticut Avenue, Lisa Banks monitored the situation with rising panic. Grassley's office was already sending messages asking to schedule a call with Katz and her client, and his aides weren't sure why Katz wasn't replying.

"I'm honestly wondering how I ever let her out of my sight," Banks half joked in a text message to Katz's wife. "This is a total shit show. And I'm trying to navigate the country's future by myself here. This would drive a lesser person to drink, or worse. Please tell her everything is fine and delete." She closed with a martini emoji.

As the day went on, #MeToo activists continued to mobilize, with no idea that Ford was unwilling to testify and that her chief public representative was lying on a hospital table.

The following morning, Tuesday, Katz woke up at her family farm in a far corner of Maryland. Katz had stitches, swelling, and doctor's orders to stay out of the office for at least a few days. But she swore off any medication that might fog her thinking, propped herself up in bed, and flipped open her laptop to review the emails from Senator Grassley's staff and begin negotiating.

As a first step, Ford's team had already requested an FBI investigation of Ford's allegation, in an attempt to have impartial law enforcement officials try to shed light on what had happened that day three decades ago. But the FBI was refusing to get involved, saying it considered Kavanaugh's background check closed. Republicans on the Senate Judiciary Committee were insisting that it had the authority and skill to investigate.

Ford's team was rejecting offers by Grassley's committee to interview Ford in private. So it was now a matter of negotiating the terms of a hearing, in effect making up the rules as they went along. That morning, in an opinion article in the *Times*, Anita Hill worried aloud about that very prospect. Twenty-seven years before, during her own testimony, the committee's members "performed in ways that gave employers permission to mishandle workplace harassment complaints throughout the following decades," she wrote. That the committee, made up of some of the exact same senators, still lacked a specific protocol for evaluating claims of sexual harassment or assault against a nominee suggested that it "has learned little from the Thomas hearing, much less the more recent #MeToo movement," she wrote. Everything about how Ford might deal with the committee was up for grabs: the timing, the format, the question of who else might participate.

Over the following days, the two sides traded carefully worded emails and terse phone calls. Katz and Banks pushed the committee to subpoena Mark Judge, Kavanaugh's old friend, and according to Ford, the other person in the room during the attack. As Ford had described in her letter to Feinstein, she remembered seeing him looking visibly uncomfortable at a neighborhood grocery store afterward, as if he felt bad about what had happened. A recovering alcoholic, Judge had written two memoirs about life at Georgetown Prep that described an extreme party culture of regular blackout drinking. One book, *Wasted: Tales of a GenX Drunk*, mentioned a Bart O'Kavanaugh, presumably a veiled reference to the judge, and a night when he "puked in someone's car" and "passed out on his way back from a party." At the very least, Ford's team thought Judge could substantiate excess drinking by his old friend.

How could the committee ascertain the truth without requiring Judge to testify in person? Katz and Banks asked. Grassley's staff refused, saying they did not take subpoena requests from witnesses as a condition of their testifying. Instead, his staff accepted a written statement from Judge in which he acknowledged being friends with Kavanaugh in high school but said he did not recall any such party and had never seen Kavanaugh act as Ford had described. The staff also accepted a similar written statement from P. J. Smyth, another friend of Kavanaugh's whom Ford recalled being at the party, saying that he had no memory of the gathering, knew Kavanaugh to be a person of "great integrity," and had never seen him engage in any improper conduct toward women.

Republicans had eliminated potential witnesses, reducing the situation to: Do you believe her, or do you believe him?

When it came to their official correspondence, Ford's team tried to curb its outrage. In dealing with an institution like the Senate, the whole world was watching. Ford had requested that her attorneys speak as collegially as possible to the committee. She insisted that coming forward was not a partisan move, and that she would still have spoken up if Kavanaugh had been from her own party. It was not clear if she understood that many others saw her differently: She was working with Democratic lawyers, whom she had learned of from the top Democrat on the Senate Judiciary Committee, and with Seidman, a Democratic operative, making an accusation that might topple a Republican Supreme Court pick. To Mike Davis, who was the Republican staff member leading the committee's negotiations, it appeared as if Ford's team had exploited her allegation for political purposes, and that dragging out the negotiation was part of a coordinated strategy to derail Kavanaugh's nomination, Davis said later.

Back in Palo Alto, stuck in a hotel, Ford was receiving reports from the negotiations but not quite keeping track of all the elements, she later explained. She had been heartened by much of the response to the *Post* article, including from colleagues who were quick to defend her character and former high school classmates who released a letter saying her alleged assault was "all too consistent with stories we heard and lived" at the time. "I can't believe the media—and friends from all times in life—Stanford facility and PAU faculty ready to help," Ford had texted Katz the day the article was published.

But by that Thursday, she still wouldn't even commit to traveling to Washington. When Katz gently pushed her, Ford resisted:

> Ford: I'm feeling way too much pressure at moment

Katz was trying to be patient, but she couldn't keep the Judiciary Committee waiting forever.

> Katz: Believe me—i don't want to be another pressure. I'm just cognizant of the time constraints. We need to get an email out to grassley and Feinstein soon

> Ford: I can't go there 😕 To DC

> Katz: That's okay. We can always pull out on the basis that they wouldn't come up with fair rules. This is the right next step

Still, the lawyer needed her client's green light to move forward with the negotiations.

> Katz: To clarify—you are okay with us sending the email which we need to do soon. But you want us to be clear that if they don't agree to fair terms that are fair and provide for your security you won't go forward

> Ford: I want you to know as you are writing that I can't guarantee I'll go to DC 🙁 Can I see final version?

> Ford: I'm so scared I can't breathe

Ford was still not acknowledging what was really happening. (This was a pattern: She had written the letter to Feinstein without fully absorbing its potential to leak; she had gone forward with the *Post* story, convincing herself it would cycle out of the news within a week.) She had started, weeks before, by trying to make a small, discreet intervention, and at every stage, things had gotten harder and larger. Now she had a life-altering choice for herself and potentially for the country, and she was trying to avoid it. Katz, Banks, and Seidman were nudging Ford through the process by saying, Leave it to us. They didn't want to operate against their client's wishes, but they were taking the reins, determined to lead Ford forward.

That Thursday night, Ford arrived in a dark French restaurant tucked along a quiet street in San Francisco. Coburn, another one of the Washington attorneys advising her, was in town and was eager to finally meet in person. As she took a seat across from him, Ford pointed to her baseball hat. "This is my disguise," she said trying to force a smile.

Over a long dinner, she made clear why she was so scared to travel to Washington. Her family had been forced to hire twenty-four-hour private security. It was uncertain when it would be safe for them to return home. Ford had already experienced enough disruption and danger.

She pressed Play on her phone at the dinner table. "You lying fucking cunt!" came a voice from her phone. The lawyer told Ford she was right to be frightened by the messages and encouraged her to share them with the FBI. "You've got three months," another voice said. Others repeated similar phrases and sounded like they might have come from the same voice-altering machine, making her think they were somehow coordinated. "Don't be messing with my boy, Brett." "Don't be messing with my boy, Trump."

The next day, Friday, September 21, Katz stopped by her doctor's office to get her stitches removed. In the waiting room, she glanced at the television. The Republicans were losing patience.

CNN was flashing a confidential list of demands that Katz had sent to Grassley's team, apparently leaked by one of the Republican staff members. Trump was now directly casting doubt on Ford's allegation, tweeting: "I have no doubt that, if the attack on Dr. Ford was as bad as she says, charges would have been immediately filed with local Law Enforcement Authorities by either her or her loving parents." At a gathering of Evangelical activists, McConnell was promising that the Senate would "plow right through" and move to confirm Kavanaugh.

That evening, the Republican Judiciary staff announced that the entire committee would vote on Kavanaugh's confirmation the following Monday, September 24. Period. If Ford wanted to appear, she needed to confirm immediately, that Friday night, by 10:00 p.m. The evening news anchors were talking as if the whole thing was already over. "We were about to get steamrolled," Katz said.

Working from their office, Katz and Banks, with cups of coffee in hand, penned a barn-burning public letter to Grassley's staff, accusing them of browbeating a vulnerable woman who was dealing with death threats.

"The imposition of aggressive and artificial deadlines regarding the date and conditions of any hearing has created tremendous and unwarranted anxiety and stress on Dr. Ford," they wrote. "Your cavalier treatment of a sexual assault survivor who has been doing her best to cooperate with the Committee is completely inappropriate."

"The 10 p.m. deadline is arbitrary. Its sole purpose is to bully Dr. Ford and deprive her of the ability to make a considered decision that has life-altering implications for her and her family," they continued. "Our modest request is that she be given an additional day to make her decision." They released the response directly to members of the media, and it was immediately broadcast on TV.

Two hours later, Grassley tweeted out word of his concession, in an odd format that made it look like he was posting a text to the judge:

> Judge Kavanaugh I just granted another extension to Dr Ford to decide if she wants to proceed w the statement she made last week to testify to the senate She shld decide so we can move on I want to hear her. I hope u understand. It's not my normal approach to b indecisive

With no road map and no Democratic control of any of the branches of government, Katz, Banks, and Seidman had positioned Ford to testify on their time frame, even though their client had not even signed on to do so. Later, the world would talk about the power of Ford's testimony without understanding the less visible role that the other women had played.

But now they needed to get their client to Washington.

By Saturday, it was clear Ford was never going to give one firm and final yes to testifying in an open hearing. Her ambivalence was paralyzing. So her advisers worked in tandem, coaxing her from one baby step to another.

A sympathetic tech executive had offered his private jet for Ford to travel to Washington. Ford warned her team that any mention of the aircraft would make her more nervous, not less. Katz texted her photos of it anyway, to convey the reality of the situation.

Next, the advisers asked Ford to consider who she would invite to Washington if she decided to move forward. The plane could accommodate some of her friends. Her husband would stay in Palo Alto to care for their sons; both parents were determined not to disrupt the boys' lives any more than necessary. Ford considered who of her friends would be steadiest. One was a mother of triplets and a fourth daughter less than two years apart, who had served as a confidante that summer, starting with the beachside talks in Santa Cruz. She would know how to help Ford keep her cool. So would Keith Koegler, her friend and confidante, who would submit a sworn affidavit to the Senate Judiciary Committee about the time years earlier when Ford had told him about being assaulted by a prominent judge. Two friends, faculty members from the Stanford School of Medicine, would also be useful to have by her side.

By talking through these hypothetical scenarios, Katz, Banks, and the other advisers convinced Ford to go to Washington to talk to the senators. By Sunday, their team and Grassley's staff finally reached consensus: The hearing would take place the following Thursday, September 27.

But that Sunday, September 23, the entire dynamic of the Kavanaugh fight shifted. The material that Ford's team had spent weeks wondering about finally arrived: two additional allegations against the judge, which surfaced almost simultaneously. Suddenly, he was being portrayed in a far darker light, as a repeat offender.

The *New Yorker* published the account of Deborah Ramirez, who alleged that Kavanaugh had exposed himself to her during a drunken party when they were classmates at Yale. She said she had been intoxicated "on the floor, foggy and slurring her words" when Kavanaugh thrust his penis in her face, and she touched it as she was pushing him away. "Brett was laughing," Ramirez was quoted saying. "I can still see his face, and his hips coming forward, like when you pull up your pants."

At practically the same moment, Michael Avenatti, a California plaintiff lawyer who represented Stormy Daniels, the porn star who had accepted a settlement from Trump, tweeted out more ominous-sounding accusations about Kavanaugh from a new client:

We are aware of significant evidence of multiple house parties in
the Washington, D.C. area during the early 1980s, during which

> Brett Kavanaugh, Mark Judge and others would participate in
> the targeting of women with alcohol/drugs to allow a "train" of
> men to subsequently gang rape them.

Avenatti didn't name his client, but published leading questions directed to the judge on Twitter, such as "Did you ever target one or more women for sex or rape at a house party?" He claimed to have multiple witnesses who were prepared to testify.

As Katz, Banks, and Seidman followed the developments, they believed that Ramirez was telling the truth about Kavanaugh exposing himself and that the allegation would help boost Ford's credibility. But they thought what Avenatti was doing felt like a sideshow, one that could potentially cause harm.

That same Sunday morning, Rebecca Corbett, working at home from Baltimore, had known the *New Yorker* story was coming, the way journalists at competing publications often know these things: through overlapping reporting and common sources. When she learned the *New Yorker* was about to publish, she assumed the magazine had nailed the story, and she had asked her reporters to begin to draft a story that would summarize the magazine's findings. That kind of article, humbling to write, had a name in journalism: a "follow."

But as soon as Corbett, Baquet, and Purdy read the *New Yorker* article that evening, Corbett told her reporters to pause. The magazine had obtained something crucial that the *Times* had not: an interview with Ramirez. Some aspects of the story were similar to Ford's: The *New Yorker* article included no eyewitnesses. (An unnamed classmate said he had heard about the incident, but not seen it.) People Ramirez recalled being at the party denied the incident ever happened or said they didn't remember the party at all.

But Ramirez's account came with other asterisks. The article acknowledged that Ramirez had been reluctant to speak, partly because she had memory gaps from the drinking, and that it had taken her six days of assessing her recollections to describe Kavanaugh's role in the alleged incident with certainty. (Ronan Farrow, a coauthor of the story, later said that many victims struggle with memory gaps and that the six days were a sign of her carefulness.) If Ramirez had named Kavanaugh as the perpetrator to others, before he was nominated, the *New Yorker* did not have any examples. Perhaps they had further, off-the-record support for Ramirez's account, but it was not in the article.

The standard practice in journalism was for competitors to try to match one another's reporting on a significant story. If the *Post* had a scoop on Trump's dealings with Russia, the *Times* would attempt to report on the same material, and vice versa, to inform their own readers but also for additional confirmation. It was like scientists performing peer reviews: If separate, even rival, teams were able to execute the same experiments with the same results, the findings were more trustworthy. In the Weinstein reporting, the *Times* and the *New Yorker* articles had mostly—if not entirely—matched up, an indication of the strength of the material.

This was a different scenario. *Times* reporters had also interviewed dozens of former classmates and hallmates in recent days and found no one with firsthand knowledge of the incident. What's more, the *Times* had learned that Ramirez had told some of her former Yale classmates that she could not be certain Kavanaugh was the one who exposed himself. The *Times* editors were not drawing conclusions about what had happened that night at the party—only that based on the *Times*'s own reporting, the allegation was not well-supported enough to publish as a stand-alone follow story.

Avenatti's tweets presented a separate and much graver set of concerns. He had made veiled allegations of gang rape against the judge without even saying who the accuser was. The lawyer seemed to have his own agenda. In representing Stormy Daniels, Avenatti had dispensed information to the media while cultivating his own presidential ambitions. As that story had played out months before, the brash lawyer had explained to Corbett that he would offer some tips to the *Times* and other news organizations, but his primary strategy was to get on television. "I'll sleep with you, but I'm not going to marry you," he said.

That Sunday, Corbett instructed the *Times* journalists to continue finding out more about the new allegations. But that evening's article about the politics of Ford's upcoming testimony only mentioned the Ramirez allegation in the fourteenth paragraph, and also pointed out the *Times*'s different findings. There was no mention of Avenatti and his unnamed client.

By Monday morning, Republicans were using the weak points in the new allegations to more fiercely defend Kavanaugh. The assumption by Ford's team that additional allegations would bolster their client's story looked like it might be mistaken. Instead, they could detract from Ford's story. A week before, Kellyanne Conway had been arguing that Ford deserved to be heard. Now, in an appearance on *CBS This Morning*, Conway said the allegations against Kavanaugh were "starting to feel like a vast left-wing conspiracy" and implied that the judge was a victim of "pent-up demand" of victims of sexual harassment and assault.

Standing on the Senate floor, McConnell accused Democrats of engaging in a "shameful smear campaign" against the judge. Emboldened, Kavanaugh released a letter saying he wasn't going anywhere.

Mike Davis, the Republican staffer on the Senate Judiciary Committee, said later that the emergence of Avenatti had been especially significant. "He jumped into this thing and turned it into a circus, undermining the credibility of the other accusers," Davis said.

By the morning of Wednesday, September 26, the day before the testimony, Ford was secretly ensconced at the Watergate Hotel, chosen less for its legacy than its location off the grid of downtown Washington.

Ford had flown in the day before, on the borrowed private jet, with prescription Ativan to help her relax, she explained later. As soon as she had disembarked, Conway, of all people, had materialized, apparently waiting to board another plane. Ford had pulled down her baseball cap while friends who had accompanied her from California flanked her protectively, but Conway had given no sign of recognition. That wasn't surprising: Though Ford was at the dead center of the news, the public did not know the sound of her voice or what she looked like. All that had been published was a photo that had been taken decades ago and the shot in sunglasses. At the Watergate, she was protected so tightly that every time she opened her hotel room door, her security guard, positioned in the room next door, opened his in unison. Until the next morning, she would still be mostly a mystery to the country.

As her friends headed out to visit Washington monuments, Ford went to a conference room on a lower floor of the hotel. Katz and Banks were there, dashing back and forth from their law office to the secret prep room. So was Larry Robbins, who had continued to counsel Ford behind the scenes, and Michael Bromwich, a former colleague of Robbins's, who had joined the team the previous Friday and helped with the final round of negotiations with the Judiciary Committee. Seidman was at work across the hall.

The narrow, unassuming room had spotty wi-fi, but someone had stocked each seat at the conference table with Watergate-logo pads, pens, and water bottles. Katz, a junior attorney in her office, and Bromwich had drafted an opening statement, drawing on the details that Ford had provided to them and the *Post*, steering clear of sexually explicit language that she knew made Ford uncomfortable. Ford read the draft and rewrote it almost entirely. "I crossed almost everything out," she said. Not because of factual errors but because it just didn't sound like her. "It wasn't my language. It wasn't in the right order. I had to make it my own." Ford wrote and rewrote, as she did when working on scientific papers, tuning out the lawyers in the room.

Bromwich and Robbins spent an hour walking Ford through some questions they thought she might face during the hearing and offered her general advice on how to handle the testimony chair: You're there to tell the truth; don't worry about the outcome, they explained. If the senators use ambiguous words, don't speculate about their meaning. If they ask a question in three parts, ask them to break down each part one at a time. Bromwich explained that he would sit next to Ford during the hearing.

When senators paused, she should look at them, breathe deeply, and not concern herself with what they were saying.

Robbins and Bromwich, both specialists in congressional testimony, knew that the key to performing well in that format was practicing ahead of time, anticipating questions, polishing replies. Everyone practiced for congressional testimony, even for cut-and-dried regulatory matters. Not practicing answers was considered incautious, even a little reckless. The lawyers would need to run Ford through those drills very quickly: Some corporate executives spent weeks, even months, preparing for their own turns in front of Congress, and they only had one day.

Ford took some notes but found it hard to concentrate because the lawyers were talking over each other. When they asked her to practice her responses, she refused. "She was very insistent," Robbins said.

In less than twenty-four hours, Ford would be giving the most sensitive testimony anyone in Washington had heard in a long time. To avoid the impression of an all-male bank of Republican interlocutors, those senators were ceding their question time to an experienced prosecutor named Rachel Mitchell. Everyone, not just the senators, would be listening for any weaknesses, inconsistencies, or awkward moments on Ford's part.

Ford wasn't fazed. To her it would have been like practicing for a test to which she already knew the answers. She was confident of which data she did and did not know. No practice would change that.

She was only worried about one aspect: "I'm not sure I can do this in front of cameras," she told the team. She reiterated a question she had been asking for days: Why couldn't she just field questions from the Senate Judiciary Committee in a closed hearing?

Now Seidman stepped in. In a one-on-one conversation with Ford, she reiterated what Katz and Banks had been saying to her for days: The only way she could ensure that her account was communicated with accuracy and integrity was in a televised hearing. That's what Kavanaugh would be doing. "Okay," Ford replied.

Seidman was finally convinced that Ford would follow through. But Katz and Banks weren't so sure.

That afternoon, Jodi took a train to Washington, looked up the address of Katz and Banks's law firm, found a coffee bar a few steps from their office, and prepared to wait there for many hours. Katz had not invited her. She had never met Banks and still had never exchanged a word with Ford. At this point, she and Megan knew only bits and pieces about what going on behind the scenes. When Jodi had told Katz she was buying a train ticket, the attorney had said she couldn't make any promises in terms of what Jodi would be able to see. But she and Megan had agreed that one of them had to be in Washington for what was about to happen, to witness it from the closest possible vantage point, as they sought to figure out what these events would mean.

Later that evening, Jodi was sitting in the same coffee bar when Katz and Banks showed up to retrieve her and take her upstairs to witness the tail end of their preparations. Upstairs the lawyers were in great spirits. Their office had been transformed into a command center, filled with reminders of the disparate reactions to the client's story. Because of the threats the lawyers had received, security guards stood at the door. But the space was also cluttered with tokens of encouragement, like flower arrangements for Ford, sent by strangers, grouped haphazardly on Katz's desk. So many cookies had arrived that they stood in stacks atop the file cabinets.

Only a small team of mostly female lawyers and strategists who were volunteering to help Ford was left in the office. Their mood was energized, optimistic, and defiant.

On her way to the elevator, Katz grabbed a print copy of the *Times* off a desk and gestured triumphantly at the headline: "Bill Cosby, Once a Model of Fatherhood, Is an Inmate." The day before, Bill Cosby had been sentenced to three to ten years in prison, a moment of accountability that many had thought would never arrive. Commentators were saying it was the first major verdict of the #MeToo era. Katz felt like history was on her side.

But at the same moment, Trump was on television, blasting the accusations against Kavanaugh as part of one big Democratic "con job," among the developments that Megan was tracking back in New York. The president was using the Kavanaugh case to reassert his own innocence and position himself as a victim. "I've been a famous person for a long time, but I've had a lot of false charges made against me, really false charges," Trump said. "So when I see it, I view it differently than somebody sitting home watching television where they say, 'Oh, Judge Kavanaugh this or that.' It's happened to me many times."

Trump once again took direct aim at Megan and Barbaro's coverage of his treatment of women, calling it "false reporting" and "fake news." Trump also described "four or five women who got paid a lot of money to make up stories about me." There was no evidence to support Trump's claim. But Lisa Bloom's efforts to line up donations to potential Trump accusers from prominent Democrats had been documented by journalists, arming him with a talking point that, once altered and exaggerated, helped him make his case.

Ford went to bed at 10:00 p.m., hoping to get a solid night's sleep. Two hours later, she was up. She took a shower and watched television until dawn. "I was waiting and ready to go do it and be done," she said later.

The morning was a haze of preparation. A stylist showed up to do her hair, and when she glanced in the mirror, she didn't really look like herself, because the ends were curled. Some of her advisers had suspected, correctly, that the California academic didn't have the type of clothes normally worn to Congressional hearings, so they had ordered eleven different suits that were delivered to her hotel the day before. To Ford, the suits had looked so dark and expensive—so East Coast. She chose the one non-black option, in midnight blue, one that she would be able to wear teaching, and a tailor had materialized to adjust it.

Two colleagues from Stanford, one who had flown on the private jet, another who happened to be in town, joined her for breakfast in her hotel room. As they discussed the scientific papers each of them had been working on, Ford felt herself transitioning into the professional mode she intended to adopt in the hearing.

A Chevy Suburban SUV was waiting. She rode in the SUV to Capitol Hill with Katz, Banks, Bromwich, Robbins, and two of her security guards. The car pulled into an underground carpark, and then she was escorted through the bowels of Congress, down a hallway and up a stairwell into a wide corridor lined with office doors. People were peeking out, trying to catch a glimpse of her. Soon she and her team were in their own space, a room that looked like an office several doors down from the hearing chamber, where they would be able to rest and regroup during breaks. Ford was still editing the opening statement she carried in a binder, obsessing over each word choice. Ford said she crossed out a "screamed" and changed it to "yelled."

When Grassley stopped by her room, Ford smiled and exchanged pleasantries with him. She was still determined to be as congenial as possible every step of the way.

Ford's advisers had pushed the Judiciary Committee to hold the hearing in one of its smaller rooms, which they thought would help minimize Ford's jitters. None of them had explicitly told Ford the extent to which the testimony would be broadcast: another move that glossed over how massive, how consequential, this dispute over one encounter in high school had grown. Katz and Banks were worried that if she knew she would freeze with fear.

As the proceedings came to order, Ford began to read her statement without much sense of the impression she was making. She had been telling this same story all summer. She had been up all night. At her first moment at the microphone, she had asked for caffeine. The room felt strange, with senators elevated above her. The lights were overwhelmingly bright, as if they were all in an operating theater.

Her voice was scratchy with emotion, but she did not break down. The words and images she had chosen so carefully were especially evocative. She spoke of Kavanaugh fumbling to get past the one-piece bathing suit she had worn under her clothes, and the sound of the boys "pinballing off the walls" on the way downstairs as she hid in a bathroom.

"I have had to relive this trauma in front of the world, and have seen my life picked apart by people on television, on Twitter, other social media, other media, and in this body, who have never met me or spoken with me," she said. "I am an independent person and I am no one's pawn. My motivation in coming forward was to be helpful and to provide facts about how Mr. Kavanaugh's actions have damaged my life, so that you could take into serious consideration as you make your decision about how to proceed."

Ford was used to question-and-answer exchanges from the many hours she had spent in scientific conferences, and now she drew on that experience, trying to speak clearly and precisely. She didn't mind her back-and-forths with Rachel Mitchell, the prosecutor to whom the Republicans had ceded their questioning. Unlike the senators, the prosecutor was seated at floor level, which helped make it feel like they were having a human-to-human interaction, she said. And her first rounds of questions felt respectful.

But as the session went on, Ford grew alarmed. The focus of Mitchell's inquiries was changing. How had Ford traveled to Washington? What were the circumstances of her polygraph test? This all seemed tangential and confusing to her, she said. By the final break, Ford was worn down. She did not want to go back in.

When her turn at the microphone was finally finished, Mitchell approached her.

"I'll be praying for your safety," the prosecutor said. That terrified Ford. Did she know about something specific that Ford should fear?

Back in their private room, Ford's advisers were smiling and commending her. She appreciated the feedback but still saw it in academic terms. "When you give a science talk, you just say what you know," she explained. "It's not 'great job!'" But in terms of transmitting her account, she felt like she had done well—left it all on the field, she said later, using one of her beloved sports analogies. When Republican senator Jeff Flake of Arizona, seen as a potential toss-up vote, stopped by to say hello, she greeted him warmly. She still had little sense of the power or resonance her voice had carried out across the land.

Jodi, who had borrowed a pass for the packed hearing room and slipped in near the end of Ford's turn, was absorbing her first impressions of Ford in person. She faced the senators, seated at a huge wooden table, flanked by Katz and Bromwich. With only the back of her head visible to Jodi, what had come through most strongly was her voice. It was unexpectedly girlish, but she had authority, in part because she was so precise. In her testimony, she seemed devoted to getting every answer right. Unlike in the Weinstein case, when the voices of victims had been mediated by journalists, the world had watched and heard unfiltered narration from the woman herself.

Many viewers thought she was such a compelling witness that the nomination was virtually dead. On C-SPAN, sexual assault survivors were calling in to share their stories. "I have not brought this up for years until I heard this testimony and it is just breaking my heart," said a seventy-six-year-old woman. Trump said he found Ford "very compelling" and "a very credible witness." At the *Times*, editors and reporters were poised to cover a Kavanaugh withdrawal if necessary.

Like many other viewers, Jodi and Megan weren't sure what to expect when it came time for Kavanaugh to speak at the hearing. Would the distinguished federal judge present himself as above it all, to remind the world how much respect he had accumulated over his career? Perhaps he would say that he sincerely could not remember any such incident but that he should be judged by his adult conduct. That tactic had helped other figures dismiss damaging reports from their youth. During the 2000 presidential race, George W. Bush had brushed away stories of excess drinking, by saying, "When I was young and irresponsible, I was young and irresponsible." It was one of the most effective lines of autobiographical spin ever, making the former party boy sound self-deprecating and sympathetic—no one wanted to be judged by their younger self's worst moments.

But it quickly became clear that that was not Kavanaugh's intention. As he took his turn at the polished wood table, he regained ground, giving a sweeping, forceful denial of Ford's accusation under oath. "I categorically and unequivocally deny the allegation against me by Dr. Ford. I never had any sexual or physical encounter of any kind with Dr. Ford. I never attended a gathering like the one Dr. Ford describes in her allegation. I've never sexually assaulted Dr. Ford or anyone," he said.

Jodi couldn't see his face either, just a brush of brown-gray hair atop square shoulders. But she could hear him, and his rush of anger, almost as if he was spitting his opening statement into the air. His demeanor was the opposite of Ford's. She had sounded measured, calm, polite, not particularly political, and eager to please, sprinkling her testimony with scientific terminology, as if to help validate what she was saying. He sounded loud, biting, and openly partisan. "This whole two-week effort has been a calculated and orchestrated political hit, fueled with apparent pent-up anger about President Trump and the 2016 election," he said.

Over the course of several minutes, he put the listener in his shoes, describing a life of hard work upended by an escalating and out-of-control series of complaints. Over the previous week, Avenatti's client, Julie Swetnick, had finally come forward; in a sworn statement to the committee and then in a TV interview, she contradicted herself and was widely seen as not credible.

"The Swetnick thing is a joke," he said. "That is a farce."

"I wanted a hearing the day after the allegation came up," he said, referring to Ford's account. "Instead, ten days passed where all this nonsense is coming out," he said, mentioning some of the vaguer rumors that had circulated: "I'm on boats in Rhode Island, I'm in Colorado, you know, I'm sighted all over the place. And these things are printed and run, breathlessly, by cable news," he said.

"My family and my name have been totally and permanently destroyed by vicious and false additional accusations," he said. That word—*additional*—was telling.

He was driving a larger argument, making himself a focal point for male grievance, saying that he was the victim, that his entire lifetime of dedication and care, down to the hours he spent coaching his daughters in basketball, was being destroyed by women making irresponsible claims.

"If every American who drinks beer or every American who drank beer in high school is suddenly presumed guilty of sexual assault, we'll be in an ugly new place in this country," he said.

The Republican senators used their own question time to amplify his message. They sidelined Rachel Mitchell, who had been pressing Kavanaugh on the particulars of the alleged incidents, abandoning their plan to let a woman serve as their public voice. Instead, the all-male group of Republicans took turns expressing outrage at what they called the victimization of an upstanding man.

"It just keeps getting worse," said Senator John Cornyn of Texas. "It's this story that not even the *New York Times* would report, the allegation of Ms. Ramirez. And then Stormy Daniels's lawyer comes up with this incredible story, accusing you of the most sordid and salacious conduct. It's outrageous, and you're right to be angry."

"A disgrace," said Senator Orrin Hatch of Utah. "This has been sadly one of the most shameful chapters in the history of the United States Senate," echoed Senator Ted Cruz of Texas.

During the testimony, the judge made some improbable statements. He called "Devil's Triangle," a term in his yearbook that had received media attention, a drinking game, when most people knew it as high school slang for a three-way liaison between two men and a woman. He claimed that Ford's story had been "refuted by the very people she says were there, including by a longtime friend of hers." That was not true: the friend, Leland Keyser, whom Ford recalled being at the party, had told the Judiciary Committee in a letter written by her attorney that she didn't remember the gathering and didn't know Kavanaugh, but she also had told the *Washington Post* she believed Ford was telling the truth. When Senator Amy Klobuchar, a Democrat from Minnesota, asked Kavanaugh if he had ever partially or fully blacked out from drinking, he countered by asking if *she* ever had, sounding defensive.

In the hearing room, Jodi was struck by something that wasn't as palpable on television: the small size of the room, packed not just with Ford and Kavanaugh supporters, but leaders and critics of #MeToo. When Ford had finished her testimony, cries of "Thank you, Doctor Ford" had mingled with a shout of "Confirm Brett!" The seats for visitors ran only eight abreast, not that much bigger than airplane rows. Women in Kavanaugh T-shirts were right up against those who had come for Ford. Tarana Burke, the founder of the #MeToo movement, had come in sneakers, so she could walk to the protest events happening all over Capitol Hill. She was sitting not far from Ashley Kavanaugh, the judge's wife, who wore an expression of horror. All of them were crammed into an official-looking box, with wood paneling and brass seals, for a fight with improvised rules and no impartial referee.

The next morning, Jodi met Katz in the lobby of the Watergate Hotel. In the narrow conference room where Ford had huddled with her team, the preparation gear was still lying around, neat arrangements of highlighters and peanut M&M's. A second later, Ford walked in.

She seemed completely similar, and utterly different, from the day before. The first words out of her mouth were the exact same thing she had said at the start of the hearings: She requested caffeine. She was as eager to please as she had been in the hearing, asking Katz if she had been gracious enough when Senator Flake had said hello. ("You were lovely," Katz reassured her.) But the formal suit was gone, replaced with a turquoise hoodie and blue rubber Birkenstock sandals, reminders that this person came with an identity and life that was only partially represented in her few hours on the public stage. She looked like a Californian again, her hair still mussed from sleep. Around her wrist, she wore a thin silver bracelet that said "Courageous."

Since she had left Capitol Hill the day before, she finally allowed herself to collapse somewhat. She had not watched Kavanaugh's testimony. The previous night, her friends and family had congregated in a room at the Watergate for a little thank-goodness-it's-over gathering, her Palo Alto guests meeting her high school friends. One was going on television to be interviewed about Ford, and she thanked her for doing that. Her parents were there too. As everyone else was chatting and drinking, Ford had laid down on the little upholstered bench, right there in the party room, and closed her eyes.

Ford's airplane was leaving soon, and she was eager to return West, to fly away from the Washington ordeal. As she talked about when she could move back into her house, she focused on slipping back into her old life and routine. That hardly seemed possible: Her story was now having a seismic national, cultural, and political effect.

A few hours later, as the Judiciary Committee geared up to vote on whether to send the nomination to the full Senate, Katz and Banks watched the minute-by-minute television coverage from the conference room of their office. Jodi sat with them, observing the attorneys as they waited to find out if their client's testimony would truly influence the outcome of the nomination.

Katz paced the length of the conference table, texting with Ford, who was airborne. The wait was agonizing, and the outcome the lawyers wanted—for Senator Jeff Flake or another Republican to vote no—was unlikely. So as the headlines and images flicked by, without any real news yet, Jodi asked the lawyers a broader question: How much had really changed in the past year, and what would the legacy of Ford's testimony be?

"If he's confirmed, I question whether we're any better off," said Banks, the pessimist of the pair.

Katz, still the believer in the possible, could not let that answer stand. She felt Ford had challenged outdated social norms and had only been able to do so because the #MeToo movement had given her a window, because standards had already shifted. "A year ago she would never have been given an opportunity to testify," she argued.

"Things *have* qualitatively changed," she continued. "The institutions have *not* changed. The Senate has *not* changed. The power of this country is aggregated in the White House and in the Senate. But that doesn't say that this movement is a failure." Katz added that many of Ford's adversaries had not directly called her a liar, but, instead, floated an eccentric theory that she had been mistaken about the identity of the perpetrator. That was an odd form of progress, she said, but it was progress nonetheless.

"I'm not saying the movement's a failure," Banks retorted. "I'm saying despite the power of the movement, the results seem to be the same."

In the end, the television didn't offer clear answers. After being dramatically confronted by two sexual assault survivors in a Capitol Hill elevator, Flake negotiated a pause in the process, asking for an FBI investigation of Ford's allegation, as well as Ramirez's, before the full Senate voted on Kavanaugh's nomination. This was exactly what Katz and Banks had tried and failed to obtain weeks before. Now the Republicans on the committee and the White House signed off, eager to do whatever necessary to solidify Flake's support for the judge.

Jodi returned to New York and Megan arrived to continue shadowing the lawyers. On television and online, some observers were heralding the postponement of the vote and the launch of the FBI investigation as a victory for Ford, but Katz and Banks were skeptical. "We still don't know how all this will play out," Katz told Megan.

A few hours later, back in California that Friday, September 28, Ford had an emotional reunion with her husband and her two sons. The boys jumped up and down, smothering her with hugs, she said.

For the first time in months, Ford felt almost serene. There had been some embarrassment, sitting in front of all those cameras, and some awkwardness with Rachel Mitchell. But no one had actually tried to destroy her family or academic career. She assumed Kavanaugh would be confirmed, as she always had. Her victory had been telling her story to the world with dignity, she said. Maybe that would make it easier for the next generation of victims to come forward. And maybe the people vetting candidates for the court would be more careful next time.

Finally, Ford thought, she could return to her life. She turned down every interview request, telling her team: "I don't want to be *that* person, I just want to go back to teaching."

Instead, she came under attack, as Republicans sought to push Kavanaugh's confirmation through.

On Sunday night, Rachel Mitchell sent a five-page memo to the Senate Republicans taking aim at her credibility. ("A 'he said, she said' case is incredibly difficult to prove. But this case is even weaker than that.") Three nights later, Trump mocked her gleefully at a campaign rally in

Southaven, Mississippi, letting loose more than ever before. ("'How did you get home?' 'I don't remember.' 'How did you get there?' 'I don't remember.' 'Where is the place?' 'I don't remember.' 'How many years ago was it?' 'I don't know. I don't know. I don't know.' 'What neighborhood was it in?' 'I don't know.' 'Where's the house?' 'I don't know.' 'Upstairs, downstairs, where was it?' 'I don't know.'")

As Trump spoke, Republicans on the Senate Judiciary Committee released a sworn statement from a man Ford had dated in the early 1990s claiming that he had seen Ford use her understanding of psychology to coach a roommate as she prepared to take a polygraph test as part of a job interview with federal law enforcement, a claim that appeared designed to cast doubt on the polygraph test that Ford had passed. Ford was furious. It was one thing for critics to take shots at her. But this lie also hurt her friend, Monica McLean, the former FBI agent who was forced to publicly deny having ever let Ford or anyone else prepare her for a polygraph exam.

It felt like everyone in the country had a reaction to what Ford had done. A server at Dale's restaurant in Southaven, Mississippi, the same town where Trump had just spoken, was among those who were outraged. "Any woman can say anything," she said of the #MeToo movement. "You know as well as I do, they bring it on themselves, to get up the ladder, to destroy somebody they don't care for. I think it's something that should be kept personal. Sure there's a lot of bad guys in this world doing a lot of things they shouldn't have been." Her own daughter was a rape victim, she said. "I mean, I understand it big-time. You go to counseling, for a year, two, whatever you need to do, but PTSD? No, I can't see that. That's just too much. My daughter has gone on just fine in life. You forgive, you forget. You don't carry that with you your whole stupid life."

Others were celebrating Ford as a hero. Victims of sexual violence everywhere were still pouring their hearts out in response to her testimony. She was receiving tens of thousands of letters from supporters confiding their own personal stories of abuse, assault, and harassment. Celebrities like Ellen DeGeneres and Connie Chung were going public for the first time about violations they said they had suffered, citing Ford as their motivation. Protestors were swarming Capitol Hill with an intensity that made the initial Kavanaugh demonstrations look mild. *Time* magazine created a visual testament to Ford on its cover, an image of her face made with lines from her testimony.

In speaking with the *Washington Post*, in testifying before cameras, Ford had sought to retain control over her own story, but now it was being undermined, heralded, and otherwise appropriated. Desperate for a final say, Ford turned back to her team. Was there something else she could do or say? Her team counseled her against it. She could show a video of the attack, Katz and Banks told her, and critics would still dismiss her. And there was no way she could assume the weight of every survivor's trauma.

"You can't take on all the hopes and prayers and dreams of every person who wants women to be treated respectfully," Katz later recalled telling her in a phone call. "You can't carry that."

Ford couldn't let go. On Thursday night, October 4, Ford called Katz and Banks. The next day, the Senate would finally take its first vote on whether to advance Kavanaugh's nomination. In the end, the FBI investigation of Ford's allegation had been extremely narrow; after interviewing Mark Judge, P. J. Smyth, Leland Keyser, and an attorney for one of the witnesses, the FBI had found "no corroboration." They had not interviewed Ford—or Kavanaugh. The questions about what had really happened three decades earlier had not been settled. (The investigation also found no corroboration of Ramirez's allegation.)

But Ford wanted a final say. That evening, she finished composing a secret letter she had begun drafting two days earlier. It was addressed to Senator Jeff Flake, thanking him for the kindness he had shown her.

Late that night, Banks sent the letter to the senator's private email address. The next morning, before the vote, a courier whisked a hard copy to his office.

That afternoon, Friday, October 5, the Senate advanced the nomination. The final vote would likely take place the next day. It was the exact first anniversary of Jodi and Megan's first Weinstein story, and the second anniversary of the release of the *Access Hollywood* tape almost to the day.

Megan took a train to Washington and found Katz outside her office. The lawyer's cell phone was cradled in her neck and tears were in her eyes. The vote had played out as they expected. She was talking to Ford, both women processing what was happening. Ford had done far more than she had ever planned. The judge was still going to be on the Supreme Court.

"You did your part, stay strong," Katz said into the phone.

The next day, Katz, Banks, and a junior attorney in their office walked past hundreds of protesters and into the halls of the Senate building, trailed by Megan, for the final vote on Kavanaugh's nomination. In the Senate gallery, the lawyers pushed open the wood doors, walked down the white marble stairs, and slid into the blue chairs. They were there to represent Ford right up to the very end, even if it meant simply sitting in the gallery, they said.

The lawyers watched with grim faces as Republican senators rose to talk about how innocent men everywhere were at risk of being unfairly targeted. Most of them did not directly attack Ford; they called her a pawn of those trying to defeat Kavanaugh's nomination. Democrats were doing the opposite, criticizing Kavanaugh, and praising his accusers, sympathizing with sexual assault victims everywhere. When Senator Dick Durbin, a Democrat from Illinois, heralded Ford as the definition of civic duty, and apologized for the treatment she had received, Katz bent her head, overcome.

The mounting concern on both sides of the debate had turned into fury. On Capitol Hill, anti-Kavanaugh protestors displayed massive signs that said WE BELIEVE CHRISTINE BLASEY FORD and WE BELIEVE ALL SURVIVORS and confronted Republican senators in person, and even arrived at McConnell's house with beer cans, in reference to Kavanaugh's teenage habits, yelling "Chug, chug, chug" and "What do we do with a drunken justice?" Now some worked their way into the gallery for the final vote. One by one, they rose to shout their complaints. As security dragged them out, their cries echoed down the hall: "I stand with survivors." "This process is corrupt." "This is a stain on American history."

Across the room, Don McGahn, Trump's White House counsel, sat watching the proceedings with a smile on his face. When the vote was over, Senator McConnell held a press conference. Megan noted that he too radiated delight: He had gotten a new Supreme Court majority and maybe an unexpected political bonus too. The "virtual mob that's assaulted all of us in the course of this process has turned our base on fire," he said.

Kavanaugh's confirmation was certainly not the final measure of the fate of the #MeToo movement. A few weeks before, McDonald's workers, including Kim Lawson, the woman Jodi had interviewed, had held a coast-to-coast walkout over the company's weak sexual harassment policies. Historians were calling it the country's first sexual harassment–related strike in a century. Leslie Moonves, the chairman of CBS, stepped down, becoming the first Fortune 500 CEO to lose his job in the reckoning. The day before, the Nobel Peace Prize committee had announced that its 2018 award would go to Nadia Murad and Denis Mukwage, two activists who had worked to end sexual violence. At that moment, the *Times* was finishing a shocking story about Google and secret problems among some of its top male executives, including the so-called father of Android phones, who had been paid $90 million to leave the company after another employee had accused him of forced oral sex, an allegation he denied.

The debate over Ford's allegations was helping people reassess high school behavior, even if only in private. That's where a lot of the most profound change was happening, with the cacophonous public conversations, so frequently unsatisfying, sparking more contemplative private ones.

Ford herself continued to fluctuate in her feelings over what had happened. In her interviews with Megan over the following months, she was often sad or confused, occasionally emboldened and angry, almost always still very anxious. Should she have shared her story? Would it have been better kept to herself? One day Ford was tallying all the reasons not to come forward about an assault. The next day, she would claim to have no regrets. The ambivalence she had originally felt about going public seemed like it might last a very long time.

At the height of the Kavanaugh fracas in Washington, the *Times* had asked readers if they had ever behaved toward women or girls in ways they had regretted. Hundreds replied, confessing transgressions from groping to gang rapes.

"I think 'conquering' her sexually was something I expected I needed to do," wrote Tom Lynch of forcing his hand up a girl's skirt at a prom in 1980.

Terry Wheaton, now eighty-two years old, recounted forcibly kissing a classmate around 1952.

"I'm sorry, Diane," he said.

THE GATHERING

During the final months of 2018, we returned to an idea we had first considered during the Weinstein investigation. Back then, as we struggled to persuade women to break their silence, we wondered if it might help to bring some of them together to talk in person. At the time the idea had seemed impossible, a threat to the secrecy of our reporting.

But we found ourselves thinking about the possibility again, for new reasons. We realized it might help answer lingering questions, which applied far beyond the Weinstein case: What happened to women who spoke up, and what did they make of everything that had transpired?

On January 16, 2019, twelve women who had been part of our reporting convened in Los Angeles, at our request, to try to answer those questions.

The gathering had been challenging to arrange. The women lived in three countries, and we had made many calls and sent many messages to sort through schedules and explain our intention. No, this wouldn't be a group therapy session. We wanted to conduct a joint interview, for journalistic purposes. We had looked for a hotel conference room where everyone could meet, but none seemed private enough. So Gwyneth Paltrow, who was planning to attend, offered her home in Brentwood, with us paying for the meals so as to avoid accepting anything of substantial financial value from a source. For some participants, travel expenses were a barrier, so we covered a few air tickets and hotel rooms.

It was raining at 6:00 p.m. that evening when we arrived, along with our sources and subjects. Our cars pulled past an inconspicuous gray fence, and we found ourselves inside the same kind of sheltered environment as Paltrow's house in the Hamptons, the location of our first in-person interview with her all those months ago. Inside, we congregated in the den, which would be our main meeting room for the evening and part of the next day, accepting drinks and settling on wide sofas in front of a crackling fireplace.

Around the room was a history of our reporting, come to life. Rachel Crooks, who had told Megan her account of being forcibly kissed by the president at the Trump Tower elevator, had traveled from Ohio, where she was still dealing with the fallout of sharing her story, which had brought her more opportunities and problems than she had ever imagined. Seeing the tall Midwesterner in the California home was jolting to Megan—but perhaps no more than everything else that had happened since the two had first spoken.

Ashley Judd was wearing sweats, because she had come straight from her flight from Germany, where she was living. Since the Weinstein story had been published, she had been praised as a heroine, received awards, and accepted a teaching post at Harvard University's Kennedy School, her alma mater. She was to begin in the fall of 2019, with a simple title: "Leader." She was joining the board of Time's Up, the organization to promote safe and fair workplaces that had started in Hollywood in the wake of the Weinstein scandal and spread far beyond it, and had filed her own lawsuit against the producer for harassment, defamation, and loss of career opportunities. Strangers often approached her to convey their gratitude, once even lining up to wait for her as she disembarked from an airplane.

Jodi wanted to see her shake hands with Laura Madden, the former Weinstein assistant with the account of being harassed in Dublin decades ago, who had traveled from Wales. These women were the first two who had gone on the record about the producer. For all the resolve she had shown in October 2017, Madden remained soft-spoken, tucking her soft brown hair behind her ear, explaining that she was unaccustomed to this type of sharing with strangers.

Madden had flown in with her fellow former Miramax employee Zelda Perkins, who had become an activist. A few weeks after the Weinstein story broke, she had held her breath and become the first of several women to break publicly their settlement nondisclosure agreements, speaking to the press about everything except the specific experience and identity of Rowena Chiu, the colleague she had been trying to protect. In effect, Perkins had dared Weinstein to come after her legally, and he had not. In the media and British Parliament, she had mounted a public case against confidential settlements, questioning the whole notion of hush money to silence accusations of sexual abuse and other wrongdoing. Perkins was a critic by nature—that trait had helped drive her to confront Weinstein years ago, and now to challenge accepted legal practice—and she sized up the room with an air of skepticism.

Walking into Paltrow's house felt strange to her: They had last seen one another working on *Shakespeare in Love* and other films but had never shared with each other their accounts of how Weinstein had behaved. After *Shakespeare in Love* had been released, Paltrow won her Oscar a few months after Perkins had signed the settlement papers that would erase her story for the next twenty years. Now the two blondes were seated side by side on a rug in conversation. Paltrow, still wearing a dress and makeup from a talk show taping, was an easy host, sitting back and letting us run the proceedings.

Kim Lawson, the McDonald's worker whom Jodi had first spoken to almost a year before, had come from Kansas City. Since that conversation, she had become a leader of the campaign to make the fast food giant, the second-largest employer in the nation, address sexual harassment on the job. She was accompanied by Allynn Umel, an organizer of the labor campaign. But Lawson didn't appear to need any hand-holding: She was vivacious, and judging from the laughter coming from her corner of the room, she seemed to bond quickly with others.

Christine Blasey Ford sat on the couch, flanked by Debra Katz and Lisa Banks, the two lawyers who had encouraged her to testify. This was a rare excursion: Three months after the Kavanaugh hearing, Ford remained mostly hidden. She was in a much different position than the other women in the room. She was still receiving death threats. She hadn't even returned to local shopping for fear of being approached by strangers, let alone to the teaching job she loved. But she had told Megan that coming to Los Angeles reflected her new determination to venture out.

In addition to those participants, women whom we had written about by name before, was Rowena Chiu, who joined but stood apart in an important way. Since the Weinstein story had broken, she had remained invisible, communicating with Jodi through her lawyer. She had never been publicly identified or broken her silence and wasn't sure if she ever would. We had invited her to join anyway, not in spite of her silence but because of it: So many women had kept terrible stories to themselves. Maybe Chiu would speak to the consequences of that decision. But she had come on the condition that the group keep her name confidential, if she never decided to come forward, and that her lawyer, Nancy Erika Smith, attend too.

Because Chiu had stayed hidden, we had imagined her as shy or stricken, but she was warm and confident and had an impressive camera slung over her shoulder. Her parents had moved from Hong Kong to the United Kingdom before she was born, and she spoke with a British accent. She had left her life in film behind many years ago, getting a law degree, becoming a management consultant, moving to the United States, and now wrote research papers for the World Bank while raising four children. She lived right down the road from Ford, as it happened. To Jodi's relief, Chiu and her husband were not angry about the awkward moment in the driveway; they understood how confusing the situation had been. She and Perkins had finally been in touch again, trying to figure out who they were to one another after all this time. But she wasn't sure she would speak at the gathering, she warned us. She had still never shared her story out loud with another group of people.

Beginning to mingle, the women were friendly but tentative. Almost all were strangers to one another, and the thing they had in common was so unusual. Each had obsessed over the decision to share her account of harassment or assault, in many cases with either Jodi or Megan coaxing and encouraging them on the other end of the phone. We had asked them to come to the gathering prepared to answer one central question: After the leap of faith, what had they found on the other side?

We intended the interview, which would begin that evening and stretch into the next day, to be as egalitarian as possible. What each woman had to say was equally important. But there was no avoiding disparities among the participants. At McDonald's, Lawson was now making $10 an hour. Six months before, she had been homeless. We didn't mention that to the others, but every last detail of Paltrow's house—a one-story series of soothing gray-and-white rooms, scattered with small luxuries like soft throws and gilded teacups, all connected by an expansive kitchen—was a tangible reminder of differences between the women.

We made a quick round of introductions, explaining the role that each person had played in our journalism, and soon everyone was settling in at a long table with plates of Japanese food—skewers, salads, rice. The women went around the table, each saying something about how she had decided to speak up, essentially retelling the stories of theirs we have written, and the conversation began to warm up. During Paltrow's turn, she raised a glass and toasted Judd for being the first actress to break the silence about Weinstein.

"Ashley, honestly, what you did—it's very, very hard to be first into the breach," she said, acknowledging that in speaking on the record in the first Weinstein story, Judd had gone where she had not. "You really were the one who paved the way for all of us to come forward in your wake," she said.

"I always worried about you," Judd said back to her—meaning, back in the '90s and whether she was safe from Weinstein.

As the conversation went around the table, some common experiences began to surface. Crooks explained that some of her own family members had continued to support Trump, not her. Perkins said that for all the public attention she had received for her battle against secret settlements, some relatives had never once acknowledged her efforts.

After Madden spoke, she turned to Ford, mentioning that she had been able to speak out about Weinstein in part because she was confident her encounters with him were part of a broader predatory pattern.

"To stand up on your own was quite something," Madden said.

"Yeah, I didn't know if there were other people," Ford replied.

The anticipation in the room rose a notch. The group only knew Ford—her now-famous face and her now-familiar high voice—from her public testimony. She began taking them behind the scenes, recounting her Santa Cruz beachside deliberations over the summer, including her initial idea that she might phone Kavanaugh before he was nominated and ask him to reconsider.

"I was like, 'Why don't we just call him and just be, like: *Hey, let's save our families this whole thing*,'" she said.

When we got to Chiu, Jodi gave her an out, asking if she wanted to pass.

"Sure, I will take a turn," she said: brief words, but for her, momentous ones. "I'm the only person at the table who has not yet gone public with my story, so I've had very little practice in telling it," Chiu said. Aside from her husband, her family still knew nothing, she said.

"There are very few, I feel, Asian voices that come forward with this kind of story," she continued. "It's not because this kind of thing does not happen to Asian people, but I think certainly within the U.S. we have a whole culture around a model minority that doesn't make a fuss, that doesn't speak up, that puts their head down and works really hard and doesn't cause waves."

For those reasons and others, Chiu said, she was now contemplating breaking her silence. "The whole idea of coming out and speaking about something that would undoubtedly shock my friends, and shift the whole of my life, is really terrifying," she said. "It's really helpful to be here tonight to hear each of your perspectives, especially about how you've come forward and what made you come forward."

With that, the agenda became more urgent and concrete. For us, this gathering was an interview to share with readers. For her, it was potential help in making a life-defining choice.

Chiu gestured to her camera and asked if she could take some shots that night and the next day. She had given herself a perfect job: She could hide behind the lens, remaining invisible if she preferred, observing everyone else.

The group reassembled the next morning, forming a loose circle on the same couches and chairs in the den. At the center, a huge gray-and-white ottoman held cups of coffee—and flowerpots containing microphones. This was still an interview, and we were recording, as everyone knew. The plan for the next few hours was simple: We asked the women to take turns sharing stories about what happened after they came forward and hoped the conversation would build from there. Outside, it was still raining, adding to a sense of refuge.

Laura Madden was still nervous about speaking. She was self-effacing, and she had gotten relatively little credit for her bravery, continuing to rinse dishes and supervise homework in Swansea. But in her lilting accent, she told the other women what had happened, simply in her own head, in the wake of the Weinstein story: She had rewritten the history of her adult life.

"I suppose the last year, hearing other people's stories, and also seeing a documentary that was made, and it was really about the employees in London, and seeing how young I was . . . ," she trailed off, trying to describe what it had been like to see her own experience depicted objectively on-screen. "I could reframe it and see that it wasn't actually anything that I did wrong," she said. "It was what he did wrong."

No one could restore the years Madden, now forty-eight, had spent feeling uneasy about her time at Miramax or hand her a fresh career or financial success. But "just being able to see it as *his* problem has helped get some sense of myself back," she said.

Paltrow, sitting cross-legged on the rug by the warmth of the fireplace, described a very different kind of change in understanding her personal history and career. After the story had broken of Weinstein's misconduct, she learned that the producer had used her—her name, her Oscar, her success—as a means of manipulating other vulnerable women. Starting in the fall of 2017, Paltrow had spent many hours on the phone with other women who told her that Weinstein, while harassing or assaulting them, would routinely cite her and her soaring career, falsely implying she had yielded to him. "He was pointing to my career and saying, 'Don't you want what she has?'"

Some of the women had gone public. Others had told Paltrow that because they succumbed to Weinstein sexually, they felt they could never speak out. Weinstein denied he had ever made those claims about Paltrow, but it seemed this was why he had been so worried about the prospect of her speaking up: Once others knew her story, his scheme would fall apart.

"That has by far been the hardest part of this, to feel like a tool in coercion of rape," Paltrow said through tears. "It almost makes me feel culpable in some way, even though it's completely illogical." As she spoke, her home's luxury suddenly looked a little different: Weinstein had taken Paltrow's enviable life and deployed it against other women.

Umel, the labor organizer for the McDonald's workers, passed the star a box of tissues.

As each woman spoke, the others focused intently, with few phone checks and no interruptions. Each one was a messenger from an unfamiliar world: the battleground Midwest; show business; the thunder dome of Supreme Court confirmation hearings. Those differences, rather than splitting the group, generated curiosity and drew the women together.

Kim Lawson, the twenty-six-year-old fast food worker, her hair in a neat braid, lived more than four thousand miles away from Zelda Perkins. The producer was two decades her senior, spoke with a crisp British accent, and was wearing a sweater with David Bowie's name embroidered on it. But both had thrown themselves into activism, and as they spoke in succession, their words echoed.

Perkins described how she had felt delivering testimony about confidentiality agreements to members of Parliament: "The most extraordinary thing for me was walking into the Palace at Westminster and realizing that as an individual, that this was actually mine—the Palace at Westminster was mine, the politicians were mine."

Lawson told the group about filing a complaint against McDonald's with the Equal Employment Opportunity Commission, the government agency charged with upholding workers' rights against discrimination. "I never felt so much power in my life," she said. Few women in the room had ever walked a picket line, and so she described the September strike: loud chanting and yells of solidarity, new people to meet, a sense of energy and camaraderie, and lots of men who turned out in support, deliberately marching behind the women. Lawson had delivered a speech, given interviews, and pushed her daughter the length of the march in a stroller. "Everyone's with you," she said. "It's like, you're going to hear me today if you heard me no other day, you know?" she said.

Their stories involved a kind of poetic reversal. They had suffered from harassment but gained new authority and respect from fighting it. Even at her young age, Lawson had become a kind of team coach to other female McDonald's employees across the country involved in the union push, counseling them on a text chain. Customers looked at her differently: "Weren't you on TV about sexual harassment?" they asked her.

"Since I've spoken I've been able to come into the person that I was growing into at twenty-four," Perkins said, citing the age she had been when she left Miramax.

But neither Perkins nor Lawson could report complete triumphs. Settlement laws had not changed in the UK, and Perkins did not know if they would. McDonald's was beginning to strengthen its policies, introducing new training for managers and a hotline, and making plans for posters giving employees instructions on how to report. But Lawson hadn't yet seen any of those changes materialize in her own store, and it was not yet clear how much the company's thousands of workplaces would shift.

"There's a huge part of me that can't wait for it all to be over and then to just go back to my horses, and my sheep, and never ever have to speak to a journalist, or be on TV, or do any of those things ever again," Perkins said.

Some of the women nodded. Together, they had all been part of a genuine realignment, but it was so incomplete. How much more of themselves did each want to donate to the effort?

After Rachel Crooks came forward about Trump in 2016, she suffered from crippling anxiety and self-consciousness, she said as she sat facing the others with her long legs tucked beneath her. She was the only one present who lived in a rural, conservative area—"more of a #himtoo community," as she called it.

After she got through a few television appearances and a press conference about the accusation, she received an unexpected invitation. Local Democrats wanted her to run for a seat in the state legislature—a terrible idea, she thought. Critics had already accused her of telling her Trump story for political ends. "It's confirming what everyone thought, that I was doing this for some sort of agenda," she explained.

But she cared about education and health care. As for the incumbent, he was "a rubber stamp for the Republican party," she told the group. Maybe she could use her new profile in a positive way, she thought. "Right or wrong, I would have more fund-raising potential because I now had this national voice," she said. So Crooks ran for public office, learning to lead rallies and make speeches, she said. She had joined an unprecedented wave of female candidates across the country, campaigning to seize more political power than women had ever held in United States history.

The night she lost her race, she said, she didn't even cry or feel self-pity: Democrats had, for the most part, lost across Ohio. But months later, she was struggling with the way the campaign had solidified the tendency of others to view her only through her Trump story. On television, she was sometimes just labeled "Trump Accuser" at the bottom of the screen, a phrase her mother hated. "This has become your identity," a male friend told her recently.

"It has opened doors and provided this new path, but it also ties me to this awful human being," she said.

The group silently considered her dilemma. Crooks was living out one of the most common fears about coming forward: It could label you for-ever. Ford listened particularly closely. Her current fears matched what Crooks described having faced two years before, right down to a specific detail about avoiding local stores. Sitting on the couch, with her red glasses pushed up on her head, she began quizzing Crooks, as if she held a map to what lay ahead.

"I was wondering how long that lasted before you just sort of normally jump into your car and go to a restaurant without people looking at you and wondering if that's really you," Ford said. She was also struggling on-line, including with fake social media profiles of herself saying, "I recant my whole story."

"I'm, like, 'That's not true!'" Ford said. "But I'm not brave enough to get into that with them. And there's just too many of them, so . . . the social media piece . . . I don't do well with that," she said.

"Sometimes I write the replies, and I just never post them," Crooks told her. "It's very cathartic."

The reaction wasn't all negative, Ford acknowledged. She had been offered prizes, invitations, book and movie contracts. The mail for her was still accumulating, including many private stories of violence—"175,000 letters in Palo Alto," Katz interjected. Those were only the paper letters.

There were many more electronic missives. In those, and everywhere else, the reactions to what she had done were so extreme.

For hours, the others had mostly been nodding and asking polite follow-up questions. Now they spoke up with purpose. Paltrow offered a football analogy of her own. "They only tackle you when you've got the ball," she said, explaining that she had once heard the phrase from the country singer Tim McGraw.

She and Judd—longtime experts in fielding public scrutiny and criticism—began to coach everyone else in how to deal with other people's judgments. Judd was direct: Stop reading about yourself online, she instructed Ford.

"If an alcoholic can stay away from a drink one day at a time, I can stay away from the comment section one day at a time," Judd said. "I'm participating in my own self-harm when I expose myself to that material," she continued.

"Do you just not really go on the internet much?" Ford asked Judd, incredulous.

"I'm completely abstinent from all media about myself and have been for probably almost twenty years," Judd said. She posted pictures and links on social media but tried not to read anything written about herself: that was part of why she had disappeared to the woods after the first Weinstein article had been published.

As she spoke, she was curled in a pink upholstered chair facing the group. She had sat there all day, absorbing what others had to say, speaking relatively little. She seemed like the one participant who had not really been transformed. She had always wanted to be an activist, and when she went on the record about Weinstein, the world affirmed her instincts.

"I have to know the hill on which I'm willing to die," she told the group. "The equality of the sexes is that hill for me."

————————

Throughout the discussion, Chiu sat listening, saying little, occasionally clicking her camera in the direction of the others. No one pressed her on the momentous decision of whether she would say publicly what had happened to her all those years ago.

But during the final hours of the gathering, as Ford spoke more, Chiu seemed to hang on every word. Ford had become, in Chiu's mind, a kind of proxy for what she might undergo if she went public. The fact that the two women were neighbors only heightened the connection she felt. Even as Chiu kept her story hidden, she watched as friends and neighbors had organized a candlelight vigil and meal deliveries for Ford.

For months, Chiu had pictured the controversy and criticism that engulfed Ford happening to her instead. The analogy was inexact—the Weinstein case was far more settled and less controversial—but for her, it was real. "I imagined it would all come crashing down," Chiu admitted to the rest of the group. "There'd be news vans outside my door. I was worried my children would be followed to school."

That mental exercise was having an unexpected effect. Watching Ford from nearby—and now meeting her up close—had strengthened Chiu's desire to go public. She told the group that she could feel herself getting closer to joining them, to putting her name to her story. "I can't say that being in this room with so many of you—I can't say that doesn't inspire me," she said.

"I think it's really going to change who I am," she added. That had turned out to be the strongest unifying thread after the hours of discussion: Almost every member of the group who had spoken publicly had been transformed by it, and was stunned by the impact that sharing her own intimate story had on others.

The women around the room leaped in with expressions of support. "If you decide to come forward, that's a big step and that's a step of growth," Lawson said. "No matter how long it took you to say anything about it."

"If you do it, we have your back," Paltrow said.

Ford cut in with a note of caution. "Can I just say something to you?" she asked. "When I was in your position, I had a lot of people kind of telling me, 'You should do this. It's going to be great'—kind of the same kind of thing that's happening right now." But the advice, and especially the upbeat projections about how well it would all work out, had been impossible to take in. "I just didn't even hear any of it, it was so overwhelming to me," she said.

No one could ever predict how speaking out would go. Forecasting was futile. Once a story was publicly told for the first time, there was no telling what might happen, who might read it, or what others might echo, add, or disagree with. There was no guarantee of affirmation or impact. The results could be wrenching, empowering, or both.

But this was what everyone in the room, and more people beyond it, now understood: If the story was not shared, nothing would change. Problems that are not seen cannot be addressed. In our world of journalism, the story was the end, the result, the final product. But in the world at large, the emergence of new information was just the beginning—of conversation, action, change.

"We're still here," Perkins said, to laughter, in one of the group's final exchanges. She wasn't speaking directly to Chiu but the message was clear. "We're still smiling. None of us died from stepping forward. We walked through the fire, but we all came out the other side."

"I think we're probably all proud of the scars that we received," she said.

In summing up how the reckoning might be remembered over time, Laura Madden took an even longer view. "We're not the first people who've spoken up," Madden said. "We're not the first *women* who've spoken up."

"There isn't ever going to be an end," she said. "The point is that people have to continue always speaking up and not being afraid."

A few weeks later, Chiu called: She was ready to go on the record, and for us to share her name publicly.

She understood that more than eighty women had already come

forward about Weinstein. She wasn't sure that the public would still care about her account. But she wanted to speak anyway. During the initial Weinstein investigation, she hadn't been ready, but the other women, in Los Angeles and around the world, had eased the way. She feared the legal cases against him might not be successful. So she wanted to help write the history and continue pushing for change.

"I'm not just going to let it slide away," she said.

ACKNOWLEDGMENTS

If you've read these pages, you already have some sense of the debts we owe. Those are only the beginning.

To all of our sources: Thank you for participating in our journalism. Some of you spoke with us at great personal risk or confided stories you never thought you would share with a stranger—and then shared even more for this book. Many of you submitted to lengthy, repeated questioning or uncomfortable lines of inquiry. A special measure of gratitude to everyone who provided the illuminating emails, texts, and other documents interspersed throughout this narrative. A much larger cast, from experts to silent tipsters we can never name, provided essential guidance, including stories and ideas that ring in our heads still.

In addition to the colleagues portrayed in this book, we're grateful to the *Times* journalists who joined our efforts on the Weinstein story, including Rachel Abrams, Ellen Gabler, Susan Dominus, Steve Eder, Jim Rutenberg, William Rashbaum, Barry Meier, Al Baker, Jim McKinley, and the audio team at *The Daily*. At every turn, we received crucial support from Arthur Sulzberger Jr., A. G. Sulzberger, Sam Dolnick, our colleagues on the business side of the newspaper, and from subscribers, who make this journalism possible. Dean Baquet, Matt Purdy, David McCraw, Sheryl Stolberg, Emily Steel, Carolyn Ryan, and Michael Barbaro generously provided feedback on the manuscript.

The editor who is invisible in this book yet present on every page is Ann Godoff, our galvanizing force. Ann endowed this project with her vision, clarity, and decisiveness, and notes so inspiring we hung them on our office walls. For all of that, we are forever grateful. William Heyward and Casey Denis, Sarah Hutson and Gail Brussel, Carolyn Foley and Juliann Barbato all poured many hours and years of experience into helping us tell and share this story. Thank you for your extraordinary dedication.

Rebecca Corbett, our editor at the *Times*, is our true north. She not only steered us through our investigation of Weinstein but also read and commented on several versions of these chapters, helping us capture and explain what we witnessed.

Alexis Kirschbaum, our editor and ally in London, provided essential insight, feedback, and friendship. Thank you as well to Emma Bal and Jasmine Horsey of Bloomsbury Publishing.

Elyse Cheney is our agent, matchmaker, and guide, and we are grateful for her tenacity, judgment, and hustle. We're also indebted to her colleagues Claire Gillespie, Alice Whitwham, Alex Jacobs, and Allison Devereux. Charlotte Perman and Kristen Sena of Greater Talent Network have handled our speaking engagements with grace—particularly the campus visits, with questions from students that helped us articulate what we wanted to say in these pages.

Kelsey Kudak fact-checked the manuscript with sensitivity and commitment, moving through hundreds of pages of complicated investigative work and taking direction from two different authors with equanimity. Astha Rajvanshi provided research assistance on topics large and small.

For other essential help, we'd also like to thank Joseph Abboud, Kendra Barkoff, Kassie Evashevski, Natasha Fairweather, Jonathan Furmanski, Molly Levinson, Eleanor Leonard, Priya Parker, Melissa Schwartz, Felicia Stewart, Nancy Erika Smith, and Josh Wilkinson. For our author photos, we were lucky enough to have a photographer who knows a thing or two about portraits in the extended *She Said* family; many thanks to Martin Schoeller and his team for these pictures.

Anyone who has parented young children can instantly fill in the scenes of diaper changing, bottle-feeding, and sleep training that took place in between (and occasionally during) our reporting. We were saved again and again by our babysitters, our children's teachers, and most of all, our families.

From Jodi: Not everything in life happens in the order you expect. During the period described in this book, I needed my parents, Wendy and Harry Kantor, more than I have at any time since childhood, because of the constancy of their love and the way they frequently swept in to care for, entertain, and guide my own children. Mom and Dad; Charlene Lieber, my second mother; calm, brave Fred Lieber; and the entire extended Kantor Lieber clan: Thank you for seeing us through these frantic years. Donna Mitchell, thank you for being a force of calm and goodness in the lives of our daughters, and for sharing the biggest and smallest moments with us.

Ron: Even as you unearthed stories of financial wrongdoing and reported on your own book on what to pay for college, you backed this work with full force, encouraging, feeding, and sustaining me. One of the best gifts you ever gave me was the Post-it you left on my desk, a few days before the publication of the original Weinstein story, that read "You can do this." Yes, but only with your love, help, and devotion.

Talia, you are a light, a lockbox, and an increasingly formidable discussion partner and debater. You overheard things that no tween should hear, faithfully kept secrets, helped with your little sister, and kept your cool even as I was often absorbed in broader dramas. Watching you articulate who you really are, and begin to build a life, is the thrill of mine.

Violet, you were only a year and a half old when we started, and your innocence made you my refuge. Parents are supposed to console their children, but I frequently found solace in your curls, songs, made-up words, discoveries, and above all, in the fierceness of your embrace.

From Megan: I'm indebted to my parents, John and Mary Jane Twohey, who have served as my moral compass for decades, reinforcing my values, nudging me along the pursuit of truth, and picking me up whenever I stumble. Ben and Maya Rutman, Helen and Felix Rutman-Schoeller and Martin Schoeller, I am thankful for your endless kindness and joyous laughter. Jenny Rattan-John, you are our rock, our teacher, and a cherished member of our family.

Jim: We had been married for less than a year and were brand-new parents when the Weinstein investigation began. Not once did you teeter in your support of the project and later this book, even when it meant canceled vacations, long stretches of single parenting, and fielding the intense emotions that came with this work. Your warm hugs, sharp listening skills, and encouraging texts propelled me forward, and your own expertise and judgment as a literary agent were delivered up at just the right moments.

Mira: you learned how to walk and talk during the course of this reporting, and the feistiness with which you tackled each stage of development served as a major source of inspiration. I am increasingly impressed by and grateful for your grit, cunning, and passion.

To our daughters, and to yours: May you know respect and dignity always, in the workplace and beyond.

NOTES

This book is based on three years of our reporting, stretching from the spring of 2016 through the spring of 2019, on President Donald J. Trump's treatment of women, Harvey Weinstein's decades of alleged sexual harassment and abuse, and Christine Blasey Ford's path to publicly accusing Brett Kavanaugh of sexual assault. These notes are intended to provide readers with a road map of which information in this book came from which sources.

We conducted hundreds of interviews, speaking with almost everyone depicted in this book, including Trump, Weinstein, and Ford, who detailed her experience to Megan over dozens of hours. Ford's legal team, Bob Weinstein, David Boies, Lance Maerov, Irwin Reiter, and most of the alleged victims portrayed granted us multiple interviews. Some of what we share was originally off the record, such as Jodi's early conversations with Reiter, and Weinstein's October 4, 2017, surprise visit to the *Times*, but through additional reporting, including returning to the parties involved, we were able to include the material. Over the past two years, we have sought comment from Weinstein on our findings multiple times, most recently in spring 2019. Kelsey Kudak spent five months fact-checking the book, often adding new information.

We reviewed thousands of pages of documents, cited below, including lawsuits filed against Trump, internal records from The Weinstein Company, and correspondence between Ford and her lawyers. Some text messages, emails, and other primary records are reproduced in the book so that readers can examine them directly.

We also drew on the reporting of other journalists, including Ronan Farrow, Emily Steel, and Michael Schmidt.

CHAPTER ONE: THE FIRST PHONE CALL

7 **"Here's the thing, I have been treated"**: Rose McGowan, email message to Jodi Kantor, May 11, 2017.

7 **"Because it's been an open secret"**: Rose McGowan (@rosemcgowan), "because it's been an open secret in Hollywood/Media & they shamed me while adulating my rapist. #WhyWomenDontReport," Twitter, October 13, 2016, https://twitter.com/rosemcgowan/status/786723360550035460.

7 **writing a memoir**: Rose McGowan, *Brave* (New York: HarperCollins, 2018).

7 **"tank that shows off cleavage (push up bras encouraged)"**: Rose McGowan (@rosemcgowan), "casting note that came w/script I got today. For real. name of male star rhymes with Madam Panhandler hahahaha I die," Twitter, June 17, 2015, https://twitter.com/rosemcgowan/status/611378426344288256.

7 **"It is okay to be angry"**: Rose McGowan (@rosemcgowan), "It is okay to be angry. Don't be afraid of it. Lean in. Like a storm cloud it passes, but it must be recognized. #readthis," Twitter, April 3, 2017, https://twitter.com/rosemcgowan /status/849083550448193536; "dismantle the system," Twitter, May 4, 2017, https://twitter.com/rosemcgowan/status/860322650962264064.

8 **"At some pt"**: Jennifer Senior (@JenSeniorNY), "At some pt, all the women who've been afraid to speak out abt Harvey Weinstein are gonna have to hold hands and jump," Twitter, March 30, 2015, https://twitter.com/jenseniorny /status/582657086737289216.

9 **He had even participated**: Jodi Kantor (@jodikantor), "Harvey Weinstein at the January 2017 Women's March in Park City, Utah," Twitter, October 5, 2017, https://twitter.com/jodikantor/status/916103297097961472.

12 **described what it called a horrific group sexual assault**: Sabrina Rubin Erdely, "A Rape on Campus," *Rolling Stone*, November 4, 2014. Rolling Stone retracted

the story on April 5, 2015, and commissioned a study by the *Columbia Journalism Review*, which was published by the magazine. Sheila Coronel, Steve Coll, and Derek Kravitz, "Rolling Stone and UVA: The Columbia University Graduate School of Journalism Report," *Rolling Stone*, April 5, 2015, https://www.rollingstone.com/culture/culture-news/rolling-stone-and-uva-the-columbia-university-graduate-school-of-journalism-report-44930; Ravi Somaiya, "Rolling Stone Article on Rape at University of Virginia Failed All Basics, Report Says," *New York Times*, April 5, 2015, https://www.nytimes.com/2015/04/06/business/media/rolling-stone-retracts-article-on-rape-at-university-of-virginia.html.

13 **a series of lawsuits:** Ben Sisario, Hawes Spencer, and Sydney Ember, "Rolling Stone Loses Defamation Case Over Rape Story," *New York Times*, November 4, 2016, https://www.nytimes.com/2016/11/05/business/media/rolling-stone-rape-story-case-guilty.html; Hawes Spencer and Ben Sisario, "In Rolling Stone Defamation Case, Magazine and Reporter Ordered to Pay $3 Million," *New York Times*, November 7, 2016, https://www.nytimes.com/2016/11/08/business/media/in-rolling-stone-defamation-case-magazine-and-reporter-ordered-to-pay-3-million.html; Matthew Haag, "Rolling Stone Settles Lawsuit Over Debunked Campus Rape Article," *New York Times*, April 11, 2017, https://www.nytimes.com/2017/04/11/business/media/rolling-stone-university-virginia-rape-story-settlement.html; Sydney Ember, "Rolling Stone to Pay $1.65 Million to Fraternity Over Discredited Rape Story," *New York Times*, June 13, 2017, https://www.nytimes.com/2017/06/13/business/media/rape-uva-rolling-stone-frat.html.

13 **police had called the story "a complete crock":** Erik Wemple, "Charlottesville Police Make Clear That Rolling Stone Story Is a Complete Crock," *Washington Post*, March 23, 2015, https://www.washingtonpost.com/blogs/erik-wemple/wp/2015/03/23/charlottesville-police-make-clear-that-rolling-stone-story-is-a-complete-crock; Bill Grueskin, "More Is Not Always Better," *Columbia Journalism Review*, April 5, 2015, https://www.cjr.org/analysis/rolling_stone_journalism.php; Craig Silverman, "The Year in Media Errors and Corrections 2014," *Poynter Institute*, December 18, 2014, https://www.poynter.org/newsletters/2014/the-year-in-media-errors-and-corrections-2014.

14 **were shelving rape kits, robbing victims of the chance for justice:** Megan Twohey, "Dozens of Rape Kits Not Submitted for Testing by Chicago Suburban Police Departments," *Chicago Tribune*, June 14, 2009, https://www.chicagotribune.com/news/chi-rape-kits-14-jun14-story.html; Megan Twohey, "Illinois to Test Every Rape Kit," *Chicago Tribune*, July 6, 2009, https://www.chicagotribune.com

/news/ct-met-rape-kit-law-20100706-story.html; Megan Twohey, "Doctors
Continue to Operate Unchecked," *Chicago Tribune*, August 23, 2010, https://
www.chicagotribune.com/lifestyles/health/chi-doctor-sex-charges-gallery
-storygallery.html; Megan Twohey, "The Child Exchange," *Reuters*, September
9, 2013, https://www.reuters.com/investigates/adoption/#article/part1.

15 **"That must be a pretty picture, you dropping to your knees":** *Celebrity
Apprentice: All-Stars*, Season 6, episode 1, aired March 3, 2013, on NBC; Mark
Graham, "Did Donald Trump Just Utter the Most Blatantly Sexist Statement in
the History of Broadcast Television?" VH1, March 5, 2013, http://www.vh1.com
/news/84410/donald-trump-brande-roderick-on-her-knees.

15 **Most of Trump's former employees:** Associated Press, "For Many Trump
Employees, Keeping Quiet Is Legally Required," *Fortune*, June 21, 2016, http:
//fortune.com/2016/06/21/donald-trump-nda; John Dawsey and Ashley Parker,
"'Everyone Signed One': Trump Is Aggressive in His Use of Nondisclosure
Agreements, Even in Government," *Washington Post*, August 13, 2018, https://
www.washingtonpost.com/politics/everyone-signed-one-trump-is-aggressive
-in-his-use-of-nondisclosure-agreements-even-in-government/2018/08/13
/9d0315ba-9f15-11e8-93e3-24d1703d2a7a_story.html.

15 **pieced together multiple allegations:** Michael Barbaro and Megan Twohey,
"Crossing the Line: How Donald Trump Behaved with Women in Private," *New
York Times*, May 14, 2016, https://www.nytimes.com/2016/05/15/us/politics
/donald-trump-women.html.

15 **"kissed, fondled, and restrained" her from leaving:** Ibid.

16 **conducted a lengthy interview of the candidate:** Donald Trump, interview by
Megan Twohey and Michael Barbaro, May 10, 2016.

16 **"went on *Fox and Friends* to dispute your story":** *Fox and Friends*, "Donald
Trump's Ex-girlfriend Says She Was Misquoted in the *Times*," *Fox News*, May
16, 2016, https://video.foxnews.com/v/4895612039001/#sp=show-clips.

16 **"The @nytimes is so dishonest":** Donald J. Trump (@realdonaldtrump), "The
@nytimes is so dishonest. Their hit piece cover story on me yesterday was just
blown up by Rowanne Brewer, who said it was a lie!" Twitter, May 16, 2016,
https://twitter.com/realdonaldtrump/status/732196260636151808; Donald J.
Trump (@realdonaldtrump), "With the coming forward today of the woman
central to the failing @nytimes hit piece on me, we have exposed the article as

a fraud!" Twitter, May 16, 2016, https://twitter.com/realdonaldtrump/status /732230384071680001.

17 **His argument was absurd:** Erik Wemple, "Bill O'Reilly Follows Donald Trump into the Racist Hellhole," *Washington Post,* June 7, 2016, https://www .washingtonpost.com/blogs/erik-wemple/wp/2016/06/07/bill-oreilly-follows -donald-trump-into-racist-hellhole.

17 **audiotape from the gossip show** *Access Hollywood* **from 2005:** David A. Farenthold, "Trump Recorded Having Extremely Lewd Conversation about Women in 2005," *Washington Post* (updated), October 8, 2016, https://www .washingtonpost.com/politics/trump-recorded-having-extremely-lewd -conversation-about-women-in-2005/2016/10/07/3b9ce776-8cb4-11e6-bf8a -3d26847eeed4_story.html.

18 **Trump apologized for his words:** Video, "Trump Responds in 2016 to Outrage over Comments," *New York Times*, October 8, 2016, https://www.nytimes.com /video/us/politics/100000004698416/trump-responds-to-outrage-over-lewd -remarks.html; Maggie Haberman, "Donald Trump's Apology That Wasn't," *New York Times*, October 8, 2016, https://www.nytimes.com/2016/10/08/us /politics/donald-trump-apology.html.

18 **"No, I have not":** "Transcript of the Second Debate," *New York Times,* October 10, 2016, https://www.nytimes.com/2016/10/10/us/politics/transcript-second -debate.html.

18 **two other women:** Megan Twohey and Michael Barbaro, "Two Women Say Donald Trump Touched Them Inappropriately," *New York Times,* October 12, 2016, https://www.nytimes.com/2016/10/13/us/politics/donald-trump-women .html.

18 *The Apprentice* **had gone on the air:** Rachel Crooks, interviews by Megan Twohey, October 2016 through spring 2019.

19 **Before that, the only man who had ever kissed her:** Eli Saslow, "Is Anyone Listening?" *Washington Post,* February 19, 2018, https://www.washingtonpost .com/news/national/wp/2018/02/19/feature/trump-accuser-keeps-telling-her -story-hoping-someone-will-finally-listen.

20 **"You are disgusting!" Trump shouted:** Donald Trump, interview by Megan Twohey, October 11, 2016.

20 **Minutes later, Trump stepped onstage:** Video, "Presidential Candidate Donald Trump Rally in Panama City, Florida," C-SPAN, October 11, 2016, https://www.c-span.org/video/?416754-1/donald-trump-campaigns-panama-city-florida.

20 **Some Republicans were saying he should drop out:** Jessica Taylor, "'You Can Do Anything': In 2005 Tape, Trump Brags about Groping, Kissing Women," National Public Radio, October 7, 2017, https://www.npr.org/2016/10/07/497087141/donald-trump-caught-on-tape-making-vulgar-remarks-about-women; Alan Rappeport, "John McCain Withdraws Support for Donald Trump after Disclosure of Recording," *New York Times,* October 10, 2018, https://www.nytimes.com/2016/10/08/us/politics/presidential-election.html; Jonathan Martin, Maggie Haberman, and Alexander Burns, "Lewd Donald Trump Tape Is a Breaking Point for Many in the G.O.P.," *New York Times,* October 8, 2016, https://www.nytimes.com/2016/10/09/us/politics/donald-trump-campaign.html.

21 **An explosive civil lawsuit alleged:** Josh Gerstein, "Woman Suing Trump over Alleged Teen Rape Drops Suit, Again," *Politico*, November 4, 2016, https://www.politico.com/story/2016/11/donald-trump-rape-lawsuit-dropped-230770; Jane Coaston and Anna North, "Jeffrey Epstein, the Convicted Sex Offender Who Is Friends with Donald Trump and Bill Clinton, Explained," *Vox*, February 22, 2019. https://www.vox.com/2018/12/3/18116351/jeffrey-epstein-trump-clinton-labor-secretary-acosta.

21 **as a woman tearfully recounted:** abc.com Staff, "Woman Accuses Trump of Inappropriate Sexual Conduct at 1998 US Open," ABC, October 20, 2016, https://abc7.com/politics/woman-accuses-trump-of-inappropriate-sexual-conduct-at-1998-us-open/1565005.

21 **a link to a post from a conservative news site:** Katie Mettler, "She Accused Trump of Sexual Assault, Lou Dobbs Tweeted Her Phone Number," *Washington Post*, October 14, 2016, https://www.washingtonpost.com/news/morning-mix/wp/2016/10/14/she-accused-trump-of-sexual-assault-lou-dobbs-tweeted-her-phone-number.

22 **"Failure to do so will leave my client":** Marc Kasowitz, "re: Demand for Retraction," letter from Marc Kasowitz to David McCraw, October 12, 2016, https://assets.donaldjtrump.com/DemandForRetraction.PDF.

22 **"It would have been a disservice":** David McCraw, "re: Demand for Retraction," letter from David McCraw to Marc Kasowitz, October 13, 2016, https://www.nytimes.com/interactive/2016/10/13/us/politics/david-mccraw-trump-letter.html.

23 **had covered up repeated allegations:** Emily Steel and Michael S. Schmidt, "Bill O'Reilly Thrives at Fox News, Even as Harassment Settlements Add Up," *New York Times*, April 1, 2017, https://www.nytimes.com/2017/04/01/business/media/bill-oreilly-sexual-harassment-fox-news.html.

24 **advertisers like Mercedes-Benz:** Karl Russel, "Bill O'Reilly's Show Lost More Than Half Its Advertisers in a Week," *New York Times*, April 11, 2017, https://www.nytimes.com/interactive/2017/04/11/business/oreilly-advertisers.html.

24 **other women at Fox started:** Emily Steel and Michael S. Schmidt, "Bill O'Reilly is Forced Out at Fox News," *New York Times*, April 19, 2017, https://www.nytimes.com/2017/04/19/business/media/bill-oreilly-fox-news-allegations.html.

24 **Roger Ailes, the Republican power broker:** John Koblin and Jim Rutenberg, "Accused of Sexual Harassment, Roger Ailes Is Negotiating Exit from Fox," *New York Times*, July 19, 2016, https://www.nytimes.com/2016/07/20/business/media/roger-ailes-fox-news-murdoch.html.

25 **Shaunna Thomas, a feminist activist:** Shaunna Thomas, interview by Jodi Kantor, April 2017.

CHAPTER TWO: HOLLYWOOD SECRETS

27 **red carpet photos:** "2017 Cannes Film Festival Red Carpet Looks," photos, *New York Times*, May 20, 2017, https://www.nytimes.com/2017/05/20/fashion/2017-cannes-film-festival-red-carpet-looks.html.

28 **given an interview to *Variety* in 2015:** Ramin Setoodeh, "Ashley Judd Reveals Harassment by Studio Mogul" *Variety*, October 6, 2015, https://variety.com/2015/film/news/ashley-judd-sexual-harassment-studio-mogul-shower-1201610666.

28 **"I am so sorry, my lawyer":** Judith Godrèche, email message to Jodi Kantor, June 13, 2017.

29 wasn't a Weinstein victim: Marissa Tomei, interviews by Jodi Kantor, 2017–18.

29 "You have to ask for money": Elizabeth Rubin, "Spy, Mother, Comeback Kid: All Eyes Are on Claire Danes," *Vogue,* July 14, 2013, https://www.vogue.com /article/all-eyes-on-claire-homeland-claire-danes-and-damian-lewis.

30 a gushing tweet a few months before: Lisa Bloom (@LisaBloom), "BIG ANNOUNCEMENT: My book SUSPICION NATION is being made into a miniseries, produced by Harvey Weinstein and Jay Z!," Twitter, April 7, 2017, https://twitter.com/lisabloom/status/850402622116855809.

31 made getting in touch with Ashley Judd simple: Ashley Judd and Maryanne Vollers, *All That Is Bitter and Sweet* (New York: Ballantine, 2015).

31 she had a personal story to tell: Ashley Judd, interviews by Jodi Kantor and Megan Twohey, June 2017–January 2019.

33 She yearned for playmates and company: Many of the details of Judd's upbringing are chronicled in her 2015 autobiography, Judd and Vollers, *All That Is Bitter and Sweet.*

35 a law school professor named Diane Rosenfeld: Diane Rosenfeld, interview by Jodi Kantor, May 11, 2018.

35 "I propose a model": Ashley Judd, "Gender Violence: Law and Social Justice" (master's thesis, Harvard's Kennedy School of Government, 2015), 2010.

36 "I'm not as nasty": "#NastyWoman," YouTube video, 00:06:43, Live at State of the Word, posted by Nina Mariah, December 11, 2016, https://www.youtube .com/watch?v=dvN0On85sNQ.

37 Judd was fired: Ashley Judd, interview by Jodi Kantor, 2017; Copper Fit executives, interview by Jodi Kantor, 2019.

37 The call ended with a plan: Jill Kargman, interview by Jodi Kantor, June 2017.

37 Kargman urged Jodi: Jenni Konner, interviews by Jodi Kantor, 2017; Lena Dunham, interviews by Jodi Kantor, 2017.

37 told Jodi she had delivered a similar warning: Tina Brown, interview by Jodi Kantor, September 26, 2017.

38 **Paltrow shared the unknown side of the story:** Gwyneth Paltrow, interviews by
Jodi Kantor and Megan Twohey, 2017–19.

40 **the producer's mother:** Anita Gates, "Miriam Weinstein, Mother and Backbone
of Original Miramax, Dies at 90," *New York Times,* November 4, 2016, https://
www.nytimes.com/2016/11/04/movies/miriam-weinstein-died-miramax.html.

41 **a sixty-six-dollar:** "Jade Egg," Goop, https://shop.goop.com/shop/products
/jade-egg?country=USA: Bill Bostock, "Gwyneth Paltrow's Goop settles
$145,000 lawsuit over baseless vaginal eggs health claims," *Business Insider,*
September 5, 2018, https://www.businessinsider.com/gwyneth-paltrows-goop
-lawsuit-vaginal-egg-claims-2018-9.

41 **"Organically sourced, fair trade urine pH sticks":** Jen Gunter, "Dear Gwyneth
Paltrow, I'm a Gynecologist and Your Vaginal Jade Eggs Are a Bad Idea," *Dr.
Jen Gunter,* January 17, 2017, https://drjengunter.com/2017/01/17/dear-gwyneth
-paltrow-im-a-gyn-and-your-vaginal-jade-eggs-are-a-bad-idea.

43 **She did not reply:** Uma Thurman, interviews and emails with Jodi Kantor,
2017–19.

43 **While reporting on DNA evidence:** Linda Fairstein, interview by Megan
Twohey, conducted in 2009 while reporting at the *Chicago Tribune.*

46 **liked to boast of his coziness with media:** Ryan Tate, "Why Harvey Weinstein
Thinks He Owns New York Media," *Gawker,* April 2, 2008, http://gawker.com
/5004915/why-harvey-weinstein-thinks-he-owns-new-york-media.

47 **based in part on Corbett:** David Simon, interview and email with Jodi Kantor,
2018–19.

47 **when two *Times* reporters discovered:** James Risen and Eric Lichtblau, "Bush
Lets U.S. Spy on Callers without Courts," *New York Times,* December 16, 2005,
https://www.nytimes.com/2005/12/16/politics/bush-lets-us-spy-on-callers
-without-courts.html.

CHAPTER THREE: HOW TO SILENCE A VICTIM

49 **the corresponding state agencies:** The New York Division of Human Rights,
https://dhr.ny.gov, and the California Department of Fair Employment and
Housing, https://www.dfeh.ca.gov.

49 obtained a report: Generated in 2017 by the California Department of Fair Employment and Housing.

50 On the afternoon of July 14: Meeting notes and documents from Katie Benner and Jodi Kantor.

50 Two weeks before, Katie Benner: Katie Benner, "Women in Tech Speak Frankly on Culture of Harassment," *New York Times,* June 30, 2017, https://www.nytimes.com/2017/06/30/technology/women-entrepreneurs-speak-out-sexual-harassment.html.

51 a blog post describing the harassment and retaliation: Susan Fowler, "Reflecting on One Very, Very Strange Year at Uber," *Susan Fowler,* February 19, 2017, https://www.susanjfowler.com/blog/2017/2/19/reflecting-on-one-very-strange-year-at-uber.

51 One of the men and one of the firms: Katie Benner, "A Backlash Builds against Sexual Harassment in Silicon Valley," *New York Times,* July 3, 2017, https://www.nytimes.com/2017/07/03/technology/silicon-valley-sexual-harassment.html.

51 Steel was hearing alarming accounts: Emily Steel, "At *Vice,* Cutting-Edge Media and Allegations of Old-School Sexual Harassment," *New York Times,* December 23, 2017, https://www.nytimes.com/2017/12/23/business/media/vice-sexual-harassment.html.

51 conversations with restaurant, retail, hotel, and construction workers: Catrin Einhorn, "Harassment and Tipping in Restaurants: Your Stories," *New York Times,* March 18, 2018, https://www.nytimes.com/2018/03/18/business/restaurant-harassment-tipping.html; Catrin Einhorn and Rachel Abrams, "The Tipping Equation," *New York Times,* March 12, 2018, https://www.nytimes.com/interactive/2018/03/11/business/tipping-sexual-harassment.html.

51 male blue-collar workplaces: Susan Chira and Catrin Einhorn, "How Tough Is It to Change a Culture of Harassment? Ask Women at Ford," *New York Times,* December 19, 2017, https://www.nytimes.com/interactive/2017/12/19/us/ford-chicago-sexual-harassment.html; Susan Chira and Catrin Einhorn, "The #MeToo Moment: Blue-collar Women Ask, 'What About Us?'" *New York Times,* December 20, 2017, https://www.nytimes.com/2017/12/20/us/the-metoo-moment-blue-collar-women-ask-what-about-us.html; Susan Chira, "We Asked Women in Blue-collar Workplaces about Sexual Harassment: Here Are Their Stories," *New York Times,* December 29, 2017, https://www.nytimes.com/2017

/12/29/us/blue-collar-women-harassment.html; Susan Chira, "The 'Manly' Jobs Problem," *New York Times*, February 8, 2018, https://www.nytimes.com /2018/02/08/sunday-review/sexual-harassment-masculine-jobs.html.

52 **If they received subpoenas compelling them to talk:** Emily Steel, "How Bill O'Reilly Silenced His Accusers," *New York Times*, April 4, 2018, https://www .nytimes.com/2018/04/04/business/media/how-bill-oreilly-silenced-his -accusers.html.

53 **Even the EEOC:** Chai Feldblum, interview by Jodi Kantor, May 11, 2017.

54 **relinquished control of Miramax, their first movie company:** After selling Miramax to Disney for $80 million in 1993, the Weinsteins separated themselves from Disney in 2005. Laura M. Holson, "How the Tumultuous Marriage of Miramax and Disney Failed," *New York Times*, March 6, 2005, https://www.nytimes.com/2005/03/06/movies/how-the-tumultuous-marriage -of-miramax-and-disney-failed.html.

59 **to the home of John Schmidt:** John Schmidt, interviews by Megan Twohey, September 2017 through spring 2019.

59 **One Friday evening:** Amy Israel, interviews by Jodi Kantor, 2017–19.

61 **Three weeks later:** Zelda Perkins, interviews by Jodi Kantor, 2017–19.

63 **Much later, Chiu told Jodi:** Rowena Chiu, interviews by Jodi Kantor, May–June 2019.

64 **With a more senior figure:** Donna Gigliotti, emails to Jodi Kantor and Kelsey Kudak, November 2017–June 2019.

65 **she questioned whether Gigliotti could:** Megan Twohey, Jodi Kantor, Susan Dominus, Jim Rutenberg, and Steve Eder, "Weinstein's Complicity Machine," *New York Times*, December 5, 2017, www.nytimes.com/interactive/2017/12/05 /us/harvey-weinstein-complicity.html.

68 **driven up to Chiu's house:** Andrew Cheung, interview by Jodi Kantor, July 2017.

71 **Amy Israel had recommended:** Laura Madden, interviews by Jodi Kantor, July 2017 through January 2019.

76 **Allred's autobiography:** Gloria Allred, *Fight Back and Win* (New York: HarperCollins, 2006); Gloria Allred, interviews by Megan Twohey, October 2016 through spring 2019.

76 **In 2011, she and a partner:** Emily Steel, "How Bill O'Reilly Silenced His Accusers," *New York Times*, April 4, 2018, https://www.nytimes.com/2018/04/04 /business/media/how-bill-oreilly-silenced-his-accusers.html.

76 **Allred was working on a settlement:** Rebecca Davis O'Brien, "USA Gymnastics, McKayla Maroney Had Confidentiality Agreement to Resolve Abuse Claims," *Wall Street Journal*, December 20, 2017, https://www.wsj.com /articles/usa-gymnastics-reached-settlement-over-abuse-claims-with-gold -medalist-mckayla-maroney-1513791179; Will Hobson, "McKayla Maroney Sues USA Gymnastics, Saying It Tried to Buy Her Silence on Abuse," *Washington Post*, December, 20, 2017, https://www.washingtonpost.com/sports /mckayla-maroney-sues-usa-gymnastics-saying-it-tried-to-buy-her-silence -on-abuse/2017/12/20/1e54b482-e5c8-11e7-a65d-1ac0fd7f097e_story.html.

76 **in 2004, Allred's firm had also negotiated a settlement:** Ashley Matthau, interviews by Megan Twohey, October 2017 through spring 2019.

78 **a group of consumer lawyers in California:** Consumer Attorneys of California, https://www.caoc.org.

78 **On a tense phone call with lobbyists:** Various participants on the call, interview by Megan Twohey, 2018.

CHAPTER FOUR: "POSITIVE REPUTATION MANAGEMENT"

79 **his parents' Creole restaurant:** Brett Anderson, "A History of the Baquets, New Orleans Restaurant Family: From the T-P Archives," NOLA, originally published July 20, 2004, republished May 15, 2014, https://www.nola.com/ dining/2014/05/from_the_t-p_archives_a_short.html; Brett Anderson, "The Importance of Eddie's: The Late-great Baquet Family Restaurant, Remembered," NOLA, May 16, 2014, https://www.nola.com/dining/2014/05 /the_importance_of_eddies_the_1.html.

80 **but Baquet was contacted by David Boies:** Information taken from Megan Twohey interviews, from 2017 through spring 2019, of Boies and those familiar

with his representation of Harvey Weinstein, and emails and other records that included comments made by Boies from 2015 through 2017, as well as the following articles about him: Daniel Okrent, "Get Me Boies!" *Time*, December 25, 2000, http://content.time.com/time/world/article/0,8599,2047286,00.html; Andrew Rice, "The Bad, Good Lawyer: Was David Boies Just Doing Right by Harvey Weinstein? Or Did He Cross an Ethical Line?" *New York* magazine, September 30, 2018, http://nymag.com/intelligencer/2018/09 /david-boies-harvey-weinstein-lawyer.html.

80 **"I'm not calling as Harvey's lawyer":** Dean Baquet, interviews by Megan Twohey and Jodi Kantor, 2018.

82 **On August 3:** Lanny Davis, interview by Megan Twohey and Jodi Kantor, August 3, 2017.

88 **In 2002, the *New Yorker* writer:** Auletta heard about the settlements while working on a profile of Harvey Weinstein. Ken Auletta, "Beauty and the Beast," *New Yorker*, December 8, 2002, https://www.newyorker.com/magazine/2002/12 /16/beauty-and-the-beast-2.

89 **Auletta, David Remnick, the magazine's editor:** Ken Auletta, Bob Weinstein, David Boies, interviews by Megan Twohey, 2019.

91 **The producer had long relied on private detectives:** Megan Twohey, Jodi Kantor, Susan Dominus, Jim Rutenberg, and Steve Eder, "Weinstein's Complicity Machine," *New York Times,* December 5, 2017, www.nytimes.com /interactive/2017/12/05/us/harvey-weinstein-complicity.html.

92 **Under the terms of a contract:** Alana Goodman, "Harvey Weinstein's ORIGINAL contract with ex-Mossad agents ordered them to prove he was the victim of a 'negative campaign' in what was dubbed 'Operation Parachute'— spying on actresses, close friend designer Kenneth Cole and amfAR," *Daily Mail,* November 8, 2017, https://www.dailymail.co.uk/news/article-5062195 /Harvey-Weinstein-agreed-pay-1-3m-ex-Mossad-agents.html.

92 **Seth Freedman, a British freelance journalist:** Twohey and Kantor interviews of McGowan, Kendall, and others who were contacted by Seth Freedman in 2016 and 2017, and emails sent by Freedman.

92 **Black Cube went to work on Benjamin Wallace:** Benjamin Wallace, interview by Megan Twohey, 2018, and 2016 emails between Wallace and Seth Freedman.

92 **By May 2017:** Ronan Farrow, "Harvey Weinstein's Army of Spies," *New Yorker*, November 6, 2017, www.newyorker.com/news/news-desk/harvey-weinsteins -army-of-spies.

93 **Under the contract that Boies helped revise:** "Read: The Contract Between a Private Security Firm and One of Harvey Weinstein's Lawyers," *New Yorker*, November 6, 2017, https://www.newyorker.com/sections/news/read-the -contract-between-a-private-security-firm-and-one-of-harvey-weinsteins -lawyers.

93 **Jodi received a series:** "Diana Filip," email to Jodi Kantor, August 8, 2017. The associated website, Reuben Capital Partners, has been stripped; screenshots of the website were published. Alana Goodman, "EXCLUSIVE: The SPY Who Duped Rose McGowan UNMASKED! This is the blonde Israeli military veteran who worked undercover for disgraced mogul Harvey Weinstein and tricked the actress into sharing her memoirs," *Daily Mail*, November 8, 2017, https://www.dailymail.co.uk/news/article-5064027/Israeli-military-vet-duped -Rose-McGowan-revealed.html.

95 **profile of Gloria Allred and Lisa Bloom:** Alexandra Pechman, "Gloria Allred and Lisa Bloom Are the Defenders of Women in 2017," *W*, July 21, 2017, https: //www.wmagazine.com/story/gloria-allred-lisa-bloom-donald-trump-blac -chyna-lawyer.

96 **Megan had never spoken to Bloom:** Megan Twohey, email to Lisa Bloom, November 1, 2016.

97 **Bloom convened a press conference:** Stephen Feller, "Trump Rape Accuser Cancels Press Conference after Death Threats," *United Press International*, November 3, 2016, https://www.upi.com/Top_News/US/2016/11/03/Trump -rape-accuser-cancels-press-conference-after-death-threats/2381478150421.

97 **Bloom acknowledged that she solicited money:** Kenneth P. Vogel, "Partisans, Wielding Money, Begin Seeking to Exploit Harassment Claim," *New York Times*, December 31, 2017, https://www.nytimes.com/2017/12/31/us/politics/sexual -harassment-politics-partisanship.html.

97 **spent months vetting Jane Doe:** Lisa Bloom, interview by Kantor and Twohey, 2019; Lisa Bloom email to Megan Twohey, June 2019.

97 **Steel had quietly begun interviewing:** Tamara Holder, interviews by Megan
Twohey, summer 2018 through spring 2019; emails between Tamara Holder
and Lisa Bloom; Lloyd Grove, "Clients Turn on 'Champion for Women' Lisa
Bloom after Her Scorched-earth Crusade for Harvey Weinstein," *Daily Beast*,
October 26, 2017, https://www.thedailybeast.com/lisa-bloom-has-files-on
-rose-mcgowans-history-inside-her-scorched-earth-crusade-for-harvey
-weinstein; Emily Steel, "Fox Is Said to Settle With Former Contributor Over
Sexual Assault Claims," *New York Times*, March 8, 2017, https://www.nytimes
.com/2017/03/08/business/fox-news-roger-ailes-sexual-assault-settlement
.html.

98 **As the show struggled to get off the ground:** Twohey's amfAR reporting
included interviews of amfAR board members, including its then chairman
Kenneth Cole, Harvey Weinstein, David Boies, Charles Prince, and others with
knowledge of the $600,000 raised at an amfAR charity auction that flowed to
Finding Neverland investors. It also included emails and other documents from
2015 to 2017 that outlined the financial transaction, concern about the
transaction among certain members of amfAR's staff and board, and how
Weinstein responded to attempts to investigate it; Megan Twohey, "Tumult
after AIDS Fund-Raiser Supports Harvey Weinstein Production," *New York
Times,* September 23, 2017, https://www.nytimes.com/2017/09/23/nyregion
/harvey-weinstein-charity.html.

99 **Megan was meeting Tom Ajamie:** Tom Ajamie, interviews by
Megan Twohey, summer 2017 through spring 2019.

100 **Bloom had already been working with the producer:** December 2016 billing
records from Lisa Bloom's law firm, The Bloom Firm.

104 **"Based on social media activity and comments":** Sara Ness, Draft Report
submitted to Harvey Weinstein, July 2017.

CHAPTER FIVE: A COMPANY'S COMPLICITY

108 **To keep the dialogue over email going:** Irwin Reiter emails to Jodi Kantor,
September 2017.

108 **On Monday night, September 18:** Irwin Reiter, interviews by Jodi Kantor and
Megan Twohey, September 2017 through May 2019.

110 Cosby's TV projects and tour dates evaporated: Frank Pallotta and Molly Shiels, "NBC Says It's Not Moving Forward with Bill Cosby Project," CNN, November 19, 2014, https://money.cnn.com/2014/11/19/media/cosby-nbc -sitcom/index.html; Goeff Edgers, "Bill Cosby's 'Far from Finished' Tour Pushes On: But Will It Be His Last?" *Washington Post,* March 24, 2015, https:// www.washingtonpost.com/entertainment/bill-cosbys-far-from-finished-tour -pushes-on-will-it-be-his-last/2015/03/24/d665bee4-cf1f-11e4-8a46 -b1dc9be5a8ff_story.html; Todd Leopold, "Cancellations Have Dogged Cosby's Tour," CNN, February 21, 2015, https://www.cnn.com/2015/02/20/ entertainment/feat-cosby-tour-cancellations/index.html.

111 By her second day of work: From emails and other internal Weinstein Company records from 2014 and 2015.

111 "She said he was very persistent": Ibid.

112 Shari pressed forward: Shari Reiter, interview by Jodi Kantor, October 25, 2018.

112 Rehal was Weinstein's personal assistant: Sandeep Rehal, interviews by Jodi Kantor, November 2018.

113 $2.5 million in 2015: Harvey Weinstein's contract with The Weinstein Company.

113 Reiter wrote to Tom Prince: Email exchanges between Tom Prince and Irwin Reiter, February 2015.

114 was having eerily similar conversations: Michelle Franklin, interviews by Jodi Kantor, 2017–19.

115 On the afternoon of September 19: Harvey Weinstein, Jason Lilien, Lanny Davis, Charlie Prince, Roberta Kaplan, and Karen Duffy, interview by Megan Twohey and Rebecca Corbett, September 19, 2017.

119 "I'm worse": Harvey Weinstein interview by Jodi Kantor, September 19, 2017.

120 eager to see him charged: Megan Twohey, James C. McKinley Jr., Al Baker, and William K. Rashbaum, "For Weinstein, a Brush With the Police, Then No Charges," *New York Times,* October 15, 2017, https://www.nytimes.com/2017 /10/15/nyregion/harvey-weinstein-new-york-sex-assault-investigation.html.

121 **Boies and Abramowitz shared the documents:** Ken Auletta, David Boies, interviews by Megan Twohey, 2019.

121 **Weinstein paid Gutierrez:** Twohey interviews of people familiar with the settlement and internal Weinstein Company records from 2015.

121 **copy of the audio recording:** Ronan Farrow, "Harvey Weinstein's Secret Settlements," *New Yorker,* November 21, 2017, https://www.newyorker.com /news/news-desk/harvey-weinsteins-secret-settlements.

122 **No one had more incentive to hold Weinstein accountable:** Based on Megan Twohey interviews in 2018 and 2019 of Bob Weinstein, Megan Twohey and Jodi Kantor interviews of those who worked with him, as well as emails and other internal Weinstein Company records.

123 **When Harvey Weinstein needed money:** Megan Twohey interview of Bob Weinstein; Ronan Farrow, "Harvey Weinstein's Secret Settlements," *New Yorker,* November 21, 2017, https://www.newyorker.com/news/news-desk/harvey -weinsteins-secret-settlements.

123 **One day in 2010 or 2011:** Bob Weinstein, interview by Megan Twohey, 2018; and Irwin Reiter, interviews by Jodi Kantor, 2017-19.

124 **Bob sent David Boies an email:** Bob Weinstein, email to David Boies, August 16, 2015.

128 **But Lance Maerov, who had been appointed:** Lance Maerov interviews by Megan Twohey, September 2016 through spring 2019; interviews of those who worked with Maerov; emails and other internal Weinstein Company records.

130 **Rodgin Cohen, one of the most prominent corporate lawyers:** H. Rodgin Cohen, email to Philip Richter, an attorney for The Weinstein Company board, September 4, 2015.

132 **The New York Attorney General's office:** Megan Twohey and William K. Rashbaum, "Transactions Tied to Weinstein and AIDS Charity Are Under Investigation," *New York Times,* November 2, 2017. https://www.nytimes.com /2017/11/02/nyregion/harvey-weinstein-amfar.html.

133 a long detailed complaint: Internal Weinstein Company records from 2015 and 2016.

CHAPTER SIX: "WHO ELSE IS ON THE RECORD?"

151 **At the start of his newspaper career:** Dean Baquet, interviews by Jodi Kantor and Megan Twohey, 2018.

154 **When the call itself began:** Harvey Weinstein, Charles Harder, Lisa Bloom, and Lanny Davis, interview by Jodi Kantor, Megan Twohey, and Rebecca Corbett, October 3, 2017.

154 **Harder had made a name:** Eriq Gardner, "Ailes Media Litigator Charles Harder on His Improbable Rise with Clients Melania Trump and Hulk Hogan," *Hollywood Reporter*, September 22, 2016, https://www.hollywoodreporter .com/thr-esq/ailes-media-litigator-charles-harder-930963.

154 **shut down the gossip website Gawker:** Sydney Ember, "Gawker and Hulk Hogan Reach $31 Million Settlement," *New York Times*, November 2, 2016, https://www.nytimes.com/2016/11/03/business/media/gawker-hulk-hogan -settlement.html.

154 **He had represented Roger Ailes:** Brian Stelter, "Roger Ailes Enlists Lawyer behind Hulk Hogan and Melania Trump Suits," *CNN Money*, September 5, 2016, https://money.cnn.com/2016/09/05/media/roger-ailes-charles-harder/index .html.

154 **After he negotiated a $2.9 million settlement:** Tom Hamburger, "Melania Trump Missed Out on 'Once-in-a-Lifetime Opportunity' to Make Millions, Lawsuit Says," *Washington Post*, February 7, 2017, https://www.washingtonpost .com/politics/melania-trump-missed-out-on-once-in-a-lifetime-opportunity -to-make-millions-lawsuit-says/2017/02/06/3654f070-ecd0-11e6-9973 -c5efb7ccfb0d_story.html?utm_term=.1f8e8f635b8c&tid=a_inl_manual; Emily Hell, "When They Go Low, Melania Trump Calls Her Lawyers," *Washington Post*, January 30, 2019, https://www.washingtonpost.com/lifestyle/style/when -they-go-low-melania-trump-calls-her-lawyers/2019/01/30/d3892a1e-240a -11e9-ad53-824486280311_story.html?utm_term=.09e90f097c14; Glenn Feishman, "Trump Hires Harder, Hulk Hogan's Gawker-Toppling Lawyer in

Dispute Against Omarosa," *Fortune*, August 14, 2018, http://fortune.com/2018 /08/14/trump-charles-harder-gawker-lawyer-hulk-hogan-omarosa.

154 **"the very notion of a free press":** Jason Zengerle, "Charles Harder, the Lawyer Who Killed Gawker, Isn't Done Yet," *GQ*, November 17, 2016, https://www.gq .com/story/charles-harder-gawker-lawyer.

158 **"it's going to be bad":** Lance Maerov, David Boies, and David Glasser, interviews by Megan Twohey, 2018 and 2019.

158 **"We can nip at it around the edges":** Lisa Bloom, email to Harvey Weinstein, Lanny Davis, Charles Harder, and David Boies, October 4, 2017.

CHAPTER SEVEN: "THERE WILL BE A MOVEMENT"

161 **Megan called David Glasser:** David Glasser, interviews by Megan Twohey, October 2017 and spring 2019.

162 **At 1:43 p.m., Team Weinstein's answer landed:** Charles Harder, email to Diane Brayton, Arthur Sulzberger Jr., Dean Baquet, Jodi Kantor, and Megan Twohey, October 4, 2017.

165 **At 3:33 p.m., McCraw forwarded the reporters:** David McCraw, email to Charles Harder, October 4, 2017.

168 **Jodi and Megan sat down to read about themselves:** Brent Lang, Gene Maddaus, and Ramin Setoodeh, "Harvey Weinstein Lawyers Up for Bombshell *New York Times*, *New Yorker* Stories," *Variety*, October 4, 2017, https://variety .com/2017/film/news/harvey-weinstein-sexual-new-york-times-1202580605; Kim Masters, Chris Gardner, "Harvey Weinstein Lawyers Battling *N.Y. Times*, *New Yorker* Over Potentially Explosive Stories," *Hollywood Reporter*, October 4, 2017, https://www.hollywoodreporter.com/news/harvey-weinstein-lawyers -battling-ny-times-new-yorker-potentially-explosive-stories-1045724.

170 **"My mom is just my mom":** Gracie Allen, interview by Jodi Kantor, 2018.

172 **Suddenly, Weinstein himself was on the phone:** Weinstein and Bloom, interview by Jodi Kantor and Megan Twohey, October 5, 2017.

176 **Tolan pushed the button:** Jodi Kantor and Megan Twohey, "Harvey Weinstein Paid Off Sexual Harassment Accusers for Decades," *New York Times*, October 5, 2017, https://www.nytimes.com/2017/10/05/us/harvey-weinstein-harassment -allegations.html.

178 **most of the directors would resign:** Bruce Haring, "Fifth Weinstein Company Board Member Resigns, Leaving Three Remaining," *Deadline*, October 14, 2017, https://deadline.com/2017/10/fifth-weinstein-company-board-member-resigns -leaving-three-left-1202188563.

179 **Katherine Kendall said:** The stories of Tomi-Ann Roberts, as well as Katherine Kendall, Dawn Dunning, and Judith Godrèche, were all depicted in the *New York Times* in the following weeks. Jodi Kantor and Rachel Abrams, "Gwyneth Paltrow, Angelina Jolie and Others Say Weinstein Harassed Them," *New York Times*, October 10, 2017, https://www.nytimes.com/2017/10/10/us/gwyneth -paltrow-angelina-jolie-harvey-weinstein.html; the stories of Hope d'Amore and Cynthia Burr were depicted thereafter. Ellen Gabler, Megan Twohey, and Jodi Kantor, "New Accusers Expand Harvey Weinstein Sexual Assault Claims Back to '70s," *New York Times*, October 30, 2017, https://www.nytimes.com /2017/10/30/us/harvey-weinstein-sexual-assault-allegations.html.

179 **Ronan Farrow was finishing:** Ronan Farrow, "From Aggressive Overtures to Sexual Assault: Harvey Weinstein's Accusers Tell Their Stories," *New Yorker*, October 10, 2017, https://www.newyorker.com/news/news-desk/from -aggressive-overtures-to-sexual-assault-harvey-weinsteins-accusers-tell-their -stories.html.

179 **Lauren Sivan, a television journalist:** Yashar Ali, "TV Journalist Says Harvey Weinstein Masturbated in Front of Her," *Huffington Post*, October 6, 2017, https: //www.huffingtonpost.com/entry/weinstein-sexual-harassment-allegation_us _59d7ea3de4b046f5ad984211.

180 **when Megan later revealed in the paper:** Nicole Pelletiere, "Harvey Weinstein's Adviser, Lisa Bloom, Speaks Out: 'There was misconduct,'" ABC, October 6, 2017, https://abcnews.go.com/Entertainment/harvey-weinsteins -adviser-lisa-bloom-speaks-misconduct/story?id=50321561; Megan Twohey and Johanna Barr, "Lisa Bloom, Lawyer Advising Harvey Weinstein, Resigns Amid Criticism From Board Members," *New York Times*, October 7, 2017, https://www.nytimes.com/2017/10/07/business/lisa-bloom-weinstein -attorney.htm.

CHAPTER EIGHT: THE BEACHSIDE DILEMMA

181 **When Jodi got a tip:** Melena Ryzik, Cara Buckley, and Jodi Kantor, "Louis C. K. Is Accused by 5 Women of Sexual Misconduct," *New York Times,* November 9, 2017, https://www.nytimes.com/2017/11/09/arts/television/louis-ck-sexual-misconduct.html.

183 **in search of a woman named Stormy Daniels:** Michael Rothfeld and Joe Palazzolo, "Trump Lawyer Arranged $130,000 Payment for Adult-Film Star's Silence," *Wall Street Journal,* January 12, 2018, https://www.wsj.com/articles/trump-lawyer-arranged-130-000-payment-for-adult-film-stars-silence-1515787678; Megan Twohey and Jim Rutenberg, "Porn Star Was Reportedly Paid to Stay Quiet about Trump," *New York Times,* January 12, 2018, https://www.nytimes.com/2018/01/12/us/trump-stephanie-clifford-stormy-daniels.html.

183 **in 2016, American Media Inc.:** Joe Palazzolo, Michael Rothfeld, and Lukas I. Alpert, "*National Enquirer* Shielded Donald Trump from Playboy Model's Affair Allegation," *Wall Street Journal,* November 4, 2016, https://www.wsj.com/articles/national-enquirer-shielded-donald-trump-from-playboy-models-affair-allegation-1478309380; Ronan Farrow, "Trump, a Playboy Model, and a System for Concealing Infidelity," *New Yorker,* February 16, 2018, https://www.newyorker.com/news/news-desk/donald-trump-a-playboy-model-and-a-system-for-concealing-infidelity-national-enquirer-karen-mcdougal; Jim Rutenberg, Megan Twohey, Rebecca R. Ruiz, Mike McIntire, and Maggie Haberman, "Tools of Trump's Fixer: Payouts, Intimidation and the Tabloids," *New York Times,* February 18, 2018, https://www.nytimes.com/2018/02/18/us/politics/michael-cohen-trump.html; Ronan Farrow, "Harvey Weinstein's Army of Spies," *New Yorker,* November 6, 2017, https://www.newyorker.com/news/news-desk/harvey-weinsteins-army-of-spies; Mike McIntire, Charlie Savage, and Jim Rutenberg, "Tabloid Publisher's Deal in Hush-Money Inquiry Adds to Trump's Danger," *New York Times,* December 12, 2018, https://www.nytimes.com/2018/12/12/nyregion/trump-american-media-michael-cohen.html.

184 **"He's now experiencing all the things he's put everybody else through":** Melena Ryzik, "Weinstein in Handcuffs Is a 'Start to Justice' for His Accusers," *New York Times,* October 25, 2018, https://www.nytimes.com/2018/05/25/nyregion/metoo-accusers-harvey-weinstein.html.

186 **Democrats were split:** Laura McGann, "The Still Raging Controversy Over Al Franken's Resignation, Explained," *Vox,* May 21, 2018, https://www.vox.com

/2018/5/21/17352230/al-franken-accusations-resignation-democrats-leann
-tweeden-kirsten-gillibrand.

186 **Brafman gave a radio interview:** "Defending 'Brilliant' Harvey Weinstein,"
BBC, June 15, 2018, https://www.bbc.co.uk/sounds/play/p0664pjp.

187 **Kim Lawson, a twenty-five-year-old:** Kim Lawson, interviews by Jodi Kantor,
2018–19.

188 **The attorney Debra Katz, who specialized in sexual harassment:** Debra Katz,
interviews by Jodi Kantor and Megan Twohey, 2018–19.

191 **Her name was Christine Blasey Ford:** Christine Blasey Ford, interviews by
Megan Twohey, December 2017 through May 2019, and written communication
between Ford and her friends, members of the Senate Judiciary Committee,
and one of her lawyers. The paper in question can be found at https://www
.researchgate.net/publication/327287729_Attenuation_of_Antidepressant
_Effects_of_Ketamine_by_Opioid_Receptor_Antagonism.

192 **"She said she was eventually able to escape":** "Declaration of Russell Ford,"
Senate Judiciary Committee Investigation of Numerous Allegations Against
Justice Brett Kavanaugh During the Senate Confirmation Proceedings,
November 2, 2018, https://www.judiciary.senate.gov/imo/media/doc/2018-11
-02%20Kavanaugh%20Report.pdf, 55-56.

192 **In the spring of 2016, she and a friend:** Keith Koegler, interview by Megan
Twohey, 2019; Christine Blasey Ford, interviews by Megan Twohey, 2018–19.

194 **Their second date had taken place:** Jessica Contrera, Ian Shapira, Emma
Brown, and Steve Hendrix, "Kavanaugh Accuser Christine Blasey Ford Moved
3,000 Miles to Reinvent Her Life: It Wasn't Far Enough," *Washington Post,*
September 22, 2018, https://www.washingtonpost.com/local/christine-blasey
-ford-wanted-to-flee-the-us-to-avoid-brett-kavanaugh-now-she-may-testify
-against-him/2018/09/22/db942340-bdb1-11e8-8792-78719177250f_story
.html.

196 **The next morning, July 10, Ford returned:** WhatsApp messages from Christine
Blasey Ford to *Washington Post* Tip Line, Senate Judiciary Committee
Investigation of Numerous Allegations Against Justice Brett Kavanaugh
During the Senate Confirmation Proceedings, November 2, 2018, https://www

.judiciary.senate.gov/imo/media/doc/2018-11-02%20Kavanaugh%20Report
.pdf, 46.

196 **a mother who raved:** Julie O'Brien, "I Don't Know Kavanaugh the Judge, but Kavanaugh the Carpool Dad Is One Great Guy," *Washington Post,* July 20, 2018, https://www.washingtonpost.com/opinions/i-dont-know-kavanaugh-the-judge -but-kavanaugh-the-carpool-dad-is-one-great-guy/2018/07/10/a1866a2c-8446 -11e8-9e80-403a221946a7_story.html.

197 **On July 18, she met with Karen Chapman:** Christine Blasey Ford, interviews by Megan Twohey, 2018–19; Mathew McMurray, email to Kelsey Kodak, June 17, 2019.

200 **"Got it!" the aide wrote back:** Email from Dianne Feinstein's office to Christine Blasey Ford, July 2018.

200 **"She did not try to minimize the gaps in her memory":** Lawrence Robbins, interview by Megan Twohey, January 2019.

202 **Her law partner, Lisa Banks:** Depiction of Debra Katz based on Megan Twohey and Jodi Kantor interviews of Katz from August 2017 through spring 2019; Lisa Banks, interviews by Megan Twohey and Jodi Kantor, October 2017 through spring 2019; written communications to and from the lawyers.

204 **took on another adviser:** Barry Coburn, interview by Megan Twohey, February 2019.

206 **In August, Ronan Farrow:** Ronan Farrow, "Les Moonves and CBS Face Allegations of Sexual Misconduct," *New Yorker,* August 6, 2018, https://www .newyorker.com/magazine/2018/08/06/les-moonves-and-cbs-face-allegations -of-sexual-misconduct.

206 **Louis C.K. made his first appearance:** Melena Ryzik, "Louis C.K. Performs First Stand-up Set at Club Since Admitting to #MeToo Cases," *New York Times,* August 27, 2018, https://www.nytimes.com/2018/08/27/arts/television /louis-ck-performs-comedy.html.

206 **was about to release his latest book:** Hillel Italie, "Next O'Reilly Book Coming in September," Associated Press, April 23, 2018, https://www.apnews.com /f00002d9107742b991fecb982312243b.

CHAPTER NINE: "I CAN'T GUARANTEE I'LL GO TO DC"

211 **Five days later, on Tuesday:** Christine Blasey Ford, interview by Megan Twohey, 2018–19.

211 **a reference to Margaret Atwood's dystopian feminist novel:** Sheryl Gay Stolberg, Adam Liptak, and Charlie Savage, "Takeaways from Day 1 of Brett Kavanaugh's Confirmation Hearings," *New York Times,* September 4, 2018, https://www.nytimes.com/2018/09/04/us/politics/kavanaugh-confirmation-hearing-updates.html.

211 **Republicans, unified behind Trump's pick, were lashing back:** Ibid.

212 **On Wednesday, September 12, an article appeared:** Ryan Grim, "Dianne Feinstein Withholding Brett Kavanaugh Document from Fellow Judiciary Committee Democrats," *The Intercept,* September 12, 2018, https://theintercept.com/2018/09/12/brett-kavanaugh-confirmation-dianne-feinstein.

212 **the senator announced by press release:** Dianne Feinstein, "Feinstein Statement on Kavanaugh," United States Senator for California, Dianne Feinstein, September 13, 2018, https://www.feinstein.senate.gov/public/index.cfm/press-releases?ID=FB52FCD4-29C8-4856-A679-B5C6CC553DC4.

214 **people were absorbing the article:** Emma Brown, "California Professor, Writer of Confidential Brett Kavanaugh Letter, Speaks Out about Her Allegation of Sexual Assault," *Washington Post,* September 16, 2018, https://www.washingtonpost.com/investigations/california-professor-writer-of-confidential-brett-kavanaugh-letter-speaks-out-about-her-allegation-of-sexual-assault/2018/09/16/46982194-b846-11e8-94eb-3bd52dfe917b_story.html.

215 **Kavanaugh's denial, issued the Friday before:** Seung Min Kim, "Kavanaugh Denies Decades-old Allegation of Potential Sexual Misconduct," *Washington Post,* September 14, 2018, https://www.washingtonpost.com/politics/kavanaugh-denies-decades-old-allegation-of-potential-sexual-misconduct/2018/09/14/60ee3ae8-b831-11e8-94eb-3bd52dfe917b_story.html?utm_term=.7d6c36ca93cf.

215 **"You've got to deny, deny, deny":** Bob Woodward, *Fear: Trump in the White House* (New York: Simon & Schuster, 2018), 175.

215 **the president had mocked:** Aaron Blake, "'I Don't Believe Them': Trump Doubts Sexual Abuse Accusers and Sides with an Ally—Again," *Washington Post,*

July 6, 2018, https://www.washingtonpost.com/news/the-fix/wp/2018/07/06
/i-dont-believe-them-trump-doubts-sexual-abuse-accusers-and-sides-with
-an-ally-again.

216 **"I oppose Kavanaugh's nomination":** Rosa Brooks (@brooks_rosa),"Tweet 1 of
a bunch: I oppose Kavanaugh's nomination, think senators should vote no based
on his judicial record, but am uncomfortable with asserting that his behavior as
a teen tells us anything about his "character" now," Twitter, September 16, 2018,
https://twitter.com/brooks_rosa/status/1041482381625122816.

216 **Katz was on morning news shows:** "Lawyer: Kavanaugh Accuser Willing to
Testify," CNN, September 17, 2018, https://www.cnn.com/videos/politics
/2018/09/17/kavanaugh-accuser-christine-ford-attorney-debra-katz-newday
-sot.cnn.

217 **Senate, Judiciary Committee chairman Chuck Grassley:** Descriptions of the
negotiations between Ford's team and the Republican staff of the US Senate
Judiciary Committee based on Twohey and Kantor interviews of Katz and
Banks; Twohey interview of Mike Davis; written communication included in
Senate Judiciary Committee Investigation of Numerous Allegations Against
Justice Brett Kavanaugh During the Senate Confirmation Proceedings,
November 2, 2018, https://www.judiciary.senate.gov/imo/media/doc/2018-11
-02%20Kavanaugh%20Report.pdf; additional emails provided by Katz.

217 **That summer, the Senate Judiciary Committee:** Lydia Weaver, "Senate
Judiciary Urges Response to Sexual Harassment in Federal Courts," *The Hill*,
June 13, 2018, https://thehill.com/regulation/392075-senate-judiciary-wants
-response-to-sexual-harassment-in-federal-courts.

218 **"She should not be ignored":** "Kellyanne Conway Says Kavanaugh Accuser
'Should Not Be Ignored,'" NBC, September 17, 2018, https://www.nbcnews.com
/video/kellyanne-conway-says-kavanaugh-accuser-should-not-be-ignored
-1322246211718.

219 **Anita Hill worried aloud:** Anita Hill, "How to Get the Kavanaugh Hearings
Right," *New York Times*, September 18, 2018, https://www.nytimes.com/2018/
09/18/opinion/anita-hill-brett-kavanaugh-clarence-thomas.html.

220 **Judge had written two memoirs:** Dwight Garner, "What a Book Critic Finds in
Mark Judge's 'Wasted' 21 Years Later," *New York Times*, October 2, 2018, https:
//www.nytimes.com/2018/10/02/books/wasted-mark-judge-memoir.html.

220 Instead, his staff accepted a written statement from Judge: Senate Judiciary
Committee Investigation of Numerous Allegations Against Justice Brett
Kavanaugh During the Senate Confirmation Proceedings, November 2, 2018,
https://www.judiciary.senate.gov/imo/media/doc/2018-11-02%20Kavanaugh
%20Report.pdf, 79.

220 The staff also accepted a similar written statement from P. J. Smyth: Senate
Judiciary Committee Investigation of Numerous Allegations Against Justice
Brett Kavanaugh During the Senate Confirmation Proceedings, November 2,
2018, https://www.judiciary.senate.gov/imo/media/doc/2018-11-02%20
Kavanaugh%20Report.pdf, 90–91.

221 Part of a coordinated strategy: Mike Davis, interview by Megan Twohey, June
2019.

222 "You lying fucking cunt!": Barry Coburn and Christine Blasey Ford, interviews
by Megan Twohey, 2019.

223 CNN was flashing a confidential list of demands: Transcript, "Trump's Star
Gets Bars; Kavanaugh Accuser Open to Testifying; Conway's Interview
Reviewed," CNN, September 21, 2018, http://transcripts.cnn.com/
TRANSCRIPTS/1809/21/nday.06.html.

223 Trump was now directly casting doubt on Ford's allegation: Donald J. Trump
(@realdonaldtrump), "I have no doubt that, if the attack on Dr. Ford was as bad
as she says, charges would have been immediately filed with local Law
Enforcement Authorities by either her or her loving parents. I ask that she bring
those filings forward so that we can learn date, time, and place!" Twitter,
September 21, 2018, https://twitter.com/realdonaldtrump/status/
1043126336473055235.

223 At a gathering of Evangelical activists: "'We're going to plow right through it,'
McConnell says on Kavanaugh nomination," *Washington Post*, September 21,
2018, https://www.washingtonpost.com/video/politics/were-going-to-plow
-right-through-it-mcconnell-says-on-kavanaugh-nomination/2018/09/21
/39beef50-bdac-11e8-8243-f3ae9c99658a_video.html?utm_term=.56cd2476da50.

223 the entire committee would vote: "Judiciary Committee Continues Effort to
Accommodate Testimony from Dr. Ford Next Week," Senate Judiciary
Committee, September 21, 2018, https://www.judiciary.senate.gov/press/rep

/releases/judiciary-committee-continues-effort-to-accommodate-testimony
-from-dr-ford-next-week.

224 **Grassley tweeted out word of his concession:** The time stamp on Grassley's
tweet has defaulted to Pacific Coast time, which is why the tweet reads 8:42
p.m. Pacific time, but Grassley actually published this tweet at 11:42 p.m.
Eastern time. Chuck Grassley (@ChuckGrassley), "Judge Kavanaugh I just
granted another extension to Dr Ford to decide if she wants to proceed w the
statement she made last week to testify to the senate She shld decide so we can
move on I want to hear her. I hope u understand. It's not my normal approach to
b indecisive," Twitter, September 21, 2018, https://twitter.com/ChuckGrassley
/status/1043344767684366336.

225 **the account of Deborah Ramirez:** Ronan Farrow and Jane Mayer, "Senate
Democrats Investigate a New Allegation of Sexual Misconduct, from Brett
Kavanaugh's College Years," *New Yorker,* September 23, 2018, https://www
.newyorker.com/news/news-desk/senate-democrats-investigate-a-new
-allegation-of-sexual-misconduct-from-the-supreme-court-nominee-brett
-kavanaughs-college-years-deborah-ramirez.

225 **At practically the same moment, Michael Avenatti:** Lisa Ryan, "What
'Credible Information' Does Michael Avenatti Have on Kavanaugh?" *The Cut,*
September 24, 2018, https://www.thecut.com/2018/09/michael-avenatti
-kavanaugh-judge-client-tweets.html.

228 **"I'll sleep with you":** Rebecca Corbett, interviews by Megan Twohey and Jodi
Kantor, 2018–19.

228 **that evening's article about the politics of Ford's upcoming testimony:** Sheryl
Gay Stolberg and Nicholas Fandos, "Christine Blasey Ford Reaches Deal to
Testify at Kavanaugh Hearing," *New York Times,* September 23, 2018, https:
//www.nytimes.com/2018/09/23/us/politics/brett-kavanaugh-christine-blasey
-ford-testify.html.

228 **Now, in an appearance on *CBS This Morning*:** Emily Tillett, "Kellyanne
Conway says Brett Kavanaugh allegations feel like 'a vast left-wing conspiracy,'"
CBS This Morning, September 24, 2018, https://www.cbsnews.com/news
/kellyanne-conway-says-brett-kavanaugh-accusers-allegations-feel-like-a
-vast-left-wing-conspiracy-2018-09-24.

228 **"shameful smear campaign":** "McConnell slams 'shameful smear campaign' against Kavanaugh," *Washington Post*, September 24, 2018, https://www
.washingtonpost.com/video/politics/mcconnell-slams-shameful-smear
-campaign-against-kavanaugh/2018/09/24/f739f09a-c02f-11e8-9f4f-a1b7af
255aa5_video.html?utm_term=.6d2f69646c81.

228 **Kavanaugh released a letter:** "Brett Kavanaugh defends himself in letter to Senate Judiciary Committee," CNN, September 24, 2018, https://www.cnn
.com/2018/09/24/politics/read-brett-kavanaugh-letter-senate-judiciary
-committee/index.html.

228 **"He jumped into this thing":** Mike Davis, interview by Megan Twohey, June 2019.

231 **"Bill Cosby, Once a Model of Fatherhood":** Graham Bowley and Joe Coscarelli, "Bill Cosby, Once a Model of Fatherhood, Sentenced to Prison," *New York Times*, September 25, 2018, https://www.nytimes.com/2018/09/25/arts/television
/bill-cosby-sentencing.html.

231 **Trump was on television:** Press Conference by President Trump," The White House, September 27, 2018, https://www.whitehouse.gov/briefings-statements
/press-conference-president-trump-2.

233 **As the proceedings came to order, Ford began to read her statement:** Christine Blasey Ford, Opening Statement, Kavanaugh Hearing, September 27, 2018, https://www.c-span.org/video/?c4760434/christine-blasey-ford-opening
-statement.

235 **sexual assault survivors were calling in:** "Brenda from Missouri calls into C-SPAN," C-SPAN, September 27, 2018, https://www.c-span.org/video
/?c4751718/brenda-missouri-calls-span.

235 **Ford "very compelling":** "Trump's Evolving Statements on Christine Blasey Ford," Associated Press, October 3, 2018, https://apnews.com/04e24ef006f44
87282e2f9be3faf0a01.

235 **George W. Bush had brushed away stories:** Jim Yardley, "Bush, Irked at Being Asked, Brushes Off Drug Question," *New York Times*, August 19, 1999, https://www.nytimes.com/1999/08/19/us/bush-irked-at-being-asked-brushes
-off-drug-question.html.

236 "This whole two-week effort has been a calculated and orchestrated political hit": "Kavanaugh Hearing: Transcript," *Washington Post*, September 27, 2018, https://www.washingtonpost.com/news/national/wp/2018/09/27/kavanaugh -hearing-transcript.

236 widely seen as not credible: David Bauder, "NBC Faces Scrutiny for Interview with Kavanaugh Accuser," Associated Press, October 2, 2018, https://www .apnews.com/42674fffa6dd4c108ccd908bee7c856e.

237 That was not true: Senate Judiciary Committee Investigation of Numerous Allegations Against Justice Brett Kavanaugh During the Senate Confirmation Proceedings, November 2, 2018, https://www.judiciary.senate.gov/imo/media /doc/2018-11-02%20Kavanaugh%20Report.pdf, 93; Seung Min Kim, Sean Sullivan, and Emma Brown, "Christine Blasey Ford Moves Closer to Deal with Senate Republicans to Testify against Kavanaugh," *Washington Post*, September 23, 2018, https://www.washingtonpost.com/politics/lawyers-for-christine -blasey-ford-say-she-has-accepted-senate-judiciary-committees-request-to -testify-against-kavanaugh/2018/09/22/e8199c6a-be8f-11e8-8792-78719177250f _story.html?utm_term=.296382a233b1.

240 a five-page memo: Rachel Mitchell, "Memorandum, Analysis of Dr. Christine Ford's Allegations," September 30, 2018, https://www.jimhopper.com/pdf /mitchell_memo_highlighted.pdf.

240 Three nights later, Trump mocked her gleefully: Allie Malloy, Kate Sullivan, and Jeff Zeleny, "Trump mocks Christine Blasey Ford's testimony, tells people to 'think of your son,'" CNN, October 4, 2018, https://www.cnn.com/2018/10 /02/politics/trump-mocks-christine-blasey-ford-kavanaugh-supreme-court /index.html.

241 Monica McLean, the former FBI agent who was forced to publicly deny: Gregg Re and John Roberts, "Christine Blasey Ford Ex-boyfriend Says She Helped Friend Prep for Potential Polygraph; Grassley Sounds Alarm," Fox News, October 2, 2018 https://www.foxnews.com/politics/christine-blasey-ford-ex -boyfriend-says-she-helped-friend-prep-for-potential-polygraph-grassley -sounds-alarm; Peter Baker, "Christine Blasey Ford's Credibility Under New Attack by Senate Republicans," *New York Times*, October 4, 2018, https://www .nytimes.com/2018/10/03/us/politics/blasey-ford-republicans-kavanaugh.htm.

241 A server at Dale's restaurant in Southaven: Susan Chira and Ellen Ann Fentress, "In a Mississippi Restaurant, Two Americas Coexist Side by Side,"

New York Times, October 8, 2018, https://www.nytimes.com/2018/10/08/us
/politics/trump-kavanaugh-mississippi-.html.

241 **"You don't carry that":** "Who Is Believed and Who Is Blamed?," *The Daily,*
October 10, 2016, https://www.nytimes.com/2018/10/10/podcasts/the-daily
/kavanaugh-assault-metoo-women-girls-respond.html.

241 **Celebrities like Ellen DeGeneres and Connie Chung:** Savannah Guthrie,
"Ellen DeGeneres Opens up about Being a Victim of Sexual Abuse," *Today
Show,* October 4, 2018, https://www.today.com/video/ellen-degeneres-opens
-up-about-being-a-victim-of-sexual-abuse-1336566851633; Connie Chung,
"Dear Christine Blasey Ford: I, Too, Was Sexually Assaulted—and It's Seared
into My Memory Forever," *Washington Post,* October 3, 2018, https://www
.washingtonpost.com/opinions/dear-christine-blasey-ford-i-too-was-sexually
-assaulted—and-its-seared-into-my-memory-forever/2018/10/03/2449ed3c
-c68a-11e8-9b1c-a90f1daae309_story.html.

242 **"no corroboration":** Senate.gov, "Supplemental FBI Investigation Executive
Summary," October 5, 2018, https://www.grassley.senate.gov/news/news
-releases/supplemental-fbi-investigation-executive-summary.

243 **arrived at McConnell's house with beer cans:** Jenna Amatulli, "Brett
Kavanaugh Protesters Bring Beer, Chant 'Chug' Outside Mitch McConnell's
House," *Huffington Post,* October 5, 2018, https://www.huffpost.com/entry
/brett-kavanaugh-protesters-bring-beer-chant-chug-outside-mitch-mcconnells
-house_n_5bb75543e4b028e1fe3cdc5a.

244 **A few weeks before, McDonald's workers:** Rachel Abrams, "McDonald's
Workers across the U.S. Stage #Metoo Protests," *New York Times,* September 18,
2018, https://www.nytimes.com/2018/09/18/business/mcdonalds-strike-metoo
.html.

244 **the chairman of CBS, stepped down:** Edmund Lee, "CBS Chief Executive Les
Moonves Steps Down after Sexual Harassment Claims," *New York Times,*
September 9, 2018, https://www.nytimes.com/2018/09/business/les-moonves
-longtime-cbs-chief-may-be-gone-by-monday.html.

244 **Google and secret problems:** Daisuke Wakabayashi and Katie Benner, "How
Google Protected Andy Rubin, 'Father of Android,'" *New York Times,* October
25, 2018, https://www.nytimes.com/2018/10/25/technology/google-sexual
-harassment-andy-rubin.html.

244 **At the height of the Kavanaugh fracas in Washington:** Alicia P. Q. Wittmeyer, "Eight Stories of Men's Regret," *New York Times,* October 18, 2018, https://www.nytimes.com/interactive/2018/10/18/opinion/men-metoo-high-school.html.

EPILOGUE: THE GATHERING

247 **twelve women:** This chapter is based on audio recordings of the group interview that took place over two days.

249 **the first of several women:** Matthew Garrahan, "Harvey Weinstein: How Lawyers Kept a Lid on Sexual Harassment Claims," *Financial Times,* October 23, 2017, https://www.ft.com/content/1dc8a8ae-b7e0-11e7-8c12-5661783e5589.

249 **a public case against confidential settlements:** Holly Watt, "Harvey Weinstein Aide Tells of 'Morally Lacking' Non-disclosure Deal," *The Guardian,* March 28, 2018, https://www.theguardian.com/film/2018/mar/28/harvey-weinstein -assistant-zelda-perkins-i-was-trapped-in-a-vortex-of-fear; House of Commons Women and Equalities Committee, "Sexual Harassment in the Workplace, Fifth Report of Session 2017–2019," *House of Commons,* July 18, 2018, https:// publications.parliament.uk/pa/cm201719/cmselect/cmwomeq/725/725.pdf.

256 **Crooks ran for public office:** Matthew Haag, "Rachel Crooks, Who Accused Trump of Sexual Assault, Wins Legislative Primary," *New York Times,* May 9, 2018, https://www.nytimes.com/2018/05/09/us/politics/rachel-crooks-ohio .html.

257 **an unprecedented wave of female candidates:** Karen Zraick, "Night of Firsts: Diverse Candidates Make History in Midterm Elections," *New York Times,* November 11, 2017, https://www.nytimes.com/2018/11/07/us/politics/election -history-firsts-blackburn-pressley.html.

260 **more than eighty women had already come forward:** Sara M. Moniuszko and Cara Kelly, "Harvey Weinstein Scandal: A Complete List of the 87 Accusers," *USA Today,* October 27, 2017, https://www.usatoday.com/story/life/people /2017/10/27/weinstein-scandal-complete-list-accusers/804663001.Index

INDEX